THE
BAGH O BAHAR
OR
THE GARDEN AND THE SPRING

THE
BAGH O BAHAR
OR
THE GARDEN AND THE SPRING

BEING

THE ADVENTURES OF KING AZAD BAKHT AND THE FOUR DARWESHES

LITERALLY TRANSLATED FROM THE URDU OF MIR AMMAN, OF DIHLI

WITH COPIOUS EXPLANATORY NOTES, AND AN INTRODUCTORY PREFACE

by

EDWARD B. EASTWICK,

F.R.S., M.R.A.S.

GYAN

Published by

GYAN

Gyan Publishing House
5, Ansari Road
Daryaganj, New Delhi-110002
Phone: 011-47034999, 9811692060
E-mail: books@gyanbooks.com

Distribution Network
gyanbooks.com
India, USA, Canada, UK, Australia, France

ISBN : 978-81-212-6158-6 (PB)
First Published, 1852

2nd Impression 2021

Printed at: Gyan Press, Delhi.

The
Bagh O Bahar or The Garden and the Spring
Author: Edward B. Eastwick

THE

BĀGH O BAHĀR

OR

THE GARDEN AND THE SPRING

BEING

THE ADVENTURES OF KING ĀZĀD BAKHT AND THE FOUR DARWESHES

LITERALLY TRANSLATED FROM THE URDŪ OF MĪR AMMAN, OF DIHLĪ

WITH COPIOUS EXPLANATORY NOTES, AND AN INTRODUCTORY PREFACE

BY

EDWARD B. EASTWICK, F.R.S., M.R.A.S.

TO

WILLIAM BUTTERWORTH BAYLEY, ESQ.,

A DIRECTOR OF THE HONOURABLE EAST INDIA COMPANY, AND SOMETIME GOVERNOR-GENERAL OF INDIA.

Sir,

I feel the more satisfaction in being permitted to dedicate this Translation to you, because I thus inscribe my book to one illustrious, not only for his conduct of great affairs, but for his profound knowledge of *the* language of Hindūstān. Trusting that my work, which is the fruit of an attentive study of the original for many years, may stand the test of the most penetrating scrutiny,

I am,

Sir,

Faithfully and respectfully yours,

EDWARD B. EASTWICK.

East India College,
January 16*th*, 1852.

PREFACE

TO THE

ENGLISH TRANSLATION OF THE BĀGH O BAHĀR.

THE tale of the Four Darweshes has now become a work of so much general interest—inasmuch as it is the book in which every officer in India, civil or military, must undergo an examination—that no apology seems requisite for presenting the public, for the first time, with a translation of it. I say for the first time, for the version by Lewis Ferdinand Smith, which appeared in the days of Lord Minto's Governor-Generalship, and has lately been re-edited by Professor Forbes, is not a translation, but a paraphrase. In it all the difficult expressions are passed over, *pede sicco*, and some passages, according to Mr. Smith's own statement, are altered to give an air of greater probability to the whole. Moreover, the fragments of poetry with which the tales are interspersed, are rendered in such a doleful and dissonant manner, that no amount of compassion could induce the general reader to harass his feelings by perusing more than one line. It is to be regretted, indeed, that Professor Forbes, instead of confining himself to the retouching the stories of the first and second darweshes, had not rather favoured us with a new translation. As, however, that has not been done, I feel that I have had a clear field; and if I have failed, it is from my own carelessness, and not from the superior prowess of a rival. Lest, however, what I have said of Mr. Smith's version, should seem to be a prelude to self-eulogy, I must at once distinctly state what I have aimed at in the present translation, in order that the reader may be satisfied of the humility of my pretensions. I must inform him that I have not aspired to write an elegant or an amusing book, but one that shall be useful to the student, by conveying the exact sense of the original. In that I hope I have succeeded, and that the beginner will now have the means of assuring himself, after a proper use of the dictionary, that he has arrived at the true meaning of the author. I am not one of those who would discard the use of translations in studying a language. On the contrary, I think they may greatly facilitate the learner's progress, provided that reference is made to them as a *dernier ressort*, after attacking a difficulty in the legitimate way with dictionary and grammar. In this way translations may supply the place of a teacher, who cannot always be at hand. Moreover, by perusing them one may get a general idea of the whole story, which, in Oriental works, guiltless as they often are of any division into chapters, or index of contents, is a matter of some difficulty.

After these preliminary remarks, it seems requisite to say a few words on the book itself, and its various authors or translators. First, then, it must be observed that the "Bāgh o Bahār" is not an original work, but an Urdū translation, by Mīr Amman, of the Persian romance, entitled "Ḳiṣṣah-i Chahār Darwesh," or "Story of the Four Darweshes," composed by the celebrated poet, Amīr Khusrau, of Delhi. Of him we shall speak anon; but first as to his translator. Mīr Amman has given us in his preface to the "Bagh o Bahār," a brief narrative of himself, from which we learn that his family resided for some centuries at Delhi, where they held a Jāgīr, or grant of land in free tenure, under the Mughal emperors, and were subsequently involved in the ruin of the house of Tīmūr. Their Jāgīr was seized by Sūraj Mal, the founder of the principality of Bhartpur, and their houses plundered by Aḥmad Shāh, King of Kābul, when he invaded India. Mīr Amman himself, after various vicissitudes, arrived in Calcutta, a destitute wanderer, where his good fortune introduced him, A.D. 1801, to Dr. Gilchrist, Professor of Urdū, in the College of Fort William. The Urdū language was just then beginning to be studied by Europeans, and it was desirable to supply the want of original works in that dialect, by translations from other languages. Mīr Amman was commissioned to translate the amusing romance of "The Four Darweshes," a duty which he performed with remarkable elegance and success, and in a style very superior to a former version made by ʿAṭā Ḥusain Khān, entitled "Nau ṭarz-i muraṣṣā," "The New Gold-embroidered Fashion," which was too thickly inlaid with Arabic and Persian. It must, however, be remembered that, in a language till then almost unwritten, the grammatical canons were not likely to be fixed with that rigour which the iron hand of centuries imposes. We accordingly find in the "Bāgh o Bahār," notwithstanding its other excellences, many instances of what would now be considered bad grammar, and which the most ordinary munshī would reprobate. Thus at p. 8, l. 15; p. 22, l. 17; p. 120, l. 19; p. 144, l. 14; p. 147, l. 3; p. 151, l. 11; and at p. 161, l. 16 (of Forbes' edition), we have وه *wuh*, for the plural وے *ve*. Again, at p. 145, l. 17, we have يہہ *yih* for يے *ye*; and at p. 162, l. 13, we have يہہ *yih* agreeing with a plural substantive; and at p. 44, l. 14, جن نے *jin ne* is very flagrantly made the antecedent to the relative وه *wuh*. We find also some grave faults in the collocation of words, especially in making the genitive follow the noun on which it depends, instead of preceding it. Thus, at p. 6, l. 17, we have حقيقت اُردو كي زبان كي *ḥaḳīḳat urdū kī zabān kī*, instead of اُردو كي زبان كي حقيقت *urdū kī zabān kī ḥaḳīḳat*. Again, at p. 11, l. 13, occurs عرضي بد عملي كي *ârẓī bad âmalī kī*, instead of بد عملي كي عرضي *bad âmalī kī ârẓī*. At p. 63, l. 14, we have the nominative used for the genitive by a vulgarism, يہہ امّيدوار هوں *yih ummedwār hūṅ*, instead of اس كا امّيدوار هوں *is kā ummedwār hūṅ*, "I am hopeful of this." At p. 30, l. 2, we have the postposition پاس *pās*, without the intervention of كے *ke*, joined directly to a substantive, which is very inelegant. Several sentences of pure Persian also occur, which glitter like a *purpureus pannus*, amidst the homely Hindūstānī with which they are surrounded. Thus, at p. 161, l. 6, we have از اين چہہ بہتر *az īn chih bihtar?* "What is better than this?" which might have as easily been rendered by the Urdū اس سے كيا بہتر *is se kyā bihtar?* Add to this, that occasionally sentences of great length occur, which are quite repugnant to the character of the Urdū language, whose nature is to break up long sentences into a number of shorter ones. Thus, at p. 42, l. 5, we have a sentence of five lines, over which prodigy the author has fallen prostrate, enveloped in the dust of unintelligibility. In spite of these faults, however, against which it is right to warn the student, we must pronounce the "Bāgh o Bahār" to be the most finished specimen of the Urdū language that has yet appeared. Still we must remember that the language is but yet in its infancy, and as it has originated from a similar fusion of tongues to that which has given birth to the English, so we may predict that it will, like that noble vehicle of thought, grasp the combined beauties of the several members of which it is composed, and be one day adorned with as large a number of masterpieces of prose and song.

To return to Mīr Amman, we have only to observe that he subsequently translated the "Akhlāḳ-i Muḥsinī" of Ḥusain Vāiẓ Kāshifī into Urdū, giving his translation the name of "Ganj-i Khūbī," or "Treasury of Excellence." He also composed a variety of poems, of no remarkable merit. The name which he has chosen for his translation of "The Four Darweshes" is simply a chronological one, to denote the year in which he concluded his labours. Thus, according to the Arabic system—

ب = 2
ا = 1
غ = 1000
و = 6
ب = 2
ه = 5
ا = 1
ر = 200 = 1217 A.H. = 1802 A.D.

As has been before observed, the story was originally written in Persian, and entitled, قصّهٔ چهار درویش *Ḳiṣṣah-i Chahār Darwesh*, "Story of the Four Darweshes." The author was Abū-l Ḥasan Khusrau, or Khusrū, as some write it (the word from which we have made our Chosroes), one of the greatest poets that ever appeared in Hindūstān. On account of the sweetness of his style, he was called (smile not, reader!) the طوطي هند *Ṭūṭī-i Hind*, "Parrot of Hindūstān." In this unpoetical country we might prefer to call him the "Nightingale of the East," and such, indeed, he was. His grandfather, who bore the name of Turk, came to Hindūstān from Mā-warā-u'n-nahr, or Transoxiana, in the time of Jangīz Khān. He died at Delhi, leaving a son called Amīr Maḥmūd, or, according to others, Saif-u'd-dīn, who was high in the favour of the Emperor Taglak Shāh, and perished in battle against the infidels, or, in other words, the Hindūs. His son Amīr Khusrau succeeded to the royal favour, and enjoyed the confidence and patronage of seven successive Emperors of Delhi. He seems to have devoted himself to the composition of poetry, in which he became so famous that it is said that the illustrious Sâdī, the prince of Persian bards, visited Hindūstān, for the sole purpose of seeing him. We are told that he was the author of ninety-eight works, of which by far the greater part are lost. Of those which remain, his خمسه *Khumsah*, or "Five Metrical Romances," and his نه سپهر *Nuh Sipahr*, or "The Nine Heavens," which is a panegyric on the Emperor Muḥammad Taglak Shāh; as well as his قصّهٔ چهار درویش *Ḳiṣṣah-i Chahār Darwesh*, or "Romance of the Four Darweshes," will be found in the Ouseley Collection of MSS., now deposited in the

Bodleian Library at Oxford. The names of the above-mentioned five romances are—

1. مطلع الانوار *Maṭlà-u 'l-Anvār,* "The Dawn of Light."

2. شيرين و خسرو *Shīrīn wa Khusrau,* "The Loves of Khusrau," or Chosroes, "and Shīrīn," or Irene, daughter of the Emperor Maurice.

3. هشت بهشت *Hasht Bihisht,* "The Eight Paradises."

4. مجنون و ليلى *Majnūn wa Laila,* "The Loves of the Arab Majnūn and Laila."

5. آئينۀ سكندر *Āīnah-i Sikandar,* "The Mirror of Alexander."

This list will shew that Amīr Khusrau selected the same themes for his Muse as Naẓāmī, and, in the opinion of so competent a judge as Ḥusain Vāiẓ Kāshifī, he is not excelled by him.

Khusrau (as we learn from Mīr Amman's preface, p. 4 of this translation) composed his "Romance of the Four Darweshes," in order to amuse the sick bed of his spiritual preceptor, the renowned saint, Niẓāmu'd-dīn Auliyā Zarī Zarbakhsh, or, as he is otherwise called, Shakar Ganj Shāh, "The Honeyed King." However we sceptics may doubt the efficacy of such a remedy, certain it is that the holy man recovered in a few days after the receipt of the romance, and derived such pleasure from hearing it that he pronounced the blessing of perpetual spring on the constitutions of all future listeners. Shortly after this benediction the saintly Niẓāmu'd-dīn departed this life, and his loss left Khusrau so inconsolable that he did not long survive him. He died at Delhi, A.H. 715 = A.D. 1315.

It only remains to observe that a very good notion of the "Bāgh o Bahār," as well as of Urdū literature generally, will be found in the "Calcutta Review," No. VIII. Art. I. Of the five stories which make up the "Romance," the palm is there very justly given to the Tale of King Āzād-Bakht, which bears a strong similarity to some of the stories in the "Arabian Nights' Entertainments," to which it is not inferior in interest.

Besides the advantage which a perusal of the "Bāgh o Bahār" offers to students as regards improvement in the language, it will also furnish much useful information as to the manners, habits, and feelings of the natives of Hindūstān. Though the work of which it is a translation was written five centuries ago, such is the stereotyped character of Orientals, that it affords even at this day a most vivid picture of Eastern life.

In conclusion, I may say, that if the reader receives but the one-twentieth part of the gratification in perusing this "Translation," that I have had in making it, I shall be more than satisfied, and he will be content.

East India College, December, 1851.

BĀGH O BAHĀR.

PREFACE.

IN THE NAME OF THE MOST MERCIFUL AND COMPASSIONATE GOD![1]

God be praised! what a Creator is He! who, from a handful of earth, has created forms and figures, how various, of (mere) clay. Though there be (but) two colours, one white, one black, and though He has given to all the same nose, ears, hands, and feet, He has, nevertheless, created shapes each distinct from the other, and of various kinds, so that the form and fashion of one agrees not with the shape and appearance of another. Among tens of millions of created things, whichever you desire to recognise you can. The sky is (but) a globule of the ocean of His unity, and the earth a watery bubble;[2] but the marvel is this, that the ocean rolls thousands of billows, yet it cannot so much as disorder one of His hairs.[3] In praise of Him whose power and might is such, the tongue of man is, as you may say, dumb.

---

[1] All Muḥammadan writings begin in the same manner, with an address to the Deity, glorification of the Prophet, and praise of the person to whom the work is dedicated.

[2] Here بتاشا and بلبلا are identical in meaning, but in order to vary the expression, I have slightly altered the signification of the former.

[3] I cannot help thinking that in this extraordinary expression there is an attempt at an equivoque of which the Orientals are so fond. بال بیکا *bāl bīkā* means "a disordered hair;" بال بھیگا *bāl bhīgā* would mean "wet hair," which would be suitable enough with reference to the thousand surges. The English reader must not consider such attempts at punning (wretched as they are) to be repugnant to Eastern taste.

Though he should speak, what can he say? better is it thus, that on a subject on which he is unable to utter a word he should remain silent.

From heaven, lo! to earth, whose things these are;
His praise though I would write,—what power is there?
When (e'en) the Prophet said, "I comprehend him not."
Great dolt is he who would pretend to this!
Night and day, onward moving, sun and moon survey His work.
Yea! each individual creature's form is an astonished eye![4]
He who no second[5] has, nor like, nor e'er will have;
All suitable is Godhead to this peerless One.
Thus much I know that He our maker and preserver is,
In every way on me is (shown) His favour and beneficence.

And blessing be on His friend, for whose sake he created earth and heaven, and (to whom) he gave the dignity of the prophetic office.

A Light of God was Muṣṭafa's[6] pure frame,
Whence 'tis well known no shadow from it came.[7]
Where mine the (*lit.* so great) power his praises to rehearse?
Yet this the rule, and custom prompts my verse.

And blessing and peace be on the twelve Imāms[8] who are his progeny.

Be ended here the praise to God and Aḥmad[9] due;
I now commence the theme I hold in view:
O God! for sake of thy own Prophet's progeny,
Make this my speech approved by low and high.

---

[4] *i.e.* All things survey the glorious works of God with astonishment.

[5] This is exactly the Horatian "Nec viget quidquam simile aut secundum." *Carm.* 1. I. 12.

[6] A name of Muḥammad; "chosen," "selected," from صفي the best part of a thing.

[7] The faithful have a tradition that their Prophet was shadowless.

[8] The twelve Imāms were, according to the Shīāhs:—1. Alī, son-in-law of Muḥammad. 2. Ḥasan, his eldest son. 3. Ḥusain, his younger son. 4. Alī Zainu'l-ābidīn, eldest son of Ḥusain. 5. Muḥammad Bāḳir, son of Zainu'l-ābidīn. 6. Jāfar Ṣādiḳ, son of Bāḳir. 7. Mūsā, son of Jāfar. 8. Alī Riẓā, son of Mūsā. 9. Abū Jāfar Muḥammad, son of Riẓā. 10. Alī Askarī, son of the above. 11. Ḥasan Askarī, son of the above. The 12th will be Mahdī, who is yet to appear.

[9] Aḥmad, a name of the Prophet, and equivalent to Muḥammad, as signifying "most praised."

The origin of this composition is, that in the year one thousand two hundred and fifteen of the Hijrah,[10] and eighteen hundred and one of the Christian Æra, corresponding to the year one thousand two hundred and seven of the Faṣlī Æra,[11] in the Government of the Most Noble of Nobles the Marquess of Wellesley, Governor General, and Lord Mornington,[12] (in whose praise the understanding is lost and the intellect confused. God has assembled in his person all the qualities which rulers ought to have. In short, it was the good fortune of this realm that such a Governor honoured it with his presence, from the blessing of whose footsteps a world has derived repose. No one has the power to commit violence on another;—the tiger[13] and the goat drink water at the same descent to the river;—all the poor utter benedictions, and find the means of supporting life) philosophical inquiry extended. The illustrious (English) gentlemen imbibed the desire of becoming acquainted with the Urdū language,[14] and holding discourse with the natives of Hindūstān, and (so) transacting civil matters with a perfect understanding (of what they did); wherefore in this same year several books were compiled according to order.

In the service of those gentlemen who are wise and able to speak the Hindūstānī language, I make representation that this story of the Four Darweshes was in the beginning composed by Amīr Khusrau,[15] of Dillī, on the occasion of his Holiness Niẕāmu'd-dīn Auliyā Zarī Zarbakhsh (who was his

---

[10] The Hijrah, or Flight of Muḥammad, dates from the 16th of July, A.D. 622.

[11] The Faṣlī, or Revenue Æra of Upper India, dates from A.D. 592⅞; that of Southern India from A.D. 590.

[12] The arrangement of these titles shews the indistinct notion the natives have of their meaning.

[13] The word شیر *shīr* in Hindūstān means tiger more often than lion. Shīr Afkan was so named for his prowess in slaying an animal of the former species.

[14] The reason why Hindūstānī is called Urdū will appear presently.

[15] Or Khusrū, in which case it is compounded of خوش pleasing, رو face. As I have written it the name is from خوش pleasantly, رفتن to go. This personage is supposed to have been born at Gazna, A.H. 630 = A.D. 1232–3, and by some in A.H. 634 = A.D. 1236, at Badāma town, in the province of Dillī, where he resided. He died A.H. 725 = A.D. 1325, and was buried at Dillī, close to the court of Ḳuṭbu'd-dīn.

spiritual adviser,[16] and whose shrine[17] is at Dillī, three kos[18] from the Castle outside the Red Gate, before the Miṭiyā Gate, near the Red House) falling sick (*lit.* his temperament was ailing). Then, in order to amuse the mind of his spiritual preceptor, Amīr Khusrau used continually to recite this story, and wait on him during his sickness. After some days God restored him to health. Then he, on the day of (taking) the bath of convalescence, pronounced this blessing,—that whoever should hear this Story should, through the grace of God, continue in health; and since then this Tale has been currently known in the Persian language.

Now my patron, the courteous gentleman, John Gilchrist, who rightly appreciates men of merit (so long as the Gangā and Jamunā flow, may his good fortune always increase!), of his good favour commanded, saying,—translate this Story into the pure Hindūstānī colloquial dialect, which the Urdū people, Hindūs, Musalmān, women, men, boys and girls, high and low, speak and use among themselves. According to the order of his Highness, I also began to write in this same style, just as one converses.

In the first place, this sinful and criminal person, Mīr Amman of Dillī, will relate his own circumstances, as follows:—My ancestors, from the reign of the Emperor Humāyūn,[19] continued performing devoted service in the retinue of each successive Emperor, generation after generation; while he (the prince) also with fostering eye, remained displaying towards them that appreciation of their merit which was fitting. Having exalted them by the bestowal of grants of land, and dignities, and offices, he made them to abound and be happy; and with his august tongue pronounced them his hereditary servants, born in his house, and his ancient officers; moreover, this title is enrolled in the royal register. When vicissitude befel this house

---

[16] The پیر *pīr* is a sort of living Saint, to whom offerings of all kinds are presented, and whose name, advice or intercession is invoked in perilous conjunctures.

[17] The mosque near which he was buried.

[18] کوس *kos*, a measure which varies in different provinces, but may be reckoned at two miles.

[19] Son of Baber, began to reign A.D. 1530.

(through which house all other houses flourished) as is manifest: (why explain what is evident?) then Sūraj Mal the Jāṭ[20] seized on the district which had been conferred (on my ancestors), and Aḥmad Shāh Durrānī[21] plundered their household property. After undergoing ruin such as this, I became an exile from this city (which was my native country and birth-place, and in which very place my navel-string is buried); and that ship (whose helmsman was the king) foundered. I began to be submerged in the sea of friendliness—to the sinking man the support of a straw appears (*lit.* is) a great matter. For some years I found rest in the city of Āẓīmābād, with indifferent fortune (*lit.* something succeeded, something failed). At length thence also my feet were withdrawn (*lit.* were torn up), fortune did not favour me; I left my family and having embarked alone in a vessel, contrived to support myself as far as (*lit.* arrived by the force of water and grain at) the most illustrious of cities, Calcutta. Some time passed without employment. By chance the Nawwāb Dilāwar Khān sent for me, and appointed me to the tuition of his younger brother, Mīr Muḥammad Kāẓim Khān. I stayed there almost two years, but did not see there the means of maintaining myself. Then, through the medium of Munshī Mīr Bahādur Ālī, I obtained an introduction to the presence of the valiant gentleman, John Gilchrist (may his good fortune endure!). At length (then) by the aid of fortune, I grasped the skirt of one so magnanimous. Prosperous days must come; and if not, this at least is a blessing,[22] that I have a morsel to eat, and sleep at my ease (*lit.* stretch out my feet and sleep), and in my house ten persons—small and great—find a subsistence, and utter prayers for blessing on that appreciator of merit—may God accept them! (*i.e.* the prayers).

I have heard from the mouths of my ancestors, an account of the Urdū language, as follows. The city of Dillī,[23] in the opinion

---

[20] The prince of Bhartpur.

[21] The Afghān king who mounted the throne of Kābul after the death of Nādir, A.D. 1747.

[22] غنیمت *Ghanīmat* is a word for which we have no exact equivalent. It does not exactly mean a blessing, though so rendered in the dictionaries; but rather, "a piece of luck;" "an unlooked-for piece of good fortune."

[23] *Anglicè*, Delhi.

of the Hindūs, has existed through the four ages:[24] their kings and people were dwelling (there) from old time and speaking their own language. A thousand years ago commenced the rule of the Musalmān; Sulṭān Maḥmūd of Ghaznī came; afterwards reigned the dynasties of Ghor[25] and Lodī. Through this intercourse, the languages of the Hindūs and Musalmān became somewhat mixed. At length Amīr Tīmūr[26] (in whose family the imperial name and descent still continues) took Hindūstān. By his arrival and stay, the bāzār of the army was introduced into the city, whence the city bāzār was called Urdū.[27] Afterwards, the Emperor Humāyūn,[28] being driven to great straits at the hands of the Paṭhāns, went into Persia.[29] At length having returned from thence he chastised his surviving enemies.[30] No rebel remained to set on foot sedition or rebellion.

When the Emperor Akbar[31] mounted the throne, then from (various) countries, from the four quarters, all the tribes having heard of the appreciation of merit and the munificence of this incomparable family, came and assembled in the royal presence; but the speech and dialect of each was different. From their being collected together, and owing to the trade traffic and intercourse which they carried on with one another, a single language, that of the Urdū, became established. When his Majesty Shāh Jahān,[32] Lord of the conjunction (of the two beneficent planets Jupiter and Venus), caused the royal palace and the principal *masjid*[33] and the ramparts of the city to be

---

24 According to the Hindūs, there are four ages: the Satya, Tretā, Dwāpur, and Kali; in which last we are now living. Dillī therefore, in their opinion, is as old as the world.

25 Muḥammad Ghorī mounted the throne of Ghaznī, and part of India, A.D. 1202. Belolī, the first king of the house of Lodī, began to reign A.D. 1454.

26 Tīmūr invaded Hindūstān A.D. 1327.

27 Urdū, a Tartar word signifying camp; *Urdū zabān*, "camp language."

28 Humāyūn, son of Baber, mounted the throne A.D. 1530, and fled to Persia A.D. 1542, recovered Hindūstān A.D. 1554, from the Paṭhāns or Afghāns.

29 ولايت *wilāyat*, properly "a country," but the term is now generally applied to Persia or England.

30 پسماندون *pasmāndon*. In the Calcutta Review, vol. iv. p. 321, is a strange rendering of this word, where it appears as a proper name—the *Pusmand races !!*

31 Akbar, son of Humāyūn, mounted the throne of Hindūstān A.D. 1555.

32 Shāh Jahān, third son of Jahāngīr, mounted the throne A.D. 1627.

33 *Anglicè*, Mosque.

erected, and jewels to be set in the peacock throne; and having set up on poles a tent like a mass of clouds (in extent), caused it to be drawn tight with cords, and the Nawwāb Ȧlī Mardān Khān brought (thither) the canal, then the Emperor being pleased, commanded a feast, and made the city the seat of his empire. From that time it became known as Shāh Jahānābād (although Dillī is a distinct place, *that* is called the old city and *this* the new), and he gave to its bāzār the lofty title of the Urdū (or camp).

From the reign of Amīr Tīmūr to that of Muḥammad Shāh,[34] and moreover to that of Aḥmad Shāh,[35] and Ȧlamgīr the Second,[36] the kingdom was regularly handed down generation after generation. At length the Urdū language, being continually purified, became (by degrees) so pure, that the tongue of no city can compare with it.[37] But a fair appreciator of merit is required to decide this point, to which end God has now, after a long interval, created a wise gentleman, of critical acumen, like John Gilchrist, who, by his own discernment, and creative genius, and research, and labour, has compiled books of rules. By reason of which the Hindūstānī language has become current in the various countries (of India), and its symmetry has been augmented afresh. Otherwise, no one thinks ill of his own turband,[38] and speech, and gait. If you ask a clown, he finds fault with the inhabitants of the city, and thinks himself best of all. Well, the wise themselves know how it is (*i.e.* what need of dwelling on this further?). When Aḥmad Shāh Abdālī came from Kābul and plundered the city (Dillī), Shāh Ȧlam[39] was in the Eastern provinces, and no heir or master of the kingdom remained: the city was without a

---

[34] Muḥammad Shāh, grandson of Bahādur Shāh, which latter was the second son of Aurangzīb, mounted the throne of Dillī A.D. 1718.

[35] Aḥmad Shāh succeeded his father Muḥammad Shāh A.D. 1747.

[36] Ȧlamgīr the Second, who was the grandson of Bahādur Shāh, mounted the throne A.D. 1753.

[37] ٹکّر کھانا A metaphor, taken from the encounter of rams.

[38] The natives are very nice in their manner of tying the turband, which is as great an art, and as justly valued, as that of the neckcloth with us.

[39] Shāh Ȧlam began to reign A.D. 1761, and a little before this time the Afghāns, under Aḥmad Shāh, repeatedly plundered Dillī, and massacred the inhabitants.

head. It is true the city flourished from the prosperous fortune of the empire; all of a sudden ruin fell upon it. Its great men were scattered,[40] and fled wherever they could find refuge.[41] By associating with the inhabitants of the countries into which they came, a difference arose in their dialect; and there are many who from some cause or other went into Dillī and abode there for ten or five years,—how far will they, too, be able to speak? here and there they will undoubtedly commit blunders. But the person who, having endured all disasters, has remained (immoveable) like a brick of Dillī, and ten or five generations of whose ancestors have passed their lives in this very city, and who has attended the Darbārs (audience-chambers) of the nobles, and the fairs, and assemblages of the people, and their marriage-feasts,[42] and the processions of the Saint Shāh Madār,[43] has walked about for amusement, and to witness spectacles, and has perambulated the streets of that city for a length of time, and after quitting it has carefully preserved his language; his manner of speaking will undoubtedly be correct. And this humble individual, too (having done all that has been said above), after visiting every city and seeing what was to be seen, has arrived at this place.

---

[40] Literally, "became I somewhere, you somewhere."

[41] Literally, "wherever there was room for their horns."

[42] Urs is also a festival held in honour of saints.

[43] Shāh Badī u'd-dīn, or Zindah Shāh Madār, of Syria, was a great Walī, or Saint. He lived to a great age,—nay, some think him still living, whence his name Zindah. He came to India, residing at Makhanpur, where his tomb now is. The fair held in his honour on the 17th of Jamādu'l awwal, is attended by a million of people, but women cannot enter his mausoleum. *Vide* Ḳānūn-i Islām, p. 241.

BEGINNING OF THE STORY.

I NOW commence the story, give ear a little, listen and bestow an impartial judgment. In the adventures of the Four Darweshes, it has thus been written, and the narrator has thus related, that there was formerly in the kingdom of Rūm[44] an emperor, in whose person was (united) the justice of Nūshīrwān,[45] and the generosity of Ḥātim.[46] His name was Āzād-ba<u>kh</u>t,[47] and the city of Ḳusṭunṭuniyah (which they call Istambol) was his capital. In his time the people were numerous; the treasury full; the army contented; the poor at ease were passing their time with such comfort, and living so happily, that in the house of each the day was as the festival of ʿĪd,[48] and the night as the Shab-i barāt;[49] and all the thieves,

---

[44] Rūm, Turkey or Rumelia.

[45] Nūshīrwān (sweet-flowing) was the 20th King of the 4th dynasty of Persia, *i.e.* the Sassanides or <u>Kh</u>usravians. He was contemporary with Justin and Justinian, and in his reign Muḥammad was born, A.D. 578.

[46] Ḥātim Ṭāī was an illustrious Arab, who lived one generation before Muḥammad, and was celebrated for his munificence.

[47] Literally, "free fortune."

[48] ʿĪd signifies any solemn feast, but it is especially applied to the five annual feasts of the Musalmān, viz., two principal ones, which are both فرض and سُنّت (commanded by God and the Prophet), the Ramazān-ʿīd or ʿĪd-u'l fiṭr, and the Baḳar-ʿīd, and three inferior, or سُنّت (commanded only by the Prophet). These are Muḥarram, Ā<u>kh</u>irī chahār shambah, and Shab-i barāt. The first corresponds to our Easter, and is held on the 1st of Shawwāl, the 10th month, after the fast of Ramazān, which answers to our Lent. *Vide* Ḳānūn-i Islām, p. 261. The second, Baḳar-ʿīd or Kurbān, or ʿĪd-u'ẓ-ẓuḥā, is held on the 9th of the 1st month, <u>Z</u>ī ḥijjah, in honour of Abraham's offering up Ismaʿīl. The ʿĪd of the Muḥarram was observed before Muḥammad, and till 46 A.H., when it was changed to a fast for Ḥusain and Ḥasan. The Ā<u>kh</u>irī chahār shambah is on the last Wednesday of the 2nd month, Ṣafar, on which day the Prophet had a lull in his last illness.

[49] The Shab-i barāt is held on the 14th of the 8th month, Shābān, when God records the actions of men for the ensuing year. Hence Shab-i barāt or Night of Record. The night of the 14th is passed in mirth, and especially in the discharge of fireworks.

pickpockets, early pilferers, petty larceners, and sharpers that there were, all these he annihilated and did not leave the name or trace of them in all his kingdom. All the night the doors of the houses remained unclosed, and the shops of the bāzār continued open. Wayfaring people and travellers proceeded on their way tossing up gold in the forest and in the plain; no one was asking them, saying, how many teeth are there in your mouth? and whither go ye?[50] under the rule of that king were thousands of cities, and several Sulṭāns paid him tribute. Notwithstanding so great an empire he did not suffer his heart to neglect for one moment the remembrance and the worship of God. All worldly enjoyments which he could desire, were in his possession, but a son, which is the fruit of life, was not in the garden of his destiny. On this account, he was for the most part remaining sad, and after prayers at the five appointed times,[51] he was addressing the bountiful God thus: "O God! Thou of thy favour hast bestowed on me, weak being that I am, everything, but hast alone not given me a lamp of this dark house. This one regret remains in my mind, that there is none to take my name or give me water[52] at the last moment; and in thy secret treasury everything is to be found. Bestow on me a living son, then my name and the ensign of this empire will remain firm."

In the same hope the life of the king reached forty years. One day, having performed his devotions in the palace of mirrors, he had remained reading his daily portion of the Ḳur'ān. All of a sudden, as he turned his attention towards a mirror, a white hair appeared in his whiskers, which remained glittering like a thread of brocade. Having seen it, the eyes of the king were suffused with tears, and he heaved a cold sigh. Again he reflected in his heart as follows: "Alas! thou hast to no purpose wasted so much of thy life, and in the lust of this

---

[50] Briefly, "they were not meddled with."

[51] The Muḥammadans have five times enjoined for daily prayer, which are فرض, or of divine appointment. 1. Namāz-i fajr, from dawn to sunrise. 2. Ẓuhr, mid-day prayer between one and three p.m. 3. Âsr, from four to sunset. 4. Maghrib, at sunset, or six p.m. 5. Aishab, between eight and midnight.

[52] Dying people usually ask for water, and it is the son's duty to give it. Of a very sudden death it is said, "He did not even ask for water."

world hast turned a world upside down. How wilt thou now be benefited by the vast territories thou hast subdued? At last some other person will dissipate all this wealth and property. To thee, indeed, the messenger of death has already arrived. Even if thou shouldst live some days, then the strength of thy body will decrease; whence this is apparent, that in my destiny it was not written that an heir to my canopy[53] and throne should be born. At length, one day, I must die, and abandon everything. Wherefore this is better, that I of my own accord should relinquish them, and pass the rest of my life in the recollection of my creator."

Having fixed this thing in his heart, he went into the lower garden and, after dismissing all his courtiers, said: "From to-day let none approach me; let all continue to come and go in the public half-of-audience, and remain attentively engaged in their duties." Having said this, he himself went into an apartment and sate down, and having spread his prayer-carpet, occupied himself with his devotions. He had no employment but weeping and sighing. In this same manner Āzād-ba<u>kh</u>t passed some days. At evening, at the time of breaking his fast, he was eating a date and drinking three gulps of water, and all day and night he remained stretched out on the place of prayer. Rumours of these circumstances spread abroad; by degrees the intelligence was diffused through the whole country, that the king, having withdrawn his hand from the government, had made choice of seclusion. On all sides enemies and rebels raised their heads and advanced beyond their own territories. Whoever had a mind, encroached on the kingdom and made preparations for revolt. Wherever there were governors, a vast disorder arose in their governments. From every province representations of mal-administration arrived at Court. All the courtiers and nobles assembled, and began to take counsel and deliberate. At last this decision was resolved on, to the effect that the Nawwāb Vazīr was a man of understanding and

---

[53] The چھتر *chhattar*, or umbrella, here translated "canopy," is, in the East, as is well known, the ensign of royalty, insomuch that a Rājā is called Chhattar-pati, "Lord of the umbrella."

wisdom, as well as the intimate friend and confidante of the king, and in rank, too, superior to all; to his presence they would go and see what he thought right and said. All the grandees and nobles came to the Vazīr and said, "The state of the king is this, and that the condition of the kingdom. If a little more neglect is shown, then the territories which have been acquired with so much toil will be gratuitously lost, and to recover them will be a matter of great difficulty." The Vazīr was an old man, long in office, loyal, and a man of understanding; his name also was Khiradmand (Wise), a name significant of his character. He said, "Although the king has forbidden us to approach his presence, still do ye come; I also will proceed thither. God grant that it may please the king to summon us before him." Having said this, he took all with him as far as the public hall-of-audience, and having left them there, he himself came to the private hall, and sent by the hand of a eunuch to represent in the service of a king, saying, "This aged slave is present! for some days he has not seen the world-adorning beauty. I am in hopes that having beheld (the king) for a single interview, I may kiss his feet, then I shall be satisfied." The king heard this representation of the Vazīr, and inasmuch as he was acquainted with his long service, and loyalty, and sagacity, and devotion, and generally followed his advice; he said, after reflection, "Call in Khiradmand." At length, when permission had been accorded, the Vazīr entered the presence, performed his respects, and remained standing with his arms folded. He saw then that the king's appearance had become a strange one, for from excessive weeping and emaciation, hollow circles had formed round his eyes,[54] and his face had become yellow. Khiradmand could not restrain himself; he ran involuntarily and threw himself at his feet. The king, with his hand, raised his head, and said, "There![55] you have seen me! are you satisfied? Now go! trouble me no more; do you administer the government." Khiradmand,

---

[54] Briefly, "his eyes were sunk."

[55] لو *lo*, the 2nd p. pl. imper. of لينا *lenā*, to take, is here used as an interjection, meaning, "enough," or "there!"

having heard, wept bitterly,[56] and made representation, "By your Majesty's bounty, and through your safety, empire is always attainable by your slave;[57] but from this sudden seclusion of the Asylum of the World in this manner, ruin has fallen upon the whole kingdom, and the end of this is not good. What thought is this which has entered the august mind? If you will be pleased to make this hereditary servant, born in your house, the confidante of this secret, then it is better. Whatever enters the imperfect understanding (of your slave) he will represent. These dignities have been bestowed upon your slaves on account of this very day, that the king should enjoy pleasure and ease, and that those who have been nourished by your salt should remain in deliberation regarding the kingdom. On what day will the slaves of the king be of use, save when (may God not will it to come to pass!) anxiety attaches itself to the august mind?" The king said, "Thou speakest truth, but that anxiety which is within my heart is beyond counsel.

"Hear, O Khiradmand! all my life has passed in this same headache of acquiring territory. Now I have reached this period of life, for the future, death remains; and from this, too, the message has come, since my black hair has become white. So is the proverb, 'Having slept all night, will they not wake even now when it is morning?' As yet a son has not been born, which would have satisfied me. On this account my heart has become very sad, and I have sate down abandoning everything. Whoever chooses, let him take territory or wealth; it is of no use to me; moreover, I hold this resolve for some future day, to abandon everything and issue forth into the forests and mountains, and not shew my face to any one, and in this same manner bring to an end this life of a few days. If any place has taken my fancy, then I will seat myself there and perform my devotions to my God. Perhaps the end will be fortunate, and as for the world, I have had ample experience of it; I have discovered no enjoyment in it." Having said thus much, and having heaved a sigh, the king became silent.

---

[56] Literally, "gnashing his teeth."

[57] In other words, "the royal safety is as good as a kingdom."

Khiradmand was the Vazīr of his father. From the time that this (monarch) was prince he was maintaining a friendship with him; he was, moreover, wise and well disposed. He began to say, "It is never proper to be without hope from the majesty of God. He who by a single command created eighteen thousand worlds, for him what great matter is it to bestow on you offspring? Point of adoration of the world![58] remove from your heart this vain idea; otherwise the whole world will be involved in confusion, and this empire (with what repeated toil and labour did not your ancestors and you acquire it!) will in a moment pass from your hands, and through neglect the country will become desolate. Dishonour (which God forbid) will be incurred. Regarding this, moreover, inquiry must be made at the day of resurrection, as follows: 'Having made thee a king, I had delivered over to thy charge my servants, thou didst despair of my mercy, and harassed and afflicted thy subjects.' What answer will you give to this question? Moreover, the worship of God too will on that day be unavailing, for this reason, that the heart of man is the house of God, and kings will be examined solely as to justice. Pardon the disrespect of your slave, to go forth from the house and to wander from forest to forest is the business of Jogīs[59] and Faḳīrs,[60] not that of kings. Do you pursue that employment which is suitable to you;[61] the remembrance and worship of God is not dependent on forests and mountains. Your Majesty will have heard this couplet:

Though God is near, he seeks him in the wild,
They cry him in the town while (sleeps) in arms the child!

If you will listen unbiassed, and accept the representation of this devoted servant, then it is better thus, that the Asylum of the World should direct his mind every moment and instant

---

[58] The Ḳiblah is the point to which the Jews, Christians, and Muḥammadans turn in prayer. With the two former it is in Jerusalem; with the latter, Makkah (Mecca).

[59] The Jogī is a Hindū ascetic, who passes his life in contemplation and penance.

[60] The Faḳīr is a Muḥammadan devotee.

[61] It is not improbable that a pun is here intended upon جوگا *jogā*, "fit," and جوگي *jogī*, "an ascetic."

towards his God, and seek a blessing from him. From this Court no one is excluded. By day let your Majesty attend to the government of the country and the administration of justice to the poor; thus the servants of God[62] will remain in security and ease under the shadow of your fortunate skirt. And at night be pleased to perform your devotions, and offering humble supplications, mingled with blessings to the pure spirit of the prophet, call in the aid of Darweshes, recluses, and men resigned to God. Be pleased also to bestow daily stipends on orphans, captives, those with large families, the indigent, and widows. By the blessing of such good deeds and virtuous intentions, if God wills, there is strong hope that the desires and wishes of your heart will all be accomplished, and that longing on account of which the august mind has been disturbed, will be gratified, and happiness will be restored to the exalted breast. Fix your eyes upon the bounty of the All-provider, for he in one instant performs what he wishes." At length, by such representations of the Vazīr Khiradmand, confidence was restored to the heart of Āzād-bakht. He said, "Well! what thou sayest is right; let us try this, too. For the rest, whatever is the will of God, that will be accomplished."

When the heart of the king was comforted, he then inquired of the Vazīr, saying, "What are all the other nobles and counsellors doing? and how are they?" He represented: "All the pillars of the state are offering prayers for the life and property of the Point of Adoration of the World. All have been distressed and confounded by the inquietude of your Majesty. If you would be pleased to show your auspicious beauty, then the minds of all would be put at ease. Moreover they are at this time present in the public hall-of-audience." Having heard this, the king gave commandment, saying, "If it please the Most High God, I will to-morrow hold a Court; announce it to all; let them be in attendance." Khiradmand having heard this promise, was pleased, and having raised both his hands, invoked a blessing, saying, "As long as this earth and sky keep their place, may your crown and throne remain

---

62 That is, "the people."

firm!" And having taken leave from the presence, he came forth much pleased, and repeated this good intelligence to the nobles. All the nobles departed with laughter and merriment to their homes. Joy was diffused throughout the city. The people and commonalty rejoiced, saying,[63] "To-morrow the king will hold a public Court." In the morning, all the slaves born in the house, high and low, and the pillars of the state, small and great, came and stood each in his own place and rank, and remained expecting the splendour of royalty.

When a watch[64] of the day had passed, all of a sudden the curtain rose, and the king, having come forward, seated himself on the royal throne. Glad music began to sound in the guard-house. All presented their congratulatory offerings, and performed their bows[65] and obeisances in the place of audience. Each, according to his dignity and station, received promotion; the hearts of all were pleased and tranquillized. When two watches had passed, the king having arisen (from his throne), entered the inner apartments of the palace, and having partaken of choice refreshments, reposed in his sleeping-apartment. From that day the king made this (his) fixed custom, always in the morning to hold a court, and at the third watch to employ himself in reading, or to repeat the daily portion of the Ḳur'ān, and having expressed his repentance, and sought for forgiveness in the Court of God, to supplicate for the blessing which he desired. One day he saw it written in a book also, that if grief or anxiety was so infixed in any one that no remedy could be devised for it, then it was right to submit it to Providence; and that the sufferer himself should betake himself to the cemetery, and bestow on them[66] blessing for the

---

[63] كہ *kih*, signifies "that," but I have, when it introduces words spoken, invariably translated it "saying."

[64] A پہر *pahar*, or "watch," is three hours, and the day commences at six a.m.

[65] The كورنش *kornish*, is a half-bow, with one hand to the head; the تسليم *taslīm*, is a complete bow, with both hands down, and more humble than the "kornish."

[66] On whom? the dead? or the Prophet?—*Utrum mavis.* Or is اُن کو *unko*, here used ungrammatically for اپنے تئیں *apne ta'īn*, which follows just after? The form of the Durūd is, "O God! grant blessing, prosperity, and peace to Muḥammad and his posterity." See Ḳānūn-i Islām, p. 316, *note*.

sake of the Spirit of the Prophet; and considering himself as nothing, awaken his heart from this worldly carelessness, and weep at the warnings set before him, and survey the omnipotence of God, reflecting that, "before me, what Lords of dominion and wealth have been born on this earth! but the sky having involved all in its revolution, has mingled them with the dust." This is the proverb:

Kabīrā[67] wept when he beheld the circling mill-stone roll;
Of that which passes 'twixt the stones, nought goes forth whole!

Now, if you look, no trace remains of them but a heap of earth; and having left all their worldly wealth, their families, their children and posterity, acquaintances and friends, servants and attendants, elephants and horses, they are lying alone. All this was of no avail to them. Moreover, no one now knows even their names, or who they were; and their circumstances within the tomb are unknown,—whether worms, ants great and small, and snakes, have devoured them; or what has happened to them, and how they have fared with God. Having meditated on these matters in his heart, let him consider the whole world as the sport of a comedy.[68] Then the bud of his heart will always remain blooming—in any state it will not fade. When the king had perused this admonition in a book, he remembered the words of the Vazīr Khiradmand, and he found that both were in unison. He was eager to act accordingly; but he thought that to mount his horse, and, accompanied by a multitude of attendants, to go and move about after the manner of kings, would be unfitting. "It is better thus to change my apparel, and make a practice of going by night alone to the tombs, or into the service of some recluse, a man of God, and keep vigil during the night. Perhaps by the intervention of these men my desire in this world and my salvation in

[67] Kabīrā lived in the reign of Sikandar Shāh Lodī, from A.D. 1488 to A.D. 1516. He was a simple weaver of Benāres, where he was buried. He was, however, a great religious reformer; and Nānak, founder of the sect of Sikhs, now so famous, derived his doctrines from his works. His principal dogma was the Unity of God and contempt of caste.

[68] That is, "a mere passing pageant."

the next may be attained." Having resolved on this in his heart, one day[69] at night he put on coarse soiled clothes, and having taken some rupees and pieces[70] of gold, he silently issued from the royal castle, and took the road to the plain. Proceeding on, he arrived in a cemetery, and continued reciting with much fervency the benediction called Durūd. And at that time a furious wind was blowing; indeed, you might rather call it a tempest. All of a sudden from a distance there appeared to the king the semblance of a torch, which showed brightly like the morning star. He reflected in his heart that in that tempestuous and gloomy night this light was not devoid of a mysterious significance. "Either it is a talisman, for if you sprinkle in a lamp round the wick alum and brimstone, then, however strong the wind that blows, the lamp will not be extinguished; or it is the lamp of some saint which is burning;—be it what it may, I must go and look. Perhaps from the light of this candle the lamp of my house also may be kindled, and the wish of my heart be attained." Having formed this resolve, he went in that direction. When he came near he beheld then four indigent faḳīrs, with the garment[71] belonging to their profession cast round their necks, and their heads resting on their knees; (in which position) they sate silent, in a state of insensibility. And their condition was like that of a traveller separated from his country and tribe, who remains at his wits' ends, being overtaken with the grief and affliction of friendlessness and poverty. In this same manner, these four remained like pictures on a wall, and a lamp placed upon a stone continued to give a faint light. The wind never reached it; the sky, as you might say, had become its lantern, so safely it burned.

---

69 "One day, at night," is a common expression. Oriental writers see no impropriety in it, as روز *roz*, day, is here taken for the twenty-four hours.

70 The "ashrafī," here translated "piece of gold," is worth 1*l*. 11*s*. 8*d*.

71 The كفني *kafnī*, is a cloth about fifteen feet long and a yard wide. In the centre of its breadth is a slit, through which the head passes, and a collar is there sewed on. One third hangs behind, reaching to the calf of the leg, the rest before. The superfluous length is tucked up by the belt, and forms a bag for receiving alms.

Āzād-bakht, as soon as he beheld it, felt convinced that assuredly his wish would come to pass, by the blessing of the footsteps of these men of God; and the dry tree of his hope becoming verdant, by their favour would bear fruit. Having gone into their presence, he would recount his story, and join their company. Perhaps, having taken compassion upon him, they would offer prayers, which would be accepted with the Almighty.[72] Having formed this intention, he was about to step forward. At that moment his understanding warned him, saying, "O, devoid of judgment! act not with precipitation; pause[73] a little. How knowest thou who these are? and whence they have come, and whither they are going? How can we tell whether they are Devs[74] or Ghūls[75] of the waste? who, having assumed the forms of men, have met and sate down together. In any case, to be precipitate, and to go among them and disturb them, is not good. I must now conceal myself in a corner, and learn the circumstances of these Darweshes." At length the king did this very thing—he went silently into a corner of that place and sate down, so that none perceived the sound of his footsteps in approaching. He directed his attention towards them, saying, "Let us see what communication they hold with one another." By chance one of the Fakīrs sneezed. He thanked God.[76] The three other Kalandars[77] started up at (the sound of) his voice, and trimmed[78] the lamp.

---

72 Literally, "the Being who has no wants."

73 Literally, "take a look."

74 The Devs are malignant spirits, created many thousand years before Adam, and ruled over by Jān bin Jān, and afterwards by Iblīs.

75 The Ghūl is a kind of sylvan dæmon, who devours travellers.

76 After sneezing, it is proper to say, "Alḥamdu'l illāh," "Praise to God," and to reply with "Bārak Allāh," "God prosper you!" or some such words. Ḳānūn-i Islām, p. 420.

77 A Ḳalandar is a sort of Faḳīr, living at a takiyah or straw-hut outside the town, and supported by alms. Some have wives, some not. Some are بے شرع *be sharā*, "without law," some با شرع *bā sharā*, "with law."

78 اکسانا *uksānā*, in Shakespear's Dictionary is said to mean, "to extinguish a lamp," but the word has manifestly an opposite meaning here. Forbes has omitted the word altogether. "Aliquando bonus dormitat Homerus."

The light[79] then was bright. Each on his own bed filled his ḥuḳḳah and began to smoke. One of those hermits[80] said, "O friends, partners of woe, and companions in wandering over the world! we four persons, by the revolution of the sky, and the interchange of night and day, have wandered for a length of time from door to door with dust upon our heads.[81] Praise be to God! that by the aid of fortune, and the assistance of fate, we have to-day met together in this place, and the events of to-morrow are unknown as to what will occur, whether we shall keep the same road or be separated. The night is very long.[82] From now to continue stretched out sleeping is not good. Wherefore this is better that each should recount his own history, according to the distress that has befallen him in this world (provided that there be not a kaurī's[83] worth of falsehood in it). Then the night will pass in conversing. When a little of the night is left then we will cast ourselves down to sleep." All replied, "O Spiritual Guide! to whatsoever you command we have assented. First do you yourself be pleased to commence your adventures which you have seen, then we shall be edified."

---

[79] ٹھیپ *ṭhīp*, is in all the dictionaries given as feminine, to the manifest neglect of this passage. In the Calcutta edition the reading is ٹیپ *ṭīp*, which is probably only a mispronunciation of दीप *dīp*.

[80] The Āzād is a kind of hermit "be-sharā" or unobservant of the law, who shaves every part of his body, and practises celibacy. He omits the reading of daily prayers; subsists on alms, to the quality of which he is indifferent. He has no fixed abode, but wanders from place to place. *Vide* Ḳānūn-i Islām, p. 297.

[81] That is, "in distress."

[82] Literally, "is a great mountain," *i.e.* "tedious or long."

[83] A kaurī is a small shell (cyprea moneta) used as money. From 80 to 100 = 1 pice = one half-penny.

TRAVELS OF THE FIRST DARWESH.

THE first Darwesh knelt down on his knees, with his feet under him, and began to narrate as follows the story of his travels. O servants of God![84] be attentive here a little, and listen to the history of this distressed[85] person.

To this my tale awhile attend and hear!
How Heaven has brought on me reverses, hear!
Whate'er the hardships that have fall'n on me,
Those I'll relate, throughout attentive be!

O Friends! my birth-place and the land of my ancestors is the country of Yaman (Arabia Felix). The father of this humble person was a prince of traders,[86] a great merchant, by name Kh̲wājah Aḥmad. At that time no banker or merchant equalled him. In most cities he had warehouses and agents established for the sake of buying and selling, and in his house were to be found hundreds of thousands of rupees in cash and merchandise of divers countries. Two children were born in his house; one, indeed this very faḳīr, who, clad in the kafnī (or faḳīr's garb), and the sailī or necklace of coloured threads,[87] stands, and is speaking in the presence of (you) spiritual guides. The other was a sister, whom my father[88] in his lifetime had

---

[84] معبودالله *mābūd 'allāh*, properly means "Adorable God!" but here it is probably a lapsus for معبوداء, *mābūdā*, and as two "alifs" came together one was by an error omitted.

[85] Literally, "one without head and feet."

[86] Perhaps this might be taken as part of the name, which would then be Maliku't-tujjār Kh̲wājah Aḥmad.

[87] The "sailī" is emblematic of the dress of those who turned faḳīrs through grief for Ḥasan and Ḥusain. With them it was made of hair. Kānūn-i Islām, p. 188. Shakespear pronounces it "selī": the Ḳānūn-i Islām and Forbes' text make it "sailī." Forbes' Voc., "selī"!!

[88] Literally, "place of the Ḳiblah," or point to which the face is turned in prayer,—a respectful title.

given in marriage to a merchant's son of another city. She was living in her father-in-law's house. In brief, what limit is there to the fondness and indulgence of one who has so much wealth and but one boy? I, the faḳīr, was brought up with much tenderness under the shade of my parents, and began to learn reading and writing, the profession and science of a soldier, and the ledger and accounts of mercantile business. Up to fourteen years (my life) passed in much happiness and freedom from care, no worldly anxiety entered my mind. All of a sudden, in one and the same year, by the Divine decree, both my parents died.

My grief was of an extraordinary kind, which I cannot describe. All at once I became an orphan. No elder or superior remained over my head. From this sudden calamity I remained weeping night and day. I entirely left off eating and drinking. Forty days somehow or other passed away. On the fortieth day my own relations, and strangers small and great, assembled. When the Fātiḥah[89] had been concluded, all fastened on the faḳīr (*i.e.* on me) the turban of his father, and admonished him (as follows): "In the world the parents of all (men) have continued and continue to die, and you too must one day die; have patience therefore; make an inspection of your house; now in the place of your father you have become the head; be on the alert in your business and proceedings." Having given me consolation they took leave. All the agents, managers, servants, and attendants that there were, came and were present; they presented offerings and said, "Be pleased to survey with your auspicious glance, the storehouse of treasure and goods." When my sight all at once fell on that countless

---

[89] The Fātiḥah is the offering of prayers to God for the remission of sin and acceptance into heaven of him in whose name it is desired. It consists in saying, "For such or such a one I offer this prayer," and then, repeating the first chapter of the Ḳu'rān, "Praise be to God, the Lord of all creatures, the most merciful, the king of the day of judgment, Thee do we worship, and of Thee do we beg assistance. Direct us in the right way, in the way of those to whom Thou hast been gracious; not of those against whom Thou art incensed, nor of those who go astray." It is called the Fātiḥah chapter, and is followed, when read for the dead, by the 111th chapter, called Ḳulh ullāh.

wealth, my eyes were opened. I gave orders for the preparation of the public hall-of-audience. The carpet-spreaders having spread the carpets, fastened up costly curtains and screens, and engaged as servants excellent and handsome personal attendants. At my expense they caused to be made for them splendid garments. I, the faḳīr, sate down on an ottoman, propped up with pillows. A set of men, all of the same class, fops, coxcombs, parasites, false flatterers, came, formed my acquaintance, and became my companions. I began to remain in their society during the eight watches. They spake of all sorts of matters, chattering with tales of this and that, and were saying, "In this season of youth, be pleased to extract the wine of the 'ketakī,' [90] or of the rose. Send for delicate mistresses, and with them drink and make merry."

In short, the tempter of man is man. From continually speaking and hearing, my nature also was led astray. I began to discuss wine, the dance, and gaming. After that the time arrived that I forgot my business as a merchant, and employed myself in debauchery, and in raising money on loan. My servants and companions, when they perceived this carelessness, made away with whatever fell into the hands of each. You may say they plundered me of it. I had no information as to how much money was spent, whence it came, or whither it went! Property that is got for nothing, the heart has no mercy on it. To meet this vast expenditure, had I had the treasure of Ḳārūn,[91] even then it would not have sufficed. In the space of a few years my state became all of a sudden such, that I had nothing left but my hat and a girdle for my loins. My friends and acquaintances, who were eating the bread I had bitten,[92] and in every word spoke of sacrificing [92] for me a spoonful of their own blood, vanished.[93] Moreover, if I met or encountered them anywhere in the road, or by the way, they averted their eyes, and turned away their faces; and my

---

[90] The "Pandanus odoratissimus."

[91] Ḳārūn is the Crœsus of Indian writers. He is by some said to have been Korah, the cousin of Moses.

[92] Proverbial phrases, expressive of devoted attachment.

[93] Literally, "became camphor," because that substance quickly evaporates.

servants and attendants, body-servants, huntsmen, targeteers, matchlock-men, men attired after the device of Ṣābit Khān, all forsook me and held aloof. Not a single inquirer was left to ask me, What has your condition become? No companion remained to me, but grief and regret. Now a quarter of a farthing's[94] worth of parched grain was not obtainable for me to chew and drink water. After enduring two or three severe fasts, I was unable to support the violence of my hunger. Having no resource, I cast the veil of shamelessness over my face, and made the resolve of going to my sister. But this scruple was rising in my heart, that after the decease of my father I had had no friendly communication with my sister, nor even written to her a mere letter; nay, two letters or so of condolence and affection, which she had written, I, in this waking[95] dream, had not even answered. From this sense of shame my mind, indeed, was unwilling, but I saw no other resting-place but her house. Somehow or other, on foot, empty-handed, and with great[96] difficulty, after a thousand labours, I travelled over the few stages, reached the city of my sister, and arrived at her abode. That uterine sister, when she saw this my state, having taken my calamities[97] upon her, and embraced my neck, wept much. She offered[98] for me oil, vetches (the *Phaseolus*

---

[94] The Damṛī is the one-eighth of a pice, and one pice = two farthings. According to the Kānūn-i Islām, four damṛī = one paisā. *Vide* Glossary.

[95] Literally, "sleep of a hare," because the hare is said to sleep with its eyes open.

[96] Literally, "stumbling and falling." The Persian افتان و خیزان *uftān o khīzān*.

[97] بلائیں لینا *balā'en lenā*, or taking another's evils on oneself, is a form of blessing. The ceremony is performed by drawing the hands over the head of the person blessed, and cracking one's fingers on one's own temples. It is only practised by women. Ḳānūn-i Islām, p. 92, *note*.

[98] The Ṣadḳah, or propitiatory offering, is had recourse to for the removal of disease. There are several ways. They take كلتي *kultī*, "glycine tomentosa" or Madras horse-gram (Shakespear has only كلتبي *kulthī*, which he renders "dolichos bi-florus"); مونگ *mūng*, "phaseolus radiatus" (Linn.), "phaseolus aureus" (Roxb.), green gram or rayed kidney-bean; أڑود *aṛūd*, "phaseolus mungo," or black gram; تل *tal*, "sesamum orientale or gingilie oil seed," etc., put into separate baskets, and place on the contents of one of them a cup filled with oil, into which they look as into a mirror, and drop a copper coin or two, and give them to the poor. There are three other methods of performing the ceremony. *See* Ḳānūn-i Islām, p. 96, *Glossary*.

radiatus), and copper[99] coins, and began to say, "Although my heart is greatly delighted at (our) meeting; but, brother! what state is this to which you have come?" I was unable to give her any answer. My eyes filled with tears, and I remained silent. My sister having caused a rich robe to be quickly sewed for me, sent me into the warm bath. After bathing and washing, I put on those clothes. She assigned me a good abode, handsomely furnished, near herself, for my residence. In the morning she ordered and caused me to partake, in her presence, of various delicious dainties, as sharbat[100] and almond cakes, ḥalwā[101] of sohan, pistachio nuts, kernels, for breakfast; and at the third watch (three p.m.) fruits dried and fresh, and of various kinds; and twice during the twenty-four hours pulāo,[102] leavened bread, broiled flesh, kabābs.[103] In every way she consoled and took care of me. After such distress, when I obtained this comfort, I offered thousands and thousands of thanksgivings at the shrine of God. Some months passed in this cessation from employment, and I did not step beyond that retirement.

One day that sister, who was cherishing me as a mother, began to say, "O brother! thou art the pupil of my eye, and the token of the dead clay of my parents. By thy arrival my liver[104] has been refreshed. When I look upon thee I am gladdened. Thou hast made me joyful,[105] but God has made men

---

[99] The Ṭakā is a copper coin = two pice.

[100] Sharbat, sugar and water, *eau sucrée*, with sometimes aniseed or cardamoms.

[101] حلوا *ḥalwā*, is a sweet cake, made of two pounds of flour fried in one pound of clarified butter, and five or six pounds of syrup, three tolas of cocoa-nut kernel, one tola of spices, viz., cinnamon one stick, ten cloves, ten cardamoms, and a little aniseed. Mix over a fire. Ḳānūn-i Islām, Appendix, p. 40.

[102] The Pulāo is a dish of rice and meat, for which there are various receipts. *Vide* Ḳānūn-i Islām, Appendix, p. 37.

[103] The Ḳaliyah is broiled meat dressed with anything, and usually eaten with pulāo. The Kabāb is meat cut into squares or thin lengths, dried in the sun, and roasted on live coals or fire, with clarified butter. Ḳānūn-i Islām, Appendix, p. 34.

[104] The Orientals assign to the liver those sensations which we refer to the heart, such as joy, grief, anger, etc.

[105] Another play on words. نهال *nihāl*, which here signifies "joyful," means also "a young plant," and is chosen with reference to the باغ باغ *bāgh bāgh*, which precedes, here meaning "glad," but being the reduplication of a word signifying "a garden."

for the purpose of gaining a subsistence! It befits thee not to remain seated in the house. The man who idly broods at home, on him the people of the world vent sarcasms and reproaches; and especially the inhabitants of this city, small and great, will say with reference to your causeless [106] stay, 'After destroying and consuming the wealth and substance of his father, he has come and fallen on the pittance of his sister's husband.' This is a great disgrace and cause of ridicule to me and you, and a means of discredit attaching to the name of our parents. Else I would make shoes of my skin, and cause you to put them on,[107] and would place and keep you in my heart (literally, 'liver'). Now this is my advice. Resolve on (taking) a journey. God willing, the times will change, and in place of this distress and poverty, contentment and pleasure will be obtained." Having heard this speech, my pride, too, was roused. I assented to her advice, and replied, "Very good! you are now in the place of my mother, what you say that I will do." Having obtained this my consent, she entered the house, and having caused to be brought by the hands of her maids and female slaves fifty purses [108] of gold coins, she brought and placed them before me, and said, "A caravan of merchants is going to Damascus. Do you purchase with these rupees goods for traffic. Commit them to the charge of some merchant of integrity, and cause him to write for you a full receipt, and do you yourself set out for Damascus. When you have safely arrived there, settle your accounts, and take back your money, with the profit (accruing to you), or sell (the goods) yourself." I took that money and went to the bāzār. Having purchased merchandise, I entrusted it to an eminent merchant. I satisfied my mind as to the papers.[109] The merchant embarked in a ship and set out by way of the sea. I (the faḳīr) made preparations for proceeding by land. When I was about to take leave, my sister presented

---

[106] This translation gives the better sense. According to the collocation it is rather "will causelessly say."

[107] A proverbial expression for extreme devotedness.

[108] The Toṛā is a purse or bag containing 1,000 rupees.

[109] Literally, "writing and reading."

me with a costly vest, covering the body from head to foot, and a horse with jewelled housings, and having filled a canteen with sweetmeats, suspended it from the pommel of my saddle, and caused a leathern bottle of water to be fastened in the cords (attached to the saddle for suspending game). She tied on my arm the rūpī of the protecting Imām,[110] and having made a mark on my forehead with curds, gulping down her tears, she said, "Set forward! I have entrusted thee to God; as you are departing turning your back, in the same manner, quickly shew (again) your face." I, having recited the fātiḥah[111] for the living, said, "Of you also God is the protector. I have accepted (your good wishes)." Having gone forth thence I mounted my horse, and having placed my reliance on God, making two marches in one, I arrived in Damascus.

In short, when I reached the gate of the city much of the night had passed. The gatekeepers and guard had closed the gate. I besought them much, (saying), "I am a traveller. I come from a distance, having made a hurried journey; if you will open one of the folding doors, I will enter the city and obtain the refreshment of corn and grass." They answered me surlily from within, "At this time it is forbidden to open the gate; why come you when the night is so far advanced?" When I heard a flat refusal from them, I dismounted from my horse under the wall of the rampart, and having spread out my saddle-cloth, sate down. To keep myself awake I began to walk up and down. At the time when half the night was on this side and half on that it became still. What do I see (then) but that a box is being let down from the wall of the fort. Having seen this, I was astonished, saying, "What spell is this? Perhaps God, having taken pity on my distress and perplexity, has bestowed (somewhat) on me from his secret

---

110 On undertaking a journey, or when misfortune befalls a person, they tie up a pice, a quarter or half rūpī, or a metallic ring, called a Chhallā, in a bit of cloth dyed yellow with turmeric, in the name of Imām Ẓāmin, and wear it on the left upper arm. On arrival, this coin is used to purchase food for holy men.

111 The فاتحهٔ خير *fātiḥah-i khair*, is for the living, in contra-distinction to other fātiḥahs, which are for the dead.

treasury." When the box rested on the ground, I went up to it filled with fear. I saw then that it was a chest of wood. I opened it greedily. A beautiful lady, a woman of lovely appearance, at sight of whom my senses departed, lay writhing there with closed eyes, wounded, and steeped in blood. Slowly her lips moved, and these words proceeded from her mouth, "O faithless wretch! O unjust and cruel one! was this, forsooth, that thou hast done, the return for this kindness and friendship! Well, inflict one more blow. I have committed to God the decision of what is just between me and thee." Having said this, in the same state of insensibility she drew the corner of her shawl over her face;[112] she did not direct her attention to me.

I, the faḳīr, having seen her, and heard these words, became sad.[113] It entered my mind, "What shameless tyrant, and for what cause, has wounded so delicate a beauty? what came into his heart? and why did he direct his hand against her? In her heart, indeed, affection still remains, that in this agony of death she recalls him to mind." I had continued saying this to myself; the sound reached her ears. For a moment (literally, "one time") she withdrew the cloth from her face and looked at me. When our glances encountered, a faintness came over me, and my heart grew dark. With an effort I supported myself, (and) taking courage, inquired, "Tell the truth, who are you, and what is this that has happened? If you will explain it, then my heart will be comforted." Having heard this, though she had not the power to talk, she (nevertheless) said, softly, "Thanks! my state is such as it is through wounds. What dirt shall I utter? I am the guest of a few moments; when my life departs, then, for God's sake, be generous, and be pleased to bury me, wretched, somewhere in this very chest. Then I shall find release from the tongues of both those who speak well of me and those who speak ill, and thou wilt receive the reward of thy good deed." Having said thus much she became silent.

---

[112] The Dūpaṭṭah (literally, "two breadths") is a cloth thrown loosely over the shoulders. It should have a seam in its centre to indicate its being of two breadths, whence the name; but vulgarly the name is applied to any cloth thus worn.

[113] A play on words, *sun-kar* "having heard," *sun hūā* "was sad."

It being night I could devise nothing. I lifted up the chest and brought it near me, and began to count the hours, saying, "When will this long night be ended! that having gone with morning into the city, I may procure, to the utmost of my ability, whatever remedy there may be for her." That short remainder of the night was so tedious (literally, "such a mountain"), that my heart was in perplexity. At length, when, as I continued invoking the name of God, the morn drew near, the cock crew, and the voices of men began to reach me. I, having repeated the morning prayer, bound the chest on my saddle bags. The instant the door of the city was opened I entered. I began to inquire of every person and shopkeeper for a house to let. Seeking on, I engaged a new, handsome, and spacious mansion, and went and alighted there. First, I removed the fair one from the chest, and having made a soft bed on flocks of cotton, I layed her down in a corner, and having left there a person on whom I could depend, I went out in search of a surgeon. I was going about inquiring of every one, saying, "Who is a skilful surgeon in this city, and where does he live?" A person said, "There is a barber, who has no equal in the profession of surgery and science of medicine, and who is very perfect in this business. If you were to take a dead man to him, he would, with God's permission, devise such means that all at once even he would rise up alive. He lives in this quarter of the city, and his name is Īsạ."

Having heard this gratifying intelligence, I went on eagerly (literally, "involuntarily"). Continuing to search, I arrived, according to the direction, at his door. I saw a man with a white beard seated at the portico, and several persons pounding something in order to prepare an ointment. I, to flatter him, made him a respectful salutation, and said, "I am come, having heard of your name and virtues. What has happened is this, that I left my country to trade; through affection I took my wife with me. When I arrived near this city I was still at a little distance when evening fell. I did not think it right to travel at night in an unknown country. I alighted in the plain under a tree. At the last watch I was attacked by robbers; whatever goods they found they carried off. Through the greedy desire of her ornaments they wounded the lady also. I could do nothing—what remained of the night I got through somehow or other; as soon as it dawned I came into the city and hired a house. Having left her there I have come hastening to you. God has given you this perfect skill; shew kindness to this traveller; be pleased to honour my poor house by going thither. Examine her; if she survives, then great will be your renown, and I will be your slave all my life." The surgeon, Īsạ, was very tender-hearted and pious. He took pity on my humble words, and came with me to that house. On seeing the wounds, he comforted me (and) said, "By the grace of God the wounds of this lady will be healed in forty days, (and) I will cause her to take the bath of convalescence.

In short, that man of God having washed all the wounds with the water of the Nīm tree (Melia Azadirachta) cleansed them. Those that he found proper to be stitched he sewed up. On some of the rest of the wounds he placed bandages, taking out a little box from his pocket; and on others he spread plaster, and bound them up with a fillet, and said, with much kindness, "I will come twice (a day, *i.e.* 'morning and evening'). Do thou remain watchful; let her not move in such a way that the stitches should burst. For food, pour into her throat some chicken-broth, and give her frequently the juice of the musk-willow with rose-water to keep up her strength." Having said this, he requested leave to depart. I expressed my deep obligation to him, and having joined my hands, said, "From the consolation you have given me my life also is saved; otherwise I saw nothing before me but death. May God keep you in safety!" Having presented him with extract[113] of roses and betel, I waited on that fairy[114] night and day. I forbade myself rest.[115] At the shrine of God I was daily imploring the blessing of her recovery.

It chanced that that merchant also arrived and delivered to

---

[113] It is the custom with Indians, on the departure of a visitor, to sprinkle him with ātṛ, and present him with some betel-leaf.

[114] Parī—the "Peri" of "Lālah Rukh," or Anglicè, "Lalla Rookh." From "parī" comes our "fairy."

[115] A play on words, being, literally, "I made Ārām" or "rest,"—ḥarām "unlawful."

me the goods that I had entrusted to him. I sold them for more or less (*i.e.*, for what I could get), and began to lay out money in medicines and remedies. That surgeon was always coming and going. In a short space of time all the wounds were filled, and formed granulations. After some days she took the bath of convalescence. The delight I experienced was of an extraordinary description. I placed before the barber Īsa a robe of honour and pieces of gold, and having spread a costly carpet for that fairy, seated her on an ottoman. I distributed much alms to the poor. On that day, the empire of the seven regions of the earth, as you might say, came into the possession of this faḳīr, and the complexion of that fairy brightened up to such a degree from her recovery, that her face began to shine like the sun, and to beam forth like pure gold. The sight had no power to rest upon her beauty. I waited on her commands with the utmost devotion;[117] whatever she directed, that I did. She, in the haughtiness of her beauty and the pride of her power, if at times she looked towards me, used to say, "Take care! if thou desirest to please me, then never utter a word as to what concerns me. What I say, that continue to do without excuse; do not interfere in anything; otherwise thou wilt repent." From her manner it was apparent that she undoubtedly considered what was due to me for the attention and respect I showed her. I, too, did nothing without her permission. I performed her orders with entire devotion.[116]

A long interval passed in this loving confidence. Whatever she commissioned, that I brought immediately and laid before her. Whatever property and cash I possessed, principal and profit, was all expended. In that foreign country, who would trust me, so that I might carry on matters by borrowing and (incurring) debt? At last I began to be distressed for my daily expenses. From this my heart became much perplexed. I became emaciated with anxiety. My complexion turned sallow, but to whom could I speak? What my heart suffered, that it suffered. The sufferings of a Darwesh are (known) to the heart of a Darwesh. One day that fairy having, through her

---

[116] Literally, "with my head and eyes."

quickness, discerned (this), said, "O such a one![117] the obligation of thy attentions is indelibly[118] engraved on my mind, but at this moment I am unable to requite thee for them. If anything is required for necessary expenses, have no anxiety in thy heart —bring me a piece of paper, and an inkstand and pen." I then perceived that she was a princess of some country, in that she spoke with such pride and haughtiness. I at once placed a writing-case[119] before her. That lady wrote a mandate with her own hand, delivered it to me, and said, "Near the Fort is a building with three arches. There, in that street, is a rather large house. The name of the owner of it is Sīdī Bahār: go there and convey this note." I, the faḳīr, in accordance with her commands, according to that same name and direction, went and arrived at the desired place. I sent information of the circumstance of the note, by means of a porter. Thereupon, immediately on hearing of it, an Abyssinian, young and good-looking, wearing an elegant turban, came forth. Though his colour was dark, yet he was, as you might say, all filled with salt.[120] He took the letter from my hand, said nothing, and asked nothing. He retraced his steps just as he came, and went in again. After a short interval he came out, having placed on the heads of slaves eleven trays sealed up, with purse-covers of brocade thrown over them. He said, "Go with this young man, and convey the (square) trays." I also took leave, after saluting him, and brought them to my house. The men I dismissed outside the door. The trays I carried into the presence of that fairy just as I had received them. When she saw them, she said, "Take those eleven bags of gold pieces, and disburse from them. God is the provider." I, the faḳīr, having taken that cash, began to expend it in necessary outlay: though I was gratified, still this inquietude remained (which led me to exclaim), "O God! what state of things is this? that a stranger, with whom I am entirely unacquainted, has consigned to me

---

117 A familiar expression, half contemptuous, half kind, like "thingumy," "old fellow."

118 Literally, "carved on stone."

119 Literally, "penholder."

120 That is, "he was piquant-looking, vivacious, and sprightly."

without question or inquiry so vast a sum on (receipt of) a mere scrap of paper. If I would inquire this secret of the lady (then I must recollect) that she from the very first forbade me." Through fear I could not utter a word.

After eight days, that fair one, addressing me, said, "God Most High has bestowed on man the garb of humanity, which can neither burst nor become soiled. Although old clothes make no difference in his quality as a man, yet externally he does not find credit in the eyes of the people of God. Take with thee two purses of gold pieces, and go into the centre of the market, where the four roads meet, to the shop of the merchant Yūsuf, and having purchased some valuable jewels and two magnificent dresses, return." I immediately mounted and went to the shop. I saw there a handsome youth, dressed in a yellow suit of clothes, and seated on a cushion; and such was his beauty that a multitude was standing from his shop as far as the bāzār, to look at him. I, the faḳīr, with the greatest eagerness approached him, and having made the salutation "Peace be to thee!" sate down, and asked for the things I wanted. My speech was not like that of the inhabitants of that city. That youth said with cordiality, "Whatever your honour requires, is all ready; but be pleased to tell me this—from what country have you come? or what is the cause of your stay in this foreign city? If you will be pleased to acquaint me with these circumstances, then it will be in accordance with (literally, 'not far from') kind feeling." For me to disclose my story, was not desirable. Having framed some tale, and taken the jewels and dresses, I gave the price of them and requested leave to depart. The youth was annoyed, and said, "O Sir! if you intended to act with such coldness, what necessity was there for making friends at first with such warmth? With gentlemen great regard is had to the offer of a salutation." He spoke with such taste and grace, that my heart was involuntarily conciliated, and I thought it not agreeable to politeness to get up from thence in an unfriendly manner. For his sake I again sate down, and said, "Your commands are upon my head and eyes. I am at your service" (literally "I am present"). He was much gratified by my saying thus much, and began to say, smiling, "If you would be pleased to honour my

3

poor house this day, then, by your favour, we would assemble a party of pleasure, and amuse ourselves for two or four hours; and, seated together, we will employ ourselves in eating and drinking." I had never left that fairy by herself. I remembered her solitariness, and proffered sundry excuses; but the youth would in no wise admit them. At length, having taken a promise from me that I would return, after conveying those things, and having made me take an oath, he allowed me to go. I rose from the shop, and conveyed the jewels and dresses into the presence of that fairy. She inquired the price of the jewels, and what related to the jeweller. I informed her of all the circumstances of the purchase, and of his insisting on entertaining me. She began to say, "It is incumbent on a man to fulfil his engagement. Leave me under the protection of God, and keep your promise. To accept of an entertainment is a traditionary precept of the Prophet."[121] I then said, "My heart is unwilling to go and leave you alone—yet your order is so. Having no resource, I go—until I return, my heart will be fixed here." Having said this, I returned to the shop of the jeweller. He, seated on a stool, was waiting for me. As soon as he saw me, he said, "Come, kind friend! you have kept me waiting a long time."

Forthwith he arose, took my hand, and went on. Proceeding onwards, he conducted me into a garden. This garden was of great beauty. In reservoirs and rivulets, fountains were springing up. Fruits of various kinds were growing there—each tree was bending under the weight. Birds of various kinds seated upon them continued warbling, and in every elevated place[122] fair carpets had been spread. There, on the brink of a stream, was a summer-house, into which he went and sat down.

---

[121] سُنّت *sunnat*, the traditions of Muḥammad, which by the orthodox Musālman (thence called "Sunnīs") are considered as a supplement to the Ḳu'rān, and of nearly equal authority. They are, however, rejected as apocryphal by the Shīāhs. Ḳānūn-i Islām, Gloss.

[122] "Ālīshān" generally means "magnificent," "dignified," as, صاحبانِ عالیشان *ṣāḥibān-i ālīshān* "the dignified gentlemen"; *i.e.* "European officers." Here, however, it seems to mean "elevated," a signification most rare. But no building has been spoken of, of which "makān" might be an apartment.

After a moment, he himself rose and went out. He returned, having put on another and a becoming dress. When I saw it, I said, "Praise be to God! far be the evil eye!" Having heard this he smiled and said, "It is fit that your honour, too, should change your dress." For his sake I, too, changed my clothes. The youth had prepared the entertainment with great elegance, and had brought there all the paraphernalia that were requisite for making merry. And having formed a warm intimacy with me, the faḳīr, he began to address me in an impassioned way. Meanwhile the cupbearer waited on us with a flagon and cup of crystal, and having brought relishes of various kinds, set them down. He set in order the salt-cellars,—the wine began to circulate. When it came to the time of the second or fourth cup, four beardless youths of great beauty, with flowing ringlets, came into the assembly and began to play and sing. Such was their beauty and such the harmony, that had Tān Sen[123] been there at that time, he would have forgotten his tune,[124] and Baijūbāorā[124] would have gone mad. In this delightful moment the eyes of the young man all of a sudden filled with tears. Two or three drops involuntarily fell from him, and he said to me, the faḳīr, "Now between me and you a friendship of the soul is formed; to conceal, therefore, the secrets of the heart from friends is, in no religion, (considered) right. I am about to tell you without ceremony a thing in the confidence of friendship. If you will permit me (literally, give orders), I will summon my mistress into this assembly and comfort my heart; separated from her, my heart is not at ease."

He spoke this with such fervour, that, without having seen her, my heart also longed (to behold her). I said, "Your gratification is to me indispensable—what is better than this? Be pleased to make no delay. It is true, nothing seems good without one's mistress." The young man made a sign towards a lattice. Immediately a woman of the blackest complexion, like

---

123 "Tān Sen"—a celebrated musican of the time of Akbar.

124 A play on words, "Tān Sen" being the man's name, and *tān*, "tune," and *bāorā* and *bāolā* both signifying "mad."

a she-devil, at sight of whom a man would die prematurely, came towards the youth and sate down near him. I, the faḳīr, was affrighted at the sight of her. I said, in my heart, "Is this monster (lit. calamity) the beloved one of such a fairy-born youth, and is it of her that he has uttered such praise, and for her that he has evinced such desire?"[125] I recited the deprecatory formula, "There is no power nor virtue but in God," and remained silent. In the same state for three days and nights the company remained assembled (enjoying) wine, music, and conviviality. On the fourth night I was overpowered by intoxication and sleep. Involuntarily I fell asleep in the slumber of forgetfulness. When the morning came that youth awoke me. Having caused me to drink some cups of a beverage proper for dispelling intoxication, he said to his mistress, "Now it is not right to trouble our guest any longer."

Both taking hands, arose.[126] I asked leave to depart; he readily allowed me to go. I then quickly put on my former clothes and took the way home, and having entered the presence of the fairy, waited on her. However, such an occurrence had never happened as that I should leave her alone and stay out the night anywhere. I was much ashamed at that three days' absence, and made excuses, and related the whole story of the entertainment, and of his not permitting me to go. She was well acquainted with the world. She smiled and said, "What does it matter if thou hast stopped to oblige a friend? I have pardoned thee—what fault hast thou committed? When a man goes to any one's house, then he returns at his pleasure, but will you keep quiet after receiving (literally, 'eating and drinking') these unreturned civilities, or will you return them? Now this is incumbent on you, to go and bring that merchant's son with you, and entertain him twice as well, and have no anxiety about the (necessary) furniture. By the favour of God all the requisites shall be got ready in one moment, and

---

125 With deference to Mīr Amman, this is bad grammar. It should be—جس كي اتني تعريف كركے ايسا اشتياق ظاهر كيا *jis kī itnī târīf karke aisā ishtiyāḳ ẓāhir kiyā.*

126 This might also be rendered "having grasped both my hands, they arose."

the party of entertainment shall be well adorned." I, according to her order, went to the jeweller and said, "I have obeyed your wishes with my head and eyes; now do you also in a friendly way accept my petition." He said, "I am ready with my heart and soul."

I then said, "If you will condescendingly come to the house of this (your) slave, it will be an especial favouring of the poor." The youth made many excuses and evasions, but I did not cease to urge him until he consented. I took him along with myself to my house. But on the road I was proceeding pondering this very thing, saying to myself, "Had I the power to-day, I would shew him such attention that he would be pleased. Now I am taking him along with me, let us see what occurs." In this same dilemma I arrived near the house—then what do I see? A bustle is going on at the door. The streets have been swept and sprinkled. Pursuivants and mace-bearers are standing there. I was amazed, but knowing it to be my own house, I stepped in. I saw then, throughout the mansion, costly carpets fit for each apartment spread in each place, and cushions set. Betel-boxes,[127] vials for sprinkling rose-water, and others for holding Ītr, spittoons, flower-pots, pots of narcissus, were placed in order. In the recesses are ranged various kinds of orange-trees and flowers of divers hues. On one side is the lustre of lamps in frames of variegated talc. On the other side, shrubs[128] and cypresses and lotus-plants are shining. And throughout the hall and the balconies, candles white as camphor[129] are placed on gilt candlesticks, and jewelled shades

---

[127] The Pāndān is a box of gold, silver, copper, or brass, for holding betel or its appendages. The Gulābpāsh is a bottle of glass, gold, or silver, out of which rose-water is sprinkled. The Ītrdān is a vial for containing ītr. The Pīkdān or spittoon is of gold, silver, copper, brass, etc. Ķānūn-i Islām, p. 120.

[128] The reading in the text is little better than nonsense. It should be either, جهاڙ اور سرو كنول كي روشين هين *jhāṛ aur sarv kanwal kī ravishen haiṇ*, "shrubs and avenues of the cypress and lotus;" or with the اور *aur* omitted— جهاڙ سرو كنول كے روشن هين *jhāṛ saro kanwal ke roshan haiṇ*, "shrubs of the cypress and lotus are bright."

[129] كافوري *kāfūrī*, in Forbes' vocabulary, is rendered "made of camphor," a meaning here inadmissible.

are placed over them. All persons are ready in their respective offices. In the kitchen, pots remained clattering; in the room for cooling water, there was the same preparation. Water-pots entirely new were placed on silver stands with percolators attached and covered with vessels for hot water.[130] Further on were set, on a bench, spoons, metal bowls, with salvers and covers. Adjoining, were narrow-mouthed vessels of ice, and flagons were moved briskly in saltpetre.[131]

In short, all the furniture befitting royalty was there, and dancing girls, actors, dancing boys dressed as girls, singers, performers on the Sārangī or Ṭambūrah or Ḍholak, clothed in handsome dresses, were present, playing in concert with their instruments. I conducted the youth to an ottoman, where I seated him; and was in my heart perplexed, saying, "O God! in so short an interval how were all these preparations made?" I went about looking on every side, but nowhere found a trace of that fairy. In this same search I all at once came out in the direction of the kitchen. I beheld in an apartment there, that delicate lady, with a shirt on her neck, slippers on her feet, and wearing on her head a white handkerchief, simple, nude, divested of her ornaments.

> She wants no ornaments to whom God has beauty given;
> Behold how fair the unadorned moon (in heaven).

She continued engaged in superintending the banquet, and in giving injunctions as to each dish, saying, "Take care that it is well-flavoured, and that the gravy, seasoning, and smell is correct." In this laborious occupation, that rose-like form was all bathed in perspiration.[132]

---

[130] An intolerable absurdity; yet this is the only meaning given in the dictionary. Is it not rather likely that بجهرا *bujhrā* = بدهنا *badhnā*, "a drinking vessel with a spout to it"?

[131] Literally, "flagons of saltpetre," which gives no sense; unless the شوره *shorah*, be here for آبشوره *ābshorah*, or افشره, *afshurah*, lemonade made with the juice of pomegranates, quinces, lemons, etc., for which see Ḳānūn-i Islām, Appendix, p. 41. Bottles of wine are cooled, in India, by being briskly moved round in water in which saltpetre has been dissolved.

[132] Literally, "was sweat, sweat."

I went up to her and expressed my devotion for her, and after extolling her cleverness and skill, began to utter benedictions. When she heard this flattery, she frowned[133] and said, "Sundry things are done by human beings, which an angel has not the power to do.[134] What have I done of such a nature that you are so astounded? Enough! Long speeches do not please me. Come now! tell me what sort of politeness is this, to leave your guest seated by himself, and go wandering about in this place and that? What will he be saying in his own mind? Go quickly! take your seat among the company, and pay attention to your visitor, and having sent for his mistress also, cause her to sit beside him." I[135] immediately went to the young man and began to display a warm regard for him. Meanwhile two beautiful slaves, holding in their hands a flagon and a jewelled cup, came before us and began to supply us with wine. Hereupon I said to that youth, "I am in all respects your sincere friend and servant. It is better[136] that that beautiful lady towards whom your heart is inclined, should honour us with her presence; then, indeed, it will be highly delightful.[137] If you command, then a person shall go to call her." On hearing this, he was pleased and said, "Very good! this time you have spoken the thought[138] of my heart." I despatched a eunuch (for her). When the night was half spent, that hag,[139] borne on a splendid sedan with two poles, arrived like a sudden calamity.

I, having no resource, in order to please my guest, went out to meet her, and with extreme cordiality conducted her in, and seated her beside the youth. The young man, on beholding

---

133 Literally, "mounted a frown."

134 That is "are too gross and material for spiritual beings, to which you compare me."

135 The narrator of the story generally styles himself "the faḳīr," as in this place; but instead of this oblique form, the pronoun of the first person is used in the translation, as more suitable to the English idiom.

136 Or as we say, "best." In this phrase the comparative is used in Persian for our superlative.

137 Literally, "a great thing."

138 Literally, "thing" or "word."

139 چڑیل *churail*, is, properly, the ghost of a woman deceased in pregnancy.

her, was as delighted as if he had obtained all the good things in the world. That she-devil, too, clung round the neck of that fairy-born youth; in real truth, the sight was as when an eclipse happens to the moon of the fourteenth night. All the persons who were in the assembly began to press their fingers with their teeth,[140] saying, "What! has some calamitous influence overpowered this youth?" The gaze of all was turned in that same direction. Forgetting the spectacle of the entertainment, they began to look at the spectacle of his doings. One person said, aside, "Friends! there is a contrariety between love and reason. Whatever is incongruous to reason, this infidel love is sure to display. Look at Laiḷa with the eyes of Majnūn."[141] All responded, "It is true! it is just as you say."

I, according to the order I had received, remained in attendance on my guests; but although the youth pressed me to partake of the goblet and the viands, I, through fear of that fairy, was not giving my mind to the repast or the spectacle; and, excusing myself on the ground of my duties as a host, did not partake. In this same way three nights and days were spent. On the fourth night that youth, having called me to him, very affectionately began to say, "We, too, will now take leave; for your sake I have left all my business and waited in your service for three days. Do you also, then, sit beside me for a moment and gratify my heart." I reflected in my mind that if at this time I did not assent to what he said, he would be hurt, and I felt it necessary to oblige a new friend, and one who was my guest. I then said this, "I desire to obey your commands, for a command is before manners.[142] On hearing

---

[140] A Persian phrase expressive of astonishment. In the native picture-illustrations of the "Shāh-nāmah," the spectators of Rustam's combats with dæmons, are represented as thus expressing their wonderment.

[141] "Majnūn" or "distracted" is the name of an Arabian lover, who was enamoured of one Laiḷa, perhaps so called from her dark complexion, that word signifying in Arabic "night." She had no pretensions to beauty, but he was madly infatuated with her. *See* "Gulistān," chap. v. story 19. Their loves have been sung by Niẓāmī and others, and have passed into a proverb.

[142] The meaning of this proverb seems to be here, "Good manners would keep me waiting on you as my guest, but since you command it, I will join you in the repast."

this, the youth presented me with a cup, and I quaffed it. The wine then circulated so incessantly, that in a brief space of time all the persons assembled, being intoxicated, were deprived of their senses, and I, too, became insensible.

When it was morning, and the sun had risen two spears' length, I opened my eyes. Then I beheld that neither those preparations nor that assembly were there, nor that lady; only the empty house was left; but in one corner was set a rough woollen cloth wrapped up. When I opened that and looked, then (I beheld) the young man and his mistress, both with their heads severed, lying there. On seeing this their state, my senses departed. My reason was of no use to me (to discover) what this was or what had happened. Through perplexity I continued staring about me in every direction. Meanwhile an eunuch, whom I had observed [employed] in the business of the entertainment, shewed himself. I felt somewhat encouraged at the sight of him, and inquired the details of this occurrence. He replied, "What wilt thou gain by inquiry into this matter respecting which thou hast asked?" I, too, reflected in my mind to this effect—"He, in fact, speaks the truth." Then, after meditating for a little, I said, "Well! do not tell me. However, explain this, at least—In what place is that beautiful lady?" He then said, "Assuredly, what I know that I will relate. But for an intelligent man like you to indulge eagerly in a wine-party after a friendship of two days, without permission of her Highness, showing no respect or ceremony towards her—what is the meaning of this?"

I was much ashamed at my misconduct, and at his reproof; my tongue found no utterance besides this word, "Of a truth, now indeed I have done wrong; be pleased to pardon my fault." At length the eunuch, becoming friendly, pointed out to me the direction of the abode of that fairy, and sent me away. He himself tarried behind to look after [143] the burial and interment of those two mutilated bodies. I was (thus) freed from the suspicion of that wicked deed, and was absorbed

---

[143] Literally, "in the thought."

in the desire of rejoining that lady. With much difficulty,[144] searching on, I arrived, in the evening, in the street to which I had been directed, and passed the whole night in a state of great agitation in a corner near the door. No sound of any one's movements reached me,[145] nor was there any one who inquired what I was doing. In that same friendless state, the morning dawned on me. When the sun arose, that moon-faced beauty began to look towards me from the window of an upper apartment of the house. The kind of pleasure which I then experienced my heart alone knows. I returned thanks to God.

Meanwhile an eunuch came to me and said, "Go and seat thyself in this mosque; perhaps thy desire may be then fulfilled, and thou mayest obtain the wish of thy heart." By his command I rose up thence, and went and stopped in the mosque. My eyes, however, were fixed upon the door, and I said to myself,[146] "Let us see what is disclosed from the curtain of the future." As one who fasts, expects through the whole day the time of evening, so I, too, passed that whole day in similar inquietude. At length, somehow or other, evening came and day removed like a mountain from my breast. All at once, the same eunuch who had given me the direction of the lady's house entered the mosque. After performing his evening prayers, that compassionate person, who was the confidante of all our love-affair, approached me, and after much encouragement, took me by the hand, and led me with him. Proceeding on, he caused me to be seated in a little garden and said, "Remain here until your wish is accomplished," and he himself took leave and went, perhaps, to relate my circumstances in the presence. I remained looking at the beauty of the flowers of that garden, and the fair moonlight, and the spectacle of the fountains springing up in the reservoirs and streamlets (as copiously as in) the months of Sāwan and

---

[144] Literally, "stumbling and falling."

[145] In Urdū the negative goes to the verb—"any sound did not," instead of our "no sound did."

[146] For these words we have in the original only که *kih*, "that" or "saying that."

Bhādoṅ.[147] But when I beheld the flowers, then the thought of that rose-formed one was returning to me; when my eyes fell on the moon—then I was recalling to mind the countenance of that moon-faced beauty. All this splendour, without her, was a thorn in my eyes. At length God rendered her heart kindly-disposed to me. After a short interval that fairy, covered from head to foot with pearls, advanced from the door into the avenue, and stood there adorned like the moon of the fourteenth night, wearing on the upper part of her body a gown with a flounce of brocade, to which was stitched a border of pearls, and round her head a mantle which had a fringe, a hem,[148] a waving pattern, and bells attached.[149] By her arrival that garden and the heart of this faḳīr derived fresh life. For a moment she paced up and down[150] and seated herself, supported by pillows, on a cushion embroidered with gold. I ran up, and as the moth circles round the candle, walked round her in token of devotion, then, joining my hands, stood in the attitude of a slave. On this, the same eunuch began to speak on my behalf, and entreat for me. I said to him, "This slave is guilty and has erred, let the punishment be inflicted which is due to my fault." The lady, inasmuch as she was displeased, said haughtily, "As to this person, the best thing now is, that he should take a hundred bags of a thousand gold pieces each, pack up his goods, and depart to his own country."

On hearing this speech, I was petrified,[151] and was dried up, so that if any one had cut my body, not a drop of blood would have issued; and the whole world began to grow dark before my eyes, and a sigh of despair involuntarily escaped from my breast. Tears also began to fall. At that time I had none left

---

147 "Sāwan" is the name of the fourth Hindū month (July—August); "Bhādoṅ," of the fifth (August—September). During these months the rains are at their height. The کے *ke* may be rendered, "as in."

148 The پلّو *pallū*, is a hem of gold or silver thread.

149 This is, perhaps, the longest and most involved sentence in the whole book, and its clumsiness shews how repugnant the genius of the language is to sentences of such a length.

150 This may also be rendered "she surveyed the scenery in this and that direction."

151 Literally "became wood."

to rely upon but God. In utter despair I said, "Well, please to consider a little in your heart. Had I, luckless wretch, been desirous of this world's goods, I should not then have expended my life and property for your Highness. What! have the rights of service and devotion all at once been banished from the world, that you shew such want of kindness to me, unfortunate creature that I am? Well, now life itself is no longer of any use to me. Owing to the neglect of their fair mistresses, helpless and half-expiring lovers find existence insupportable."

Hearing this, she was incensed and, frowning, said angrily, "How nice! *You* are my lover, are you? the frog has caught cold, has it? O blockhead! it is a vain thought to speak words too high for your place.[152] A little mouth and big words[153] (are not suited). Enough! be silent; cease this unprofitable discourse. Had any one else committed this breach of decorum, I swear by the Almighty I would have caused him to be cut into gobbets, and have distributed (his flesh) to the kites: but what can I do? your services return to my recollection. Now the most advantageous plan is this, for you to depart; it was in your destiny to subsist[154] thus long in my dominions." I then, weeping and sobbing, said, "If this be written in my destiny that I should not obtain the desire of my heart, and should wander about in forests and mountains, dashing my head (against the rock), then am I helpless." These words, too, annoyed her, and she began to say, "These disgusting expressions of endearment, and this enigmatical discourse, please me not. Go and address these inuendoes to those whom they befit." Then in the same angry temper she arose and entered her palace. I made many humble entreaties,[155] but she paid no attention to me. Having no resource, I too came forth from that place despairing and hopeless.

In short, for forty days this same state of things continued. When I was sick of wandering through the streets of the

---

[152] Literally "stomach."
[153] A proverb used of those who talk big, or aim at something beyond their rank.
[154] Literally "the grain and water of your destiny was thus long," etc.
[155] Literally, "dashed my head much."

city, I issued forth into the jungle. When I returned with melancholy thence, I again entered the city like one distraught. I neither ate by day nor slept at night. Like the washerman's dog, I had no rest at home or at the steps down to the river.[156] The life of man is supported by eating and drinking. Man is a creature that subsists on grain. No strength at all was left in my body. Having become a cripple, I went and fell down under the wall of that mosque, when one day that same eunuch came to repeat the Friday's prayers. He passed by me. I remained repeating this poetry, but in a low voice through weakness:

> From this heart's grief may death or patience reach my heart,
> Whate'er be written in my fate, O God! that quick impart.

Although my external appearance had become altogether changed, and my countenance had assumed such a look that even those who had seen me before could not have recognized me as the same person,—that eunuch, however, hearing a piteous voice, turned towards me. After surveying me with attention, he uttered an exclamation of sorrowful astonishment,[157] and addressed me compassionately: "This is the condition, then, to which you have at last brought yourself." I said, "Now indeed, what has happened, has happened. I was ready with my property, (with equal readiness I have) devoted my life also (for her). Thus alone could she be gratified—then what can I do?"

Having heard this, he left a servant with me and entered the mosque. When, after finishing his prayers and (hearing) the sermon,[158] he had come out, he placed me in a litter, and taking me along with him into the presence of that neglectful fairy, seated me on the outside of a screen. Although nothing of my former appearance remained, still it had happened that

---

[156] A proverb applied to unquiet persons.

[157] افسوس کیا *afsos kiyā*, signifies also "to lament," but here it is requisite to render it by the above somewhat lengthy expression.

[158] The Khuṭbah is preached every Friday, and, as with us, follows divine service. In it the preacher blesses Muḥammad, his successors, and the reigning monarch of the country.

I had lived with her both night and day for a considerable period (and she must have known me therefore), but intentionally pretending that she did not recognize me, she began to inquire of the eunuch, "Who is this?" That gentleman said, "This is the same unfortunate, ill-fated person who fell under your Highness's displeasure and incurred your reproof. From this very cause, his appearance is thus altered. He is consumed with the fire of love. Though he quenches it with the water of his tears, it nevertheless breaks out with redoubled violence. Nothing is gained, but rather through shame for his error he is perishing." The lady said, jestingly, "Why tellest thou these idle tales? It is many days since my scouts brought me intelligence of his safe arrival in his own country. God knows who this person is and of whom thou art talking!" At that moment the eunuch joined his hands and said respectfully, "If my life be granted to me, I will make a representation." She said, "Speak on! Thy life is granted to thee." The eunuch said, "Your Highness can truly appreciate. For God's sake cause the screen to be removed from between you, and recognize him, and take pity on his friendless state. Ingratitude is not good. He now deserves whatever pity you may be pleased to shew to his condition. To say more would be to transgress the limits of respect. Whatever occurs to your royal mind, that and that alone is best."

She smiled at these words and said, "Well! who waits![159] place this person in the hospital. When he shall have recovered, his circumstances shall be investigated." The eunuch said, "If you would be pleased with your own royal hand to sprinkle rose-water upon him, and would condescend to say something to him, then he would be encouraged to hope for life. Despair is a bad thing. The world is supported by hope." Even to this, that fairy returned no answer. Hearing this dialogue (as I had grown weary of life[160]) I fearlessly exclaimed, "Now my

---

159 This might also be rendered, "Whoever he may be," etc.; the translation given above, however, is most likely the correct one.

160 After these words there is a full stop in Forbes' edition, but instead of it the sentence should be put into a parenthesis, as it is only the reason for—نڈھڑک بول اٹھا *nidharak bol uṭhā*.

heart wishes not for life on these terms. I have already my feet in the grave.[161] Death must come some day, and, as for my cure, it is in the hands of the princess—let her perform it or not, she knows best (what to do)." At length the turner of hearts softened the heart of that hard-hearted one. She became kind, and said, "Summon the royal physicians quickly." The doctors forthwith came and assembled. They inspected my pulse and urine, and deliberated long. At length they decided in their prognosis as follows:—"This person is in love with some one. There is no remedy for him, except in union with his mistress. As soon as he obtains her, he will be restored to health." When the physicians also had pronounced this to be my disease, the princess said, "Conduct this youth to the warm bath, wash him, array him in a handsome robe, and bring him into my presence." They immediately led me out, and having caused me to take the bath, dressed me in good clothes, and brought me into the presence of that lady. Then that delicate fair one said, with emotion, "Thou hast, without cause, brought reproach and disgrace upon me, without my giving any reason for it, now what else dost thou purpose to do? Distinctly state what is in thy heart."

O faḳīrs! at that time such was my condition, that I had almost died of joy. Through delight I swelled so that my clothes could not contain me,[162] and my appearance changed. I returned thanks to God, and said to her, "At this moment your Highness has fully accomplished all that could be done by the physicians, for by one word you have re-animated a dead person, such as I was. Behold, then, the difference which has arisen in my state between that time and this!" With these words I walked three times round her, and coming in front of her, stood up and said, "Your Highness commands that I should tell you what I have in my heart. Your slave then regards this as more precious than the sovereignty of the seven regions of the earth, that you would condescend to accept this humble person, and grant me exaltation by permitting me to

---

161 I have not translated the لٹکا *laṭkā*, which signifies "dangling."

162 A proverbial expression, equivalent to our "bursting with joy."

kiss your feet." For a moment, after hearing this, she was plunged in thought; then, with a side-long look, she said, "Sit down! you have done me such service and evinced such fidelity, that whatever you say is agreeable to me and engraven on my heart also. Well, I accept you."

On the same day, in a happy moment and during an auspicious conjunction of the planets, the Ḳāẓī read the marriage-service.[163] After such distress and disaster, God showed me this day when I obtained the wish of my heart. But the desire my heart cherished of lying with that lady was equalled by the inquietude I felt to become acquainted with the wonderful circumstances (which had occurred). I said to myself, "Up to to-day I have no idea who this lady is, and who that dark good-looking Abyssinian was who, on the receipt of a scrap of paper, entrusted to me so many bags of gold coins? or how, after but three hours' preparation, a banquet was got ready suitable for kings; and why those two innocent persons were put to death at the entertainment; and what was the cause of the lady's anger and unkindness to me, notwithstanding all my services and endurance of her whims; and why all at once she has thus exalted this weak individual." In short, for this very reason, after the customary ceremonies which attend the tying of the nuptial knot, for eight days, in spite of my desire, I forbore from consummating my marriage. I slept with the lady at night, but at daybreak I rose just as I had lain down.

One day, in order to bathe, I said to the female domestics, "Warm a little water that I may wash." The princess smiled and said, "For what purpose warm water?" I remained silent, but that fairy was astonished at my conduct. Moreover, she shewed by her countenance that she was vexed to such a degree, that one day she said, "You, too, are a strange man. You are either so hot or so cold,—what do they call this? If you had not the power, then why did you form such a vain desire?" I then said, without hesitation, "O my life! we must have justice. A man has a right to obtain justice." She said, "What justice remains to be done? Whatever was to be

---

[163] For a description of the marriage-rites see Ḳānūn-i Islām, p. 83.

done, has been done." I replied, "In truth my great wish and desire was this very thing which I have obtained; but my heart is kept in doubt, and by doubtfulness a man's mind is disturbed; whence nothing can be done—he is thrust out of his powers as a man. I had determined in my heart that after marriage (which was the true delight[164] of my heart) I would inquire of your Highness sundry matters (which I cannot comprehend, and which are hidden from me), which, if I hear explained by your royal tongue, then my heart will be comforted." That fairy frowned and said, "How good! have you already forgotten? Remember that I have repeatedly warned you not to interfere in my matters, and oppose in nothing. How, is it proper to shew this unwonted disrespect?" I laughed and said, "Just as you allow other disrespectful actions to stand excused, suffer this also." The fairy changed countenance, and, falling into a passion, became like a whirlwind of fire, and said, "Now thou hast become too bold! Go! mind thine one business! what advantage will result to thee from these matters?" I said, "The shame which attaches to our bodies is the greatest in the world, but one has even these secrets revealed to him. Now when you bring your mind to allow even of such a thing, what other secret requires to be concealed?"

By this allusion that fairy, having, with her natural quickness, comprehended the matter, began to say, "This is true, but my heart experiences this inquietude, lest, if the secret of this wretched person[165] should be disclosed, a great calamity should result." I said, "What discourse is this? Let not your heart entertain this thought of your slave, and with a mind at ease relate all the circumstances which have occurred. Never—never shall my tongue produce them from my heart; what possibility is there of their reaching any one's ears?" When she saw that there was no escape except by telling me,[166] then, having no resource, she said, "There are many disadvantages

---

[164] A play on words, the word signifying "delight," implying also "marriage."
[165] Literally, "one without feet."
[166] Literally, "this dear person."

in repeating these things; thou, whether I would or not, hast pressed me. Well! thy interests are dear to me. For this cause I will relate my history. It is necessary for thee to keep it secret. Take care!"

In short, after many injunctions, she began to say, "I, unhappy, am the daughter of the Sulṭān of Damascus, and he is a great king among kings. Except myself, he had in his family neither boy nor girl. From the day of my birth I was brought up under the shadow of my parents with tenderness and indulgence, and in pleasure and contentment. When I became intelligent, I then gave my mind to beautiful persons and delicate girls. Accordingly, very lovely fairy-born playmates, daughters of the nobility, remained with me as companions, and beautiful attendants and handmaids of the same age as myself waited upon me. I continually witnessed the spectacle of dancing, music, and festivity. I had no intercourse with the world, either for good or ill. Surveying my state, so free from care, nothing but thanks to God issued from my lips.

"It chanced that my mind of itself became so sad that I took pleasure in no one's companionship, nor were the parties of pleasure pleasant to me. My temper became like that of a deranged person—my heart dejected and ill at ease. No one's appearance gratified me, nor did my mind desire conversation. Seeing this my state, my nurses[167] were all overwhelmed with anxiety, and began to throw themselves at my feet. This same eunuch had been from of old my faithful confidante and partner of my secrets. Nothing had been hid from him. Seeing my distracted state, he said, 'If the Princess will drink a little sharbat made from the *cannabis sativa*,[168] then it is probable that your temper will recover its former equilibrium, and ease of mind will return.' From his speaking to me in this manner,

---

[167] In the text four kinds of nurses are enumerated—the دائي *dā'ī*, ددا *dadā*, چھوچھو *chhochho*, and انگا *angā*. In the Ḳānūn-i Islām (Glossary, p. 66), the names of the four kinds slightly differ. *Dadā* and *angā* do not there occur. *Dā'ī* seems to be the wet-nurse; *chhochho* the dry; and *dadā* and *angā*, nursemaids.

[168] This extract of hemp is called "bhang," and is very intoxicating, or, rather, exhilarating.

I too felt desirous (to taste it). I then ordered him to bring it quickly.

"The eunuch went out, and having carefully prepared a flagon of that same drink, iced it, and caused it to be brought to me by the hand of a boy. I drank it, and experienced just the beneficial effects which he had represented. I instantly bestowed on the eunuch a sumptuous robe in requital of that service, and directed him to send to me a cup of it always at the same hour. From that day this became the fixed custom, that the eunuch caused a cup to be conveyed to me by the hands of the same boy, and I, your handmaid, quaffed it. When its intoxicating influence took possession of me, then in its whirl I was amusing my mind by playing and jesting with that boy. He, too, when he had lost his shyness, began to address to me choice and sweet expressions, and to relate marvellous stories. Moreover he began to give vent to sighs and exclamations. His form, indeed, was graceful and worthy notice; my heart involuntarily grew fond of him. Owing to my passionate fondness for him, and the delight I took in his playfulness, I began to bestow on him daily gifts and rewards. That unfortunate, however, made a practice of coming into my presence with the same clothes that he always had been in the habit of wearing, nay, those garments, moreover, became soiled and filthy.

"One day, I said to him inquiringly, 'Thou hast received from the imperial bounty so much, and yet thou hast left thy person just in the same state it was at first. What is the reason of this? Where hast thou expended those rupees? or hast thou hoarded them up?' When the boy heard those words of encouragement, and found me inquiring into his condition, he began to say, with eyes suffused with tears, 'All that your Highness bestowed on this slave, my master has taken; he has not left me one farthing, whence should I get other clothes made, to dress in when I enter your presence? I am not to blame in this; I have no alternative.' At this humble speech of his, I felt pity for him, and immediately gave orders to the eunuch saying, 'From to-day educate this boy under your own eye,[169] and cause good clothes to be made

[169] Literally, "in your own society."

for him, and dress him in them, and do not suffer him to indulge in idle play and romping with the male slaves. Moreover, my pleasure is, that he should learn manners suitable for the royal service, and wait upon me.' The eunuch acted in obedience to my command, and seeing the way in which my inclination turned, began to take an especial care of him. In a few days, owing to his now enjoying easy life and being well-fed, his complexion and filling-out wonderfully improved[170] and he, as it were, cast his slough. Though I kept a guard over my heart, still the person of that caitiff[171] so impressed itself on my mind that my soul through tenderness for him desired nought but this, to place him in my heart, and not to suffer him to be absent from my eyes for a moment.

"At last I admitted him among my intimate companions,[172] and used to dress him in robes of honour of various kinds, and jewels of divers colours, and gaze upon him. At length, his being near me became a solace to my eyes and a source of comfort to my heart. Every moment was spent in encouraging him. Things at last came to this point with me, that if for a moment he left me for some necessary purpose, I felt ill at ease. After some years he reached the age of puberty. His young moustache began to grow. His stature reached its full size. The gate-keepers then, outside, began to talk about him. The porters, and men stationed to purchase goods at the women's apartments,[173] the Mewaṛās,[174] the relief-guard, and the pursuivants and mace-bearers, began to oppose his

---

170 Literally, "became something of something." روغن *raughan*, here translated "filling-out," signifies generally, "grease," and hence, "stoutness," "sleekness."

171 Literally, "infidel," but here merely an abusive term, like "miscreant," "caitiff."

172 The مصاحبان *muṣāḥibān* of princes are their favourites, confidential advisers, those who have the *entrée*.

173 The word روننا *rawannā* is rendered by this long periphrasis of nine words.

174 The word میوڑا *mewaṛā*, in Forbes' vocabulary, is rendered, "a kind of attendant," which explains nothing. In Shakespear's dictionary it is said to be the name of a robbing tribe of Mewāt. These robbers are used even under our Government and by our officers, as house-guards, *e.g.* the Ramūsīs in Bombay.

entering the seraglio. At length his visits were stopped. I indeed was restless without him. One moment seemed a mountain.[175] When I heard these tidings of despair, I felt as much consternation as though the direst calamity[176] had befallen me, and my condition was such that I could neither utter a word nor continue without him. I had no power to effect anything. (I exclaimed,) 'My God! what shall I do?' My perturbation was excessive. Owing to my disquietude I sent for the eunuch (who was my confidante), and said, 'I wish to take care of the boy. At present, the plan to be adopted is, that you should give him a thousand pieces of gold as capital, and make him open a jeweller's shop in the centre bāzār, whereby he will be able to trade, and with the profits pass his life in ease. And for his residence cause a handsome mansion to be built for him near my palace. Purchase the necessary slaves and attendants; fix their monthly salaries, and place them in his service, that he may not want for comfort in any way.' The eunuch made all the preparations for his residence and his business as a jeweller and trader. In a short time his shop made such a splendid and conspicuous appearance that all the sumptuous robes and costly jewels which were required for the use of the king or his nobles[177] were procured at no other house but his. By degrees he laid in such a stock that whatever rarities from whatsoever country were required, were to be found there. In comparison with his, all the jewellers' business was suspended. In a word no one was able to compare with him in this city,[178] nay, there was no such jeweller in any country.

"In this same traffic he indeed gained lākhs of rupees, but his separation from me began to make daily inroads in my

---

[175] That is, "of prodigious length." A similar expression occurs, p. 29, l. 6, *q.v.*

[176] Literally, "the day of resurrection," and hence used for anything surprising and terrible.

[177] سرکار *sarkār* is here pleonastic. It is merely introduced honorifically when speaking of great personages.

[178] By a lapsus of Mīr Amman, or of the transcriber, we find in the text, "in that city," which does not suit the speaker, who was living in the city at the time.

frame. No device succeeded for me to console my heart by a sight of him. At length I summoned that same experienced eunuch for a consultation, and said to him, 'No such plan succeeds that I should behold his form[179] for a little, and tranquillize my heart. There is however this method, for you to cause a subterraneous passage to be dug from his house and unite it with my palace.' Upon my giving the command, such a tunnel was prepared in a few days, and when evening came the eunuch brought in the youth by that passage in profound silence. The whole night was passed in wine, feasting, and merriment. I obtained repose by meeting him; he was gratified by seeing me. When the morning-star arose and the Mu'azzin proclaimed the summons to prayer, the eunuch conveyed the youth by the same way to his house. Beside the eunuch and two nurses who had given me suck and brought me up, no fourth person was acquainted with the matter.

"A long interval passed in this manner. One day this incident occurred. The eunuch, according to custom, had gone to call him, and saw the youth sitting silent like one absorbed in thought. The eunuch inquired of him if he was well, and why he was so sad to-day? and bade him come, for he was sent for to the presence. He returned no answer at all. He never moved his tongue.[180] The eunuch returned alone and disappointed,[181] and related how he found him. That the devil might bring me to ruin, my heart did not even then forget its love for him. Had I known that my love and affection for such a traitor and ingrate would in the end bring me to disgrace and dishonour, and stain my character and fame, I would that very moment have abandoned the affair and repented of it. I would never have mentioned his name again, nor given my heart to that shameless one. But it was to be thus. I took no notice, therefore, of his not coming, looking on it as merely the coquetry

---

179 A play on words, the same word, صورت *ṣūrat*, being used to express "plan" and "form."

180 Or as we say, "never opened his lips."

181 اپنا سا منھ لیکر *apnā sā munh lekar*. Literally: "taking a face like his own," a strange expression. We use just the reverse, "out of countenance."

of lovers.[182] Of this the result which I have now experienced is, that thou, too, though no eye-witness, hast become acquainted with this story. Else, how great the difference between me and you![183] Well! what has happened has happened. I overlooked the perverseness of that ass, and twice sent a message by the eunuch, saying, 'If thou wilt not come to me, I somehow or other will come to thee; but my coming will be highly indecorous, and fraught with danger.[184] If this secret be divulged, then it will be very bad for thee. Then do not act so that the result can be nothing but disgrace. This is best, that thou come quickly, otherwise consider me already arrived.' When I had despatched this message, and he saw that my loving desire of him was excessive, he came with an affected coquettish manner, dressing himself so as to look as miserable as possible.

"When he had seated himself beside me, I asked him, 'What is the cause of thy backwardness and ill-humour to-day? Thou hast never shewn so much petulance and boldness, but always presented thyself without excuse.' He then said, 'I, nameless and humble individual, by the favour of your Highness, and by reason of your august protection, have reached this affluence. My life has been spent in much ease. I offer my prayers for the life and fortune of your Highness. This fault has been committed by this guilty person, in the confident expectation that the Princess will pardon me. I hope for your forgiveness.' I indeed loved him with my heart and soul. I believed his hypocritical speeches, and did not observe his villany. On the contrary, I again asked him encouragingly, 'What such grievous embarrassment has befallen thee, that thou hast continued so pensive? relate it. We shall devise some remedy for it also.'

"In short, he replied in his usual cringing way, 'All things

---

182 Instead of معشوقون *māshūḳon*, a word applicable only to females, we should have expected عاشقون *āshiḳon* here. Is this a lapsus of Mīr Amman's making?

183 Lit.: "I where? and thou where?" The speaker being a princess, and the person addressed a merchant.

184 I have been unable to express قباحت *ḳabāḥat*, but by this periphrasis of five words.

are difficult to me; in the presence of your Highness all become easy.' At length, from the tenor of his discourse and conversation, this became apparent, that there was a lofty edifice, and a garden of great verdure with reservoirs, lakes, and wells of solid masonry near his house in the centre[185] of the city, to be sold, and along with the garden, a female slave also, a singing-girl, who possessed a very fine taste for music. The two, however, were to be sold together, not the garden alone; like a cat on the neck of a camel. Whoever took the garden, was also to pay the price of the female slave. And this was the wonder, that the price of the garden was five thousand rupees, and the sum demanded for the slave-girl five hundred thousand. The youth[186] represented that he could not at present raise so large a sum. I found that his heart was altogether absorbed[187] in the eager desire of purchasing those things, and that it was on this very account that his head was disturbed and his mind distracted. Although he was sitting in my presence, still his countenance was sad and his mind dejected. To cheer him up was to me a matter of hourly and momentary necessity. I instantly commanded the eunuch saying, 'To-morrow morning pay the price of that garden and slave-girl, and cause a title-deed for the garden and a receipt for the slave-girl to be written out, and hand them over to this person, and pay the cost-money to the owner out of the imperial treasury.'

"Immediately on hearing this permission the youth made obeisance to me, and his countenance recovered its usual appearance.[188] The whole night was spent in laughing and merriment, in the very same manner as it had been always wont to pass. As soon as it dawned, he took his leave. The

---

185 Literally: "navel."

186 All the description of the garden and slave-girl, to the close of this sentence, is given in the direct form, but it is requisite to use the oblique form in English.

187 Literally, "without choice."

188 I hazard this translation, notwithstanding that the dictionaries give only "tears" as the English of روهٹ *rohaṭ*, which they derive from رونا *ronā*, "to weep." I cannot think this meaning applicable, and would derive it from رو *rū* "face." If this be regarded as inadmissible, the sense will be, "he wept with joy."

eunuch, as he was ordered, purchased the garden and female slave, and gave them to him. Afterwards the youth, according to custom, was coming and going at night. One day in the season of spring, when the place, too, was pleasant to the heart, the clouds were circling round, small drops of rain were falling, and the lightning also was flashing,[189] and a soft, soft breeze was blowing. In short, at that moment the season was one of wondrous delight. As soon as I looked upon the liquors[190] of various colours, and the flagons arranged in the recesses, my heart desired to take one draught. When I came to the second or third cup, I forthwith bethought myself of that newly purchased garden. I felt an intense desire to take a walk there for one moment during this state of things. When ill-fortune is to happen the dog will bite you though you be mounted on a camel.[191] Quite of my own accord[192] and free-will I proceeded, taking a nurse along with me, by way of that subterraneous passage to the abode of that youth, and thence I went on to the garden. I beheld then that the beauty of that garden completely equalled that of Paradise. The drops of rain which had fallen on the green leaves of the trees, were like pearls set in leaves of emerald; and the redness of the flowers in that gloom blushed like the redness of the evening sky, while the streamlets filled to the brim resembled carpets of glass, and waves continued rippling.

In short, I was walking about in that garden gazing in every direction, when the day closed, and the darkness of evening made its appearance. Meanwhile that youth shewed himself in an avenue, and when he saw me, advanced with much respect and eagerness, and, taking my hand in his, led me to a summer-house with twelve doors. When I arrived there, the appearance

---

[189] This description of exhilarating weather does not accord with European notions. To appreciate it we must have experienced the heat of the sultry season in India.

[190] Literally, "bubbles."

[191] A proverb signifying that no precautions can save you from the disasters which are fated to occur to you.

[192] بیٹھے بٹھائے *baiṭhe biṭhā'e,* literally signifies "seated and having caused to sit;" but it has come to mean "ultro, sponte suâ."

of the place obliterated from my mind all the scenery of the garden. The abundance of lights was this (which I will describe). In every direction cypress lanthorns, lotus lamps, and lanthorns revolving by the smoke of the candles within, and having on their sides figures of various animals,[193] and lights astonishing the assembly,[194] and shaded lights were kindled, insomuch that the night of Barāt,[195] notwithstanding its moonlight and its lamps, was dark in comparison with it. On one side fireworks were let off, Roman candles with flowers issuing forth, and fireworks resembling pomegranates, and others like the Chrysanthemum Indicum, and like the Kæmpferia rotunda, and like pearls, and blue-lights, and rockets, and Catherine wheels, and fireworks like flowers held in the hand, and others like the Jasminum grandiflorum, and crackers, and stars. Meanwhile the clouds parted, and the moon came forth just as a mistress appears dressed in a suit of purple robes. The scene was one of marvellous beauty.[196] As soon as the moonbeams were shed abroad, the young man said, 'Now come and take your seat in an upper room of the garden-house.' I had become so bereft of sense that whatever that wretch said, to that I assented. He now led me the following dance:—He took me up stairs. That building was so lofty that all the houses of the city, and the lamps of the market-place, were as it were the lower garden to it. I was seated in a state of pleasurable emotion, with my arms round the neck of the youth,

---

[193] This periphrasis of eighteen words is used to translate the words فانوس خیال *fānūs-i khiyāl.*

[194] All these are various kinds of devices for illumination.

[195] Shab-i Barāt, which latter word signifies "Register." This is the book in which all the actions which men are to perform during the ensuing year are written. The feast is held on the 14th of Shâban, the eighth month, and on the 15th God records the actions. Owing to this circumstance the feast has obtained the name of the Shab-i Barāt, "Night of Record." It is also called—2. Lailatu'l-mubārik, "the Blessed Night." 3. Raḥmat, "Night of Mercy." 4. "Night of Discernment." —Kānūn-i Islām, p. 251.

[196] کیفیت *kaifiyat* is here used in a very idiomatic sense. The meanings given in the vocabulary of Forbes' edition are none of them applicable here. The proper meaning is in some degree given by Shakespear's "deliciousness."

when, meanwhile, a woman excessively ugly, with no shape or comeliness, coming, as it were, out of the hearth,[197] advanced holding a cup of wine in her hand. Her coming at that time displeased me excessively, and from beholding her appearance, horror arose in my heart. Then in confusion I inquired of the youth, 'Who is this filthy monster? Whence hast thou got her?' The youth, clasping his arms in a reverential posture, said, 'This is the same female slave that was purchased along with the garden, by the bounty of your Highness.' I perceived that that simpleton had purchased her with extreme eagerness. Perhaps (thought I) his heart is attracted to her. Suffering inward vexation on this account, I remained silent, but my heart from that very time became gloomy, and uneasiness spread over my temper. Furthermore, that low fellow added this annoyance, that he caused this strumpet to act as cup-bearer. At that time I was drinking my own blood, and as, when some one has enclosed in the same cage a parrot and a crow, I had no means of escape, while my heart would not suffer me to remain seated there.

"To make the story short, that wine was double distilled, such that a man would become a beast by drinking it. She gave to the youth two or four cups of the same potent liquor in succession, and half a cup I too, at the entreaty of that youth, drank off, though as unwillingly as if it had been poison. At last that shameless harlot, also becoming wanton, began to use silly and indecorous gestures to that abandoned youth, and that foolish boy also, losing all respect through intoxication, began to commit improprieties. I was overpowered with such a sense of shame that, at that time, had the earth opened, I would have engulphed myself, but, through affection for him, I kept silence, notwithstanding his senseless conduct. But he indeed was by nature vile; he understood not my thus overlooking (his behaviour). In the whirl of intoxication he drank off two more cups, so that he lost what sense he had left, and swept away all reverence for me from his mind. Overpowered by

197 The meaning is, "She was as black as if she came out of the hearth" (or as we should say, "black as a sweep, or as a coal").

lust, that shameless one, breaking through all decency, had connexion with that female slave before my face; and that goblin of a woman, too, lying beneath him in that condition, began to indulge in the blandishments of love, and kisses, and close embraces took place between the two. There was no fidelity in that faithless man, nor shame in that shameless one —as is the spirit, so is the angel.[198] My state at that time was like that of a female singer,[199] singing out of time a tuneless tune. I was invoking curses on myself, and crying, 'Wherefore came I here for which I have got this punishment?' At length, how long should I endure this? I was on fire from head to foot, and began to roll upon hot coals.[200] In this angry and exasperated state I started up from thence, repeating this proverb, 'The bullock leapt not but the sack,[201]—did ever one behold a sight like this.'[202]

"That drunkard perceived in his heart his own danger, thinking, 'if the princess is now displeased, what will be my state to-morrow? and in the morning what disasters will result? Now it is better that I slay the princess.' Having, by the advice of that harlot, made this resolve in his mind, he cast his sash about his neck,[203] and came and fell at my feet, and having taken off his turban from his head, began to entreat and supplicate. My heart was enamoured of him. I followed wherever he led me, and, like a stone for grinding moved with the hand,[204] was in his power. What he said, that I was doing.

---

198 A proverb somewhat resembling "An evil man, out of the evil treasure of his heart, bringeth forth evil things." Matt. xii. 35.

199 The ڈومنی *ḍomnī* is a female of a low caste of Musalmān called *Dom*, and sings and plays in the company of females only, using the instruments dhol or drum, and manjīre, a kind of cymbal.

200 In plain words, "I was excessively disquieted."

201 The گون *gon*, is a sack for carrying grain. The Anglo-Indians, with their usual happy patois, call them "gunny" bags.

202 This proverb applies to those guilty of such insolence and audacity, as, from their low position, could little have been expected from them.

203 This is done in token of supplication.

204 A periphrasis of seven words to express چکّی *chakkī*.

Somehow or other, having persuaded and cajoled me,[205] he caused me to be seated again, and having filled two or four cups of the same fiery liquors, he himself drank, and gave me also to drink. For one thing I was burned to a cinder[206] with anger, and next, I drank such wine. I quickly lost my senses, so that I was utterly bereft of them. Then that pitiless, disloyal, and stony-hearted caitiff wounded me with a sword, and moreover, in his own opinion, killed me outright. At that moment my eyes opened, when these words issued from my mouth, 'Well! as I have done, so it has been done to me—but do thou save thyself from this my innocent blood.

> Forbid it some tyrant should seize and arrest thee for this,
> Wash my blood from thy robe, what has been, that has been, and is.

To none make known this secret. I have not held back even my life from thee.' Having again recommended him to God, my spirit sank within me. I lost all sense and recollection. Perhaps the butcher, thinking me dead, thrust me into the box and let me down from the wall of the fort, where you saw me. I wished ill to no one, but these disasters were written in my destiny. The writing of fate is not to be obliterated. Because of these eyes I have seen these adventures; had my eyes not found pleasure in beautiful persons, then that wretched man would not have been a chain round my neck. God brought it about that thou arrivedst there, and made thee the instrument of my surviving. I now feel such shame in my heart, that, after enduring these indignities, I would either not survive, or I would hide my face from all; but what can I do? death is not in one's own power. God, after slaying me, restored me to life. Let us see what is fated in my destiny. It is evident that thy exertions and attentions were the means of my being cured from such wounds. Thou hast expended life and wealth in preserving me, and hast supplied me with

---

205 The word پنڈھلانا *pandhlānā*, occurs in Forbes' vocabulary, but not in his dictionary, nor in that of Shakespear. It is perhaps from पिण्ड *pind*, as پنڈ پڑنا *pind parnā*, is "to pursue."

206 Literally, "roast meat."

all thou possessedst. In those days, seeing thee without money, and perplexed, I wrote that letter to Sīdī Bahār, who was my treasurer. The contents were as follows:—'I am in health and safety in such a place. Convey to my mother tidings of me, unfortunate.'

"He sent with thee for thy expense those trays of money, and when I sent thee to the shop of Yūsuf, the merchant's son, to purchase the jewels and dresses, I confidently expected that as that mean person[207] quickly struck up an acquaintance and took his seat with any one, it was probable that, regarding thee also as a foreigner, he would in his affected way give you an invitation, and entertain thee. Which design of mine succeeded. He did exactly as I had imagined in my mind. When thou camest after making him a promise of returning, and told me the circumstance of his (proffered) entertainment and of his insisting upon it, I was pleased in my heart, thinking that when thou shouldest go and eat at his house, then, if thou, too, shouldst invite him to an entertainment, he would come speedily. On which account I readily gave thee leave. After three days when thou camest back thence, after concluding the entertainment, and with shame madest excuses before me for thy absence, I said, in order to encourage thee, 'Never mind! when he gave thee leave then thou camest, but it is not well to show that indifference to opinion as to keep thyself under an obligation to another and not return it. Now do thou also go and invite him, and bring him along with thyself.' When thou hadst gone to his house, I then perceived that there were no articles for his entertainment ready, and were he to come, what could I do? But this opportunity presented itself to me, in that it has been the custom of the monarchs of this country from old time to remain abroad eight months[208] in ordering their territories and transacting

---

207 كم حوصله *kam ḥauṣilah*, is rendered in Forbes' vocabulary, "unaspiring," "unambitious," a meaning altogether foreign to the sense of this passage.

208 The author here refers to the custom of the former kings of Delhi. The progress may well be called ملك گيري *mulk gīrī*, "taking territory," for refractory chiefs were reduced, their castles stormed, and sometimes new conquests were made.

their political and revenue matters, and for four months during the rainy season they reside in the royal castle. In those days the king, that is, the father of me unfortunate, had two or four months ago departed to make a royal progress through his territories in order to establish order in them.

"While you were bringing with you the youth, Sīdī Bahār[209] stated to the queen (who is the mother of me, impure,) what had befallen me. Then I, ashamed of the error and fault I had committed, went and stood before her, and related all that had occurred. Although she, from her judicious foresight, and maternal affection for me, had concealed the circumstance of my disappearance, saying to herself, 'God knows what will be the end of this: at present to disclose this disgraceful affair would not be well,' and had (as it were,) in my place deposited and hidden my fault within herself;[210] still she was in search of me. When she saw me in this state, and heard all my story, she wept and said, 'O unfortunate (girl), deserving never to have been born![211] Thou hast, with thine eyes open, and of set purpose, destroyed all the honour and dignity of the imperial house. A thousand pities! and thou hast washed thine hands of thine own life. Would that in thy stead I had given birth to a stone, then I could have endured it with patience. Even now repent. What wilt thou do? Wilt thou live or die?' I, with a feeling of deep shame, said, 'In the fate of me unfortunate this very thing was written, that after escaping from such various calamities, I should continue to survive in this dishonoured and wretched state. Than this, even death were better; but though the stain[212] of disgrace adheres to my forehead, yet I have done no such deed that dishonour should

---

209 To preserve the connexion of the sentence ايسا هوا *aisā hū'ā*, "it was so," or some such words, must be understood before كه *kih*.

210 In the text it is, "in her stomach." In other words, "Instead of being in travail with me, she was now so with my faults."

211 Forbes translates this نا شدني *nā shudanī*, "unfit to live," and Shakespear renders it, "one from whom no good is to be expected."

212 The ٹيكا *ṭīkā* is the sectarial mark made on the forehead by Hindūs.

attach to the name of my parents. My present chief anguish is this, that those two shameless ones should escape from my power, and indulge in mutual dalliance and delights, while I endure this degree of suffering at their hands. It is a shame that I am unable to effect anything. My hope is this, that the household steward be ordered to prepare the necessary requisites for an entertainment, with the utmost elegance, in the abode of this unfortunate one. Then, having summoned those two wretches, on the pretence of inviting them to a feast, I will give them the reward of their actions, and take my revenge. As he directed his hand against me and wounded me, I, too, will cut them in pieces. My heart will then be soothed, else I am consumed [213] in the flame of this resentment, in which I shall at length be burned to ashes.'

"When my mother heard this, her mental grief rendered her compassionate, and she threw a veil over my faults, and gave into the charge of the eunuch (who was my confidante), all the things requisite for the entertainment. All the persons (I required) arrived, and were present in their respective offices. At evening thou camest, bringing that man now dead, but I required the presence of that foul slave also. Accordingly I gave thee fresh injunctions, and summoned her too. When she also had come, and the company had assembled, all with repeated draughts of wine became intoxicated and insensible, and with them thou also, being intoxicated, fell down like a dead person. I then gave orders to one of the female Kilmaks in attendance to go and decapitate them with a sword. She in an instant drew forth her weapon, and having cut off their heads on the spot, made their bodies red (with blood). And my anger against thee was caused by this, that I had given thee permission to go to the entertainment, but not to rely implicitly on a friendship of but two days, and make thyself an associate of a drunken party. This folly of thine was assuredly displeasing to me, because when, after much drinking, thou be-

---

213 The word پهکنا *phuknā*, gives the idea of a thing in the forge, in the fierce flame excited by the bellows.

camest insensible, then what confidence could I have in thee as a companion? But the obligation of thy services is so fixed round my neck, that, in spite of such improper actions of thine, I pardon thee. Thus I have related to thee, from beginning to end, my adventures. Now there is one other wish remaining in my heart. Just as, to gratify thee, I have complied with all thou hast said, even so do thou also perform my directions in the way I shall tell you. The step advisable for the present crisis is, not to continue in this city, which is good neither for me nor for you. For the rest thou art master."[214]

O Servants of God! having said thus much, the princess was silent. I with my heart and soul regarded her orders as taking precedence over everything, and I was entangled in the net of love for her. I said, "Whatever is your royal pleasure, that is best. This, your devoted servant, will perform it unhesitatingly." When the princess perceived that I was altogether obedient and at her command, she said, "Send for two swift and spirited coursers (which may match the wind in speed) from the royal stable." I selected just such fairy-born highly-mettled[215] steeds, and having caused them to be saddled, sent for them. When but little of the night remained, the princess put on man's apparel, and, fully armed, mounted one of the steeds, and I, well provided with weapons, seated myself on the other, and we set off in one direction.

When the night was over, and it began to dawn, we arrived on the border of a lake. We dismounted and washed our hands and faces, and, taking a rapid breakfast, mounted and went on. At times the princess conversed a little, and thus spake, "For thy sake I have left shame, modesty, country, wealth, parents, all. Forbid it that thou, too, shouldst act like that faithless and cruel one." At times I was recounting some chit-chat, in order to shorten the journey, and was replying to her, saying, "Princess! All men are not alike. There was something wrong in the seed from which that base wretch

---

[214] This may mean, "I have said my say, do as you please;" or, "comply with this one request, the rest I leave to you."

[215] Literally, "with four kidneys."

sprang, that he committed such a deed; and as for me, I have devoted property and life in thy service, and thou hast bestowed upon me every kind of exaltation. I am now your slave, though not bought with money. If thou shouldest cause shoes[216] to be made of my skin, and put them on, I would not utter a single sigh." Such conversation was carried on between us, and we employed ourselves in travelling night and day. At times when, from fatigue, we alighted anywhere, we made prey of the beasts and birds of the forests, and having slain them in the due form,[217] and having taken salt from our salt-cellar, and struck fire with our flints, and broiled (the flesh), we ate it, and let loose our horses. They grazing on the grass and leaves, with their own mouths filled their bellies.

One day we came out into such a flat and unbroken[218] plain as possessed not even the name of a habitation, and where the form of man was nowhere to be seen. Even here, owing to the princess being my companion, day appeared to me like the feast of Īd,[219] and night like the night of Barāt. As we proceeded, our road was unexpectedly crossed by a river, at sight of which the liver became water.[220] When, as we stood on the bank, we looked about us, we found that as far as the eye could reach, there was nothing but water. Neither dry land nor raft[221] was to be seen. (We ejaculated,) "O God! now how shall we cross this ocean?" For a moment we stood absorbed in this thought. At length this idea entered my mind, that I would make her sit down there, and go myself in search of a boat or vessel, and that until I could get the means of crossing, that lady might also repose herself. I then said, "O queen! with your per-

---

[216] A proverbial expression which we have had before at page 26, line 10.

[217] An animal is lawfully slain by Muḥammadans when the throat is held up, and severed with the words, "Bism 'illāh," "In the name of God."

[218] Literally, "flat as the palm of the hand."

[219] For an explanation of Īd and Barāt, see page 9, note 48, and page 58, note 195.

[220] A most insipid attempt at wit.

[221] The dictionaries unite these words and render them thus, تبل بیڑا *thal berā*, "means of obtaining one's wishes," a most doubtful interpretation, and not at all required here.

mission I will examine the ford, and way of passing this river." She said, "I am much fatigued, and am suffering from hunger and thirst; I will rest a little, and meantime do thou devise some expedient for crossing."

At that place there was a pīpal-tree (Ficus religiosa), which formed such a shade that if a thousand horsemen had come, they might have reposed safe from heat and rain beneath it. Having seated her there, I went on and was looking in all directions to find some trace of a human being on the earth, or in the water. I exerted myself much, but found no such vestige. At length I came back thence in despair, and found that that beautiful lady was no longer under the tree.[222] How can I relate what I then experienced, for my senses departed? I became crazed and insane.[223] At times I ascended the tree, and wandered from branch to branch, from leaf to leaf. Sometimes I let go my hands and feet, and fell to the ground, and walked (in token of devoting myself for her) round the root of that tree. At times uttering shrill screams, I was bewailing my helplessness. Now I rushed from east to west, now I turned from north to south. In short I gave myself much fruitless labour,[224] but I discovered no trace of that unattainable jewel. When all my efforts were unavailing, I then began to search in all directions, weeping, and casting dust on my head.

The thought occurred to my mind that perhaps some Jin[225] had carried off that fair one, and inflicted this injury upon me; or that some one from her own country had pursued her, and finding her alone, had persuaded her, and carried[226] her off

---

[222] The selection of the Pīpal as the tree from under which the lady disappeared, perhaps arose from the popular notion among the Hindūs that that tree is the abode of sprites and goblins.

[223] There should be a full stop here; the text is wrongly pointed in Forbes' edition.

[224] Literally, "I sifted much dirt."

[225] The Jins are the genii of oriental tales.

[226] Shakespear renders ابھرنا *ubharnā*, by "to swell, to rise up, to overflow, to unlade a cart or boat," all which meanings are altogether irrelevant here. He also makes the word of Sanskṛit origin. Forbes' vocabulary makes it Hindī, and renders it "to go, to depart." His dictionary makes it "to overflow." Strange contradictions these!

again towards Syria. Distracted with my thoughts, I cast away my clothes,[227] and, naked as at my birth, I became a faḳīr, and from morn to night went on searching the country of Syria (for her I had lost), and at night cast myself down anywhere. I travelled over the whole world, but learned from none tidings of my princess, nor discovered the reason of her disappearance. Then it entered into my mind that since I found no trace of her who was my life, to live was now odious to me. In a thick forest appeared a mountain, which I then ascended, and resolved to throw myself down, that my head and face being dashed repeatedly against the rocks, might be crushed to pieces, by which means I should escape from a grief so excessive.

Saying this in my heart, I was about to cast myself down, nay my feet were already off the ground, when some one caught me by the hand. Meanwhile, my senses returned, and I then beheld a horseman in green clothing, with a veil thrown over his face, who addressed me, saying, "Why dost thou purpose thy own death? to despair of the grace of God is infidelity. As long as there is breath, so long is there hope.[228] Now in a few days three Darweshes situated[229] like thyself, involved in an exactly similar calamity, and who have beheld similar adventures, will meet thee in the land of Rūm, and the king of that country, whose name is Āzād-Bakht, to him also a grievous difficulty has occurred. When he meets you four faḳīrs there, the heart's desire and wish of each will be completely accomplished."

I seized his stirrup and kissed it, and said, "O Saint of God! these few words of yours have brought consolation to my heart, filled as it was with trouble; but, for God's sake, be pleased to

---

[227] A good instance this of the delight the Hindūstānīs have in jingling words. ویڑے *wapṛe* means nothing, and is, in fact, no word at all, but is added to jingle with کپڑے *kapṛe*, and for a like reason the no-word پھانک *phāṅk*, is added to پھینک *pheṅk*.

[228] This is exactly the Latin proverb, "Dum spiro, spero."

[229] An unusual sense of رکھے *rakhe*.

tell me this, who you are? and what is your august name?" He then said, "My name is Murtaẓa[230] Ālī, and my business is this, that, whenever a difficulty occurs to any one, I relieve him." Having said thus much, he disappeared from my sight. At length this fakīr having found solace in the good tidings of my spiritual guide, who disentangled me from my perplexity, set out for Constantinople. After enduring in the road the hardships I was fated to suffer, I, by the grace of God, arrived thus far, in the hope of meeting with my princess, and owing to my good fortune obtained the exaltation of waiting upon you. Thus our meeting with one another has taken place. We have obtained the privilege of associating and discoursing with one another, it now remains that we become known to, and acquainted with, King Āzād-Bakht.

After that we shall all five assuredly arrive at the desire of our hearts. Do you also pray that it may be so, and say, Amen! O Spiritual Guides! such is the history of this afflicted and distressed person, which I have related in the presence of you Darweshes. Let us now see hereafter when this labour and grief of mine will be exchanged for happiness and contentment, by meeting with the princess.

Āzād-Bakht, seated silent and concealed in a corner, having attentively listened to the Story of the First Darwesh, was pleased.

He then began to listen to the Story of the Second Darwesh.

---

230 Murtaẓa signifies "chosen," "approved."

TRAVELS OF THE SECOND DARWESH.

WHEN the turn came to the second Darwesh to relate his tale, he sat down cross-legged,[231] and said,

> O friends! awhile to this my tale attend,
> Which from commencement I'll relate to th' end.
> Hear, friends, my irremediable grief,
> Physicians cannot heal it, nor bestow relief.

O clothed in rags! this weak person is the prince of the country of Fārs.[232] Men skilled in every art are produced there, just as "Isfahān, half the world,"[233] is a well-known proverb. In the seven regions of the earth there is no country equal to that region, for the star of that region is a sun, and among the seven planets it is the chief luminary. The water and air of that place is pleasant, and the people of clear intellect, and men of taste. My father (who was the king of that country) selected very illustrious and wise teachers in every science and art, to instruct me from my childhood in the rules and regulations of government, and appointed them as tutors; in order that, having received a complete education in every branch of knowledge, I might become clever. By the grace of God, at the age of fourteen years I became proficient in every science. I acquired the proper manner of conversing, approved manners,[234]

---

[231] Literally, "on four knees."

[232] Fārs has a more limited signification than "Īrān," being the country bounded on the east by Karmania, by Khuzistān on the west, the Persian Sea on the south, and the desert of Naubandijān, which separates it from Khurāsān to the north. Īrān is the whole country of Persia, and seems to spring from the word Ārya, the ancient Aria.

[233] In the original "Iṣfahān" rhymes with "niṣf jahān," "half the world." The neatness of the expression is lost in English.

[234] Literally, "sitting down and rising up."

and all that is suitable and requisite for kings. And my chief pleasure, by day and by night, was to be in the company of clever persons, and to listen to tales of every country, and the deeds of magnanimous princes and illustrious men.

One day a wise associate, who was well versed in history, and acquainted with the world, began to discourse, saying, "Although there is no reliance to be placed on the life of man, there are, however, certain qualities such that through them, the name of a man is handed down with commendation by the tongues of men to the resurrection." I said, "If you would enter into a detailed explanation upon these points, I too would listen, and act in accordance with what you say." Then that person began to relate, as follows, the story of Ḥātim Ṭā'ī[235]:—"In the time of Ḥātim there was a king of Arabia, whose name was Naufal. He was a bitter enemy of Ḥātim, through jealousy of his fame. Having collected a large army, he advanced to give him battle. Now Ḥātim was one who feared God, and a good man. He considered that if he too should prepare for war, God's creatures would be slain, and much blood would be spilt, the punishment of which would be written against his name. Having thus reflected, he withdrew quite alone, seeking merely his personal safety, and concealed himself in the cave of a mountain. When the intelligence of Ḥātim's disappearance reached Naufal, he confiscated all his property and effects, and sent round a proclamation, saying, whoever should search for and apprehend Ḥātim, should receive as a reward from the king's government five hundred gold ashrafīs. Hearing this, all felt their covetousness excited, and began to search for Ḥātim.

"One day an old man and his aged wife, accompanied by two or three little children, came to break wood near the cave where Ḥātim was concealed, and began to pick sticks from that forest. The old woman said, 'Had we had good fortune, we should have got a sight of Ḥātim somehow or other, and, having seized him, have carried him to Naufal, who would then have given us

---

[235] Ḥātim Ṭā'ī was an Arab, of the tribe of Ṭaī, whence his name. He lived somewhat before Muḥammad, in the sixth century A.D.

five hundred gold ashrafīs, and we should have lived at ease, and have been released from this wearisome employment.' The old man said, 'What art thou chattering about? In our destiny this alone was written, that we should daily break sticks, place them on our heads, and sell them in the bāzār, and thus provide bread and salt, or one day a tiger from the forest should carry us off. There! mind thy own business! Why should Ḥātim fall into our hands, and the king cause his money to be given to us?' The old woman heaved a cold sigh, and remained silent.

"The words of these two were overheard by Ḥātim. He thought it far removed from magnanimity and kind feeling to conceal himself, and save his own life, and not gratify the wish of those two helpless individuals. It is true that the man in whom there is no pity, is not human; and he who feels no pain (for the distressed) is a butcher.

> For pity God created man! else He
> Of cherubs had no lack to bow the knee.[236]

"In short, the magnanimous spirit of Ḥātim would not allow him to hear this with his own ears and keep silence. He instantly came forth, and said to the old man, 'Dear friend! I, and no other, am Ḥātim; conduct me to Naufal. When he beholds me, he will give to thee whatever money he has promised to bestow.' The old man said, 'It is true that in this manner my welfare and advantage is undoubtedly secured, but how will he treat thee? how is one to know that? Should he slay thee, what shall I do? I can never do this and, for the sake of my own lucre, give thee into the hands of thy foe. How many days shall I enjoy that wealth? and how long shall I live? At length I shall die, then what answer shall I give to God?' Ḥātim besought him much, saying, 'Take me along! I bid you do it of my own free will, and I always continue in this desire, that my life and property should be useful to some one—that is best.' But the old man would in

---

[236] طاعت *ṭāāt*, "obedience," is thus somewhat freely rendered, for the sake of he rhyme.

nowise consent to lead away Ḥātim and receive the reward. At length, Ḥātim, having failed in all his endeavours, said, 'If thou dost not take me thus, I will go of my own accord to the king and say, "This old man placed me in concealment in a mountain cave."' The old man laughed and said, 'If in return for kindness, we meet with ill-treatment, then (all we can say is) "O Fortune!"' During this altercation and discussion, more persons came up, and a crowd was formed. They perceived that that very person was Ḥātim. They immediately seized him and carried him off. The old man, too, accompanied them, following in the rear, and lamenting. When they had brought Ḥātim into the presence of Naufal, he asked, 'Who seized and brought him?' One rascally cruel-hearted fellow said, 'Who besides myself could do such a thing? This victory belongs to my name. I have set up a banner in the ninth heaven.' Another swaggerer[237] began to vaunt, saying, 'I have for several days laboured and exposed myself in the forest, and seized him, and brought him thence. Be pleased to look upon my labour, and bestow what you have agreed upon.' In this same manner each, from the desire of the ashrafīs, was saying, 'This thing was done by me.' The old man, remaining silent in a corner, listened to the boastings of all, and stood and wept for Ḥātim. When all had finished recounting their valour and prowess, Ḥātim said to the king, 'If you ask the truth, it is this. The old man, who is standing apart from all, brought me. If you are acquainted with physiognomy, then make your observations, and fulfil what you promised for my capture, since, in the whole body, the tongue is the most lawful[238] (or perfect) member. What a man

---

[237] لن ترانی *lan-tarā-nī* is an Arabic word compounded of لن *lan*, "not," ترا *tarā*, "thou shalt see," نی *nī*, "me." How it came to mean "boasting" is doubtful. Forbes, in his dictionary, explains it, "Thou shalt never see the like of me."

[238] The meaning may be "that which renders a thing lawful," *i.e.* "prohibited," or the reverse; or, that which is حلال *ḥalāl* (lawful), discriminates between man and beast, is the distinction between them, for to beasts all things are indifferent, to man alone lawful, or the reverse. The tongue is the most lawful, or perfect member, as being the greatest difference between man and beast.

says that he ought to perform. Otherwise to animals also God has given a tongue,[239] then what would be (literally, is) the difference between the brute and man?'

"Naufal called the old wood-cutter to him, and inquired, saying, 'Tell the truth. What is the real state of the case? Who seized and brought Ḥātim?' That poor fellow narrated truly what had happened from beginning to end, and said, 'Ḥātim came of his own accord, for my sake.' When Naufal heard this magnanimous deed of Ḥātim, he was astonished, (and exclaimed), 'I say Bravo! to thy generosity—thou hast not withheld even thy life!' He gave orders that the hands[240] of all those who had falsely pretended to the capture of Ḥātim should be tied behind their backs, and that in place of the five hundred ashrafīs, five hundred blows with a shoe should be inflicted on the heads of each, so that the life might be driven out of them. Immediately the slippers began to fall crack! crack! so that in a single moment their heads were rendered bald. It is true,[241] false speaking is so great a crime, that no other crime equals it. May God preserve every one from this calamity! and not impart to him a taste for lying. Many people go on chattering lies, but in the time of trial they meet with punishment.

"In short, having bestowed on all of them such a reward as they merited, Naufal bethought himself that to entertain enmity against a person like Ḥātim (whose bounty extended to a whole world, and who grudged not his own life for the sake of the needy, and who walked wholly in the way of God), and to be his adversary, was far removed from a chivalrous and manly spirit. He immediately grasped the hand of Ḥātim

---

239 Here a distinction seems to be drawn between the words زبان *zabān* and جیبھ *jībh*. Both signify "tongue," but the former applies to men, and the latter to animals.

240 The meaning of this singular expression ٹنڈیاں کسنا *ṭunḍiyān kasnā*, seems to be "to tie the hands in such a way as to render them as useless as a *ṭunḍ*," *i.e.* a hand that has been cut off.

241 This is a moral reflection on the part of the author, and is singularly out of place in the middle of a story.

with much friendship and affection and said, 'Why should it not be so? Since you are so good, why should you not be so famous?'[212] He showed him courtesy and respect, and seated him near himself, and his territory, and effects and property, and furniture which he had seized, he immediately gave up. He bestowed on him anew the chieftainship of the tribe of Ṭai, and caused five hundred ashrafīs to be bestowed from his own treasury on the old man. He, uttering benedictions, went his way."

When I had heard this story of Ḥātim to an end, a spirit of emulation arose in my mind, and this thought passed through it, that Ḥātim was chief only of his own tribe, and yet by the single quality of generosity, he acquired such a name as was renowned even to that day. (I reflected that) I was, by the decree of God, King of all Īrān,[213] and that if I remained excluded from this blessing[214] it would be a great pity,—that, in fact, there was nothing in the world greater than munificence, for this reason, that whatever a man bestows in this world he receives the reward of it in the world to come. If he sows but one grain, how great a harvest he reaps from it! Having determined this in my mind, I sent for the superintendent of buildings, and ordered him to erect with all speed, outside the city, a lofty edifice, with forty high and very wide doors. In a short space of time just such a spacious building as my heart was wishing for, was completed and made ready; and in that place, at all hours, from morning to evening, I was giving out rupees and ashrafīs to the indigent and friendless, and whoever demanded anything, whatever it might be, I gave it to him in abundance.

In short, through the forty doors the necessitous were coming and taking away with them whatever they asked for. This is the account of what befel one day. A faḳīr came in from the

---

[212] This sentence is elliptical. In the text there is only, "If you are so, why should you not be so?" which is little better than nonsense.

[213] Īrān and Fārs are here used indifferently for "Persia," but for the general distinction between the words, *vide* Note 232.

[214] Namely, "renown." The whole passage is in the direct form in the original.

opposite door and begged. I gave him an ashrafī. Again, the same fakīr passed through the second door and came in. He asked for two ashrafīs. Though I knew him to be the same man, I overlooked it and gave them. In the very same way he began to come in through each door, and to increase his demand by an ashrafī at a time, and I too, intentionally, feigned ignorance, and gave him according to his demand. At length, having come in through the fortieth door, he asked for forty ashrafīs, and that also I bestowed upon him. Having received so much, he again pushed in through the first door, and begged. I was highly displeased, and said, "Hearken! O greedy one! what sort of fakīr art thou? who art not even acquainted with the three letters[245] of poverty. The practice of a fakīr should be in accordance with these." The fakīr said, "Well! Benefactor! do you yourself shew me (what they are)." I said, "From f. comes 'fasting,' from k. 'contentment,' from r. 'rigid abstinence.' He in whom these things are not is no fakīr. After receiving so much, consume that (thou hast), and return and then receive what thou shalt ask for. This alms is for removing want—not for hoarding. O covetous one! at the forty doors thou hast received from one ashrafī to forty; do thou compute that sum, viz. how many ashrafīs it makes by way of arithmetical progression;[246] and even after this, avarice brought thee in again by the first door. What wilt thou do with all this wealth after thou hast collected it? A fakīr ought to take thought but for one day. After that, God is ready for the next day to provide him with a fresh subsistence. Now take shame to thyself, and make use of patience and contentment. What sort of austerity is this, that thy spiritual preceptor has taught thee?" Having heard this speech from me, he became incensed and insolent, and threw down on the ground all he had received of me, and said, "Enough, Sir! be not so

---

[245] In Arabic "faḳr" is "poverty," or the practice of a fakīr, and consists of three letters, f. k. r. with the vowel mark. In English it is impossible to preserve the point of the sentence.

[246] Literally, "by turn of the sweetmeat," alluding to a game at which some one bets he will eat so many "rewṛīs," or sweetmeats, so many times doubled, and is confounded at the amount.

warm! Take your pelf and put it by. Assume no more the name of generosity. To be generous is very difficult. You cannot support the weight of being generous. When will you arrive at this stage? Delhi[217] is still far. There are three letters in generous also. First act upon them, and then call thyself generous." Then indeed I felt abashed and said, "Well! kind Sir! explain the meaning of this to me." He began to say, "From s. comes (*samāī*) 'endurance,' and from kh. (*khauf-i Ilāhī*) 'the fear of God,' and from y. (*yād*) 'recollection of one's own birth and death.' Till thou hast acquired thus much, take not the name of generosity. And the dignity of the generous man is this, that even if he be an evil-doer, still he is the friend of God. This faķīr has travelled over many countries, but he never saw a generous person except the Princess of Baṣrah. God has cut out the robe of generosity for that woman, and all desire the name, but do not act accordingly." Having heard this, I made many entreaties and conjured him saying, "Pardon my fault, and take what you require." He constantly refused my gifts, and departed with these words, "Now if you would bestow your whole kingdom upon me, I would not spit or squat upon it." He truly departed, but from hearing this praise of the Princess of Baṣrah, my heart became disquieted. I was left without repose. I now felt a desire which urged me to proceed somehow or other to Baṣrah and behold her.

Meanwhile the king died, and I ascended the throne. I obtained the kingdom, but that thought did not leave me. I consulted with my ministers and nobles, who were the pedestals of the throne of my kingdom, and the pillars of the state, telling them that I desired to make a journey to Baṣrah, that they should remain diligent in the discharge of their duties, and that if I survived, the duration of my journey would be short, and that I would quickly return. None of them assented to my departure. Having no alternative, I continued dejected, One day, without addressing myself to the rest, I summoned a vazīr skilled in counsel, and appointed him my viceroy and representative, with full powers, and created him absolute

---

[217] A proverb applied to those who fall short of their mark in what they undertake.

director of the State. I then put on clothes coloured with red ochre, took the guise of a faḳīr, and set out alone for Baṣrah. In a few days I arrived on its confines, and thenceforward I began to witness the following spectacle. Wherever I arrived and halted for the night, the servants of that same queen met me, and caused me to alight in a handsome abode, and supplied me abundantly with all things necessary for my entertainment, and with folded hands waited in my service the whole night. On the next day and at the next stage the same style of things was maintained. In this comfort I traversed a journey which occupied months. At length I arrived in Baṣrah. Immediately a graceful youth, handsomely attired, of good disposition, and polite manners (whose intelligence was discernible in his countenance), came up to me and in very sweet language began to say, "I am the servant of faḳīrs; I am constantly engaged in this same inquiry, that whatever traveller —be he a faḳīr or a man of the world—enters this city, should take the trouble of stepping into my house. There is but one place for the abode of strangers here. Let your honour be pleased to proceed thither and adorn that place with your presence, and bestow exaltation upon me."

I inquired, "What, Sir, is your illustrious name?" He said, "They call the name of this ignoble person, Bedār Bakht."[248] Perceiving his goodness and courtesy, this humble person went with him and entered his house. I saw then that it was a lofty edifice, furnished with regal state. He led me into a hall and caused me to be seated, and having called for hot water, had my hands and feet washed, and having caused the cloth to be laid, the steward arranged before me a number of trays. There were four large dishes. In one was Yakhnī pulāo;[249] in the second, Ḳormā pulāo;[250] in the third,

---

[248] That is, "wakeful"—or "happy—fortune."

[249] The recipe for Yakhnī is as follows:—Take a pound of mutton, four or five onions whole, one piece of green ginger, two dried cassia leaves, eight corns of black pepper, twelve pounds of water; boil these together in an earthen vessel till three or four pounds of fluid remain. Take the pot off the fire, mash the meat, etc., with the liquor, and strain it through a towel. Set aside this Yakhnī or broth. Take rice eight ounces, wash it well, and dry it by squeezing it firmly in a towel, etc. *Vide* Ḳānūn-i Islām, p. 28, App. 5.

[250] The Ḳormā pulāo is similar to the Yakhnī, except that the meat is cut into very thin slices. Ḳānūn-i Islām, p. 28, App. 5.

Mutanjan pulão;[251] in the fourth, Kūkū pulāo.[252] And there was one dish of zardah,[253] and several sorts of kaliyahs and meat boiled with onions, nargisī and bādāmī, and cakes fried in clarified butter, and several kinds of bread, such as that called after Bāḳir Khān and Tunkī, Shīr-māl, Gāo-dīdah and

---

[251] The Mutanjan pulāo is made with rice, meat, particularly that of kid, sugar, clarified butter, and occasionally pine-apples or nuts. Ḳānūn-i Islām, p. 28, App. 5. The Mutanjan pulāo, according to information received direct from India, is the same as the Ḳormā, except that the meat is venison. According to the same authority, the Yakhnī is made of eight pounds of rice, four of butter, four of meat, all boiled together; and the recipe for the Ḳormā is as follows:—Take a piece of meat, cover it with butter and hot spices, boil it in a pot, then mix it with rice and boil it over again.

[252] The Kūkū pulāo is not given in the Ḳānūn-i Islām, but the authority already quoted gives the following recipe:—Boil eggs till hard, mix with rice and the gravy of meat. (The writer adds, "This I can confidently recommend, having tasted it.")

[253] The dishes here mentioned are described by the same authority (a gentleman in India, who kindly caused them to be all prepared in his presence, at my request) to be as follows:—Zardah is a dish of the yolk of eggs.—For the Ḳaliyah, boil meat with sour milk, hot spices, and butter, in a large kettle, adding sufficient water to soften the flesh.—For the Do piyāzah, boil meat in water for a long time, cutting into the pot slices of onions from time to time. When the meat is softened, throw away the water; then melt butter in another pot till it becomes clarified; into this put onions; then put the meat into the same, with coriander, and boil the whole for a short time, five or ten minutes.—The Nargisī is a biscuit like the narcissus in flavour or odour.—The Bādāmī is flour with pounded almonds kneaded and baked.—The Raughan-josh is, as the name imports, a cake fried in "ghī"—*i.e.* clarified butter.—Bāḳir Khān and Tunkī, according to the same informant, were two celebrated bakers. I should doubt the latter being the name of a man, but would rather derive it from तनुक *tanuk*, "slight."—Shīr-māl, as its name denotes, is bread kneaded with milk instead of water.—Gāo-dīdah and Gāo-zabān are, the former small, the latter long, bread, and have their names from the fancied resemblance to the eye and tongue of a cow, as we say "bull's eyes."—Nān-i niʿmat are very small pieces of meat fried or boiled, then pounded, then fried again in butter, mixed with bread, and baked.—The Parūṭhā is thus made: Make a "chau-pattī," *i.e.* a thin cake of baked flour, spread it with butter, knead it, spread butter again, repeat kneading and spreading ten or twelve times; then bake it well, and it will come out in slices thinner than paper.—Kabāb kofte-ke are fried lumps of pounded meat.—Kabāb tikke-ke are fried balls of chopped or minced meat. The text of Forbes' edition here requires to be repunctuated. There should be a stop thus — between each dish, else nothing is more natural than to take کباب کوفتے کے تکے کے *kabāb kofte-ke tikke-ke* together. The Murgh-ke kabāb are the same as the preceding, only made of fowl.—The Khāgīnah is undoubtedly an omelet, though my informant takes it with Murgh-ke, and makes it "devilled fowl."—Malghūbah is thus made:—

Gāo-zabān, bread mixed with meat, wafers, pounded meat, minced meat and minced fowl, omelets, Malghūbah, Shabdeg, Dam-pukht, Ḥalīm, Harīsā, Samosah, Waraḳī, Ḳabūlī, Firnī, Shīr-i birinj, Malāī, Ḥalwā, Fālūdah, Pan batthā, Nimash, Ābshorah, Sāk-i ūrūs, almond-cakes, preserves, pickle-pots, small glasses filled with curds. Having beheld these danties, my spirit was filled, and when I had taken a mouthful from each dish, my stomach also was filled, and then I withdrew my hand from the repast.

That person was pressing me, saying, "What has your honour eaten? the dinner truly is all left, just as it was brought in. Be pleased, without ceremony, to eat some more." I said, "What shame is there in eating? May God keep your repasts plentiful! I have eaten as much as I could contain in my stomach, and how shall I (sufficiently) commend its flavour! for I am still licking my lips,[254] and my eructation is perfumed. Enough! now take away.[255] When the table-cloth[256] was removed, they spread a brocaded hukkah carpet

---

Boil gently two kids in twenty pounds of water all night, then put in almonds, pistachio nuts, dates, raisins, walnuts, etc., then boil again.—Shabdeg is meat and turnips cooked together all night.—The Dam-pukht is thus made:—Boil fish, take out the bones, mix it with spices and butter, then fry it; cut open a brandule (?) and having scooped it out, place fish inside, and then fry again. There is another kind of Dam-pukht. A fowl is covered all over with paste of flour, and thus boiled. The paste is taken off as soon as the fowl is sufficiently boiled.—Ḥalīm is barley pudding, with milk.—Harīsā is liquid jelly.—Samosah is sandwiches toasted with spices.—Waraḳī is the Persian name for the Parūṭhā because it peels off, ورق بورق *warak ba-warak*.—Ḳabūlī is sweet-bread.—For Firnī mix rice powdered with hot milk and a little camphor.—The Shīr-i birinj is rice-pudding.—Malāī is a cream.—Ḥalwā is a pudding of butter, flour, and milk.—Fālūdah is almost the same as the preceding.—Pan bhattā is boiled rice kept one day in water, and boiled next day in fresh water.—Nimash is jelly in a shape.—Ābshorah is thus made:—Mix tamarinds, rose-water, sugar and cold water, and cool in saltpetre and water. This is tamarind sharbat.—Sāk-i ūrūs, or brides' legs, is a sort of double bread.—Lauziyāt are almond cakes.—The curious inquirer into Oriental cookery may compare this list with the description given in the Ḳānūn-i Islām, p. 28, etc., Appendix 5; but for ordinary appetites this, perhaps, will be sufficient.

[254] Literally, "licking my tongue."

[255] It being thought unlucky to say "Take away," the expression used instead is, "Make more."

[256] Dastar khwān literally signifies "the turband of the table."

of velvet of Kāshān,[257] and brought in a basin and ewer of gold, and from a box made for its reception, presented me with perfumed flour of pulse to rub the body, and caused my hands to be washed with warm water. Afterwards they brought in, and placed before me, in a jewelled betel-box, betel-leaf prepared and folded up, and encased in leaves of gold, and rolls of betel and betel-nuts prepared by boiling, in boxes with four partitions, and cloves, and cardamoms, covered with leaves of silver. When I called for water to drink, the person who had charge of the water department came bringing a flagon dipped in ice. When it was evening, candles, white as camphor, and placed in shades, were lit. That friendly person took his seat and conversed with me, and when a watch of the night had passed, he said, "Now be pleased to repose in this bedstead, with curtains, before which a screen is standing." I replied, "O sir! for us faḳīrs a mat, or the skin of a deer, is more than enough for a bed. God has made these things for you men of the world."

He commenced saying, "All this furniture is for darweshes; none of it is my property." At his pressing entreaty, I went and lay down on the bed (which was softer even than a bed of flowers). On each side of the side-frames of the bedstead were pots of roses, and other flowers ranged in order, and burning censers of aloes, and other perfumes. To whatever side I turned, my brain was filled with fragrance. In this way I fell asleep. When the morning came he brought into my presence for breakfast almonds, pistachio-nuts, grapes, figs, pears, pomegranates, raisins, dates, and fruit sharbats. In this same manner I passed three days and nights. On the fourth day, I requested leave to depart. He then joined his hands and began to say, "Perhaps this guilty person has in some point failed in attendance on your honour, from which cause your mind is displeased!" I was amazed and said, "For God's sake what discourse is this? But the term for entertaining a guest is three days, which I have stayed. To remain longer is not well; and, besides, I have come out to travel.

---

257 Kāshān, a town of Persia, in 34° N. lat., 51° 25′ E. lon., famous for its velvets.

To tarry in one place would be improper. I therefore desire permission to go; otherwise your good qualities are not of such a nature that one's mind would desire to be separated from them."

He then said, "As you will, but be pleased to wait for a moment, that I may go into the presence of the princess and make representation, and as you desire to depart [you must know] that all the wearing apparel, carpets, etc., and gold and silver and jewelled services for meals, which are in this house for the entertainment of guests, are all your property. Measures shall be taken for obeying your instructions, whatever they may be, as to the mode of carrying these things with you." I replied, "Repeat the deprecatory formula called the 'Lā ḥaul!'[258] Have I become not a faḳīr, but a bard?[259] Had I felt this desire of lucre, then why should I have become a faḳīr? What is there amiss in a worldly life?" That dear person replied, "If the Queen should hear this affair, then God knows, after dismissing me from her service, how she will treat me. If you really feel such indifference, then fasten up all these things in a room as a deposit,[260] and seal up the door. Afterwards, do with them whatever you wish."

I was continuing to withhold my consent, and he, too, was persisting in disregarding my excuses. (At last), having no alternative, this same plan was agreed upon, to shut up all the things, and put a lock upon them, which we did, and I awaited my permission to depart. Meanwhile a eunuch, a confidential person, with an aigrette on his head and an ornament in his ear, and a sash tied round his waist, holding a golden staff of office, set with jewels, in his hand, and accompanied by several respectable[261] attendants, filling their respective offices, approached me

---

258 This is at length, لا حول و لا قوة الا بالله *lā ḥaula wa lā ḳuwata illa bi-l-lāhi*, "There is no power or goodness but in God," but they generally say, "Lā ḥaul," when they wish to deprecate anything.

259 These are distinguished in Hindūstān, as in other countries, by the exorbitant value which they place on their performances. Like the old Welsh bards, they chaunt the heroic deeds of warriors.

260 Or perhaps rather, "untouched, just as they are."

261 Thus we must render معقول *mȧḳūl*, according to Forbes, but I should prefer making it agree with عہدے *ûhde*, and translating the whole sentence, "and accompanied by several attendants holding suitable offices."

with the state I have described.[262] He began to address me with such kindness and courtesy as I am unable to express, and added, "O, Sir! if you will show favour and condescension, and bestow ornament on the poor house of this person, who eagerly desires your presence, by blessing it with your footsteps, it will be an act in accordance with a feeling which will confer exaltation on your slave, and will be consistent with a cherishing of the poor.

"Perhaps the Princess may hear that a traveller has come here, and that no one showed him politeness and courtesy. He departed just as he came. God knows what calamity she may bring upon me on this account, and what trouble she may cause. Moreover my life even may be endangered." I did not assent to these words. Then he besought me, and led me, whether I would or not, into another residence (which surpassed the first house). Like the same first host he gave me for three days and nights, twice in the twelve hours, just such repasts, and in the morning and at the third watch, sharbat and fruit for dessert, and with reference to all the dishes of silver and gold, and the carpets and furniture, which were there, he said to me, "You are absolute master of all these; do with them what you will."

When I heard these words, I was amazed and wished somehow or other to take my departure thence and fly. The eunuch remarked my countenance and said, "O slave of God! tell me thy desire or wish, whatever it may be, and I will go into the presence of the Queen and state it." I said, "Why should I, in the dress of a faḳīr, ask for worldly wealth, that you should give it me without my asking, and I refuse it?" He then said, "Desire of worldly good has departed from the minds of none, just as a poet has said in this stanza:—

Ascetics have I seen who never pare their nails, and those with matted hair,
[Self-torturing] Jogī with split ears, who his nude limbs with ashes smears.
And hermits who ne'er break their silence dread, and Jain faḳīrs with shaven head,
And in the forests wild of Ban Khaṇḍī, I have seen the sportive devotee.

---

[262] I have been obliged to use these six words to translate اِس *is*.

Heroes I have seen,—I have seen the brave, the wise, the fool, and riches' slave.
Those who in sorrow drew their breath, and those who passed from birth to death,
Successful—but I've not seen those, whose mind no taint of avarice knows."

When I heard this, I made answer, saying, "This is true, but I have no desire for it. If you permit me, I will write and deliver to you a sealed letter, containing my wish, which convey into the presence of the Queen, this will be a great kindness, you will have given me as it were the whole wealth of the world." He said, "With my head and eyes, of course." I wrote a letter, beginning with praise to God, and afterwards proceeding to business, stating that "this slave of God arrived a few days ago in this city, and every kind of attention has been shown and is shown to me by the Government. And I have found the virtues and illustrious qualities of the Queen (the hearing of which has caused me this strong desire to see her) four-fold greater than I had heard. Now the high officers of your Majesty bid me make known my wish and inclination; wherefore I without reserve represent the wish of my heart, for I am not in want of worldly wealth. I too am a king in my own country. My coming hither and the labour I have undergone has been entirely out of affection for your Highness. (From this cause alone) I have arrived here quite alone in my present condition. I now hope that by the favour of your Highness this sitter in the dust may arrive at the desire of his heart—thus it is fitting. For the rest, let your royal will be done. But if the representation of this lowly person be not accepted, he will then return in this same manner, sifting dirt and offering up his afflicted life as a sacrifice, through love for your Highness. Like Majnūn and Farhād,[263] he will remain and die in the forests or on the mountains."

Having written this request, I delivered it to the eunuch, and he conveyed it to the Princess. After a moment he returned

---

[263] A celebrated Persian statuary, who fell in love with Shīrīn, or Irene, the daughter of the Emperor Maurice, and wife of Khusrau Parwīz, and to please her, it is said, he dug through an immense mountain, and afterwards destroyed himself for her sake by casting himself down from a rock.

and called me, and took me with him to the ante-chamber of the palace. Having gone there, I perceived that an elderly woman, a dignified personage, wearing a profusion of ornaments, was seated on a golden chair, and several eunuchs and attendants, dressed in rich apparel, were standing before her with hands folded in a respectful manner. Believing her to be invested with the chief power, and regarding her as a person venerable for her age, I placed my hand upon my head. That matron saluted me with much kindness, and addressing me authoritatively, said, "Come! be seated! It is well you have come. It was yourself, then, who has written a love-letter to the Queen?" Ashamed and silent, I held down my head and seated myself.

After a moment she said, "O youth! the Princess sends you her compliments, and says that she has no objection to take a husband, and that you have asked her in marriage, but to make mention of your kingdom, and in this your condition as a faḳīr to look upon yourself as a king, and to pride yourself upon it, is very out-of-place, because in point of fact all men are the same—one like another, but of course there is a superiority in the religion of Islām. And [the Queen says] that for a long time she has been desirous of marrying, and just as you are indifferent to worldly riches, so God most High has given to her also so much wealth as to be incalculable. But there is one condition—that you first complete the marriage portion, and the marriage portion of the Princess is a certain thing if you can do[264] it." I said, "I am in all respects ready. I will not withhold my life or property—what is that thing? Tell it, that I may hear." She then said, "Wait to-day—to-morrow I will tell you." I gladly assented, took leave, and came out.

The day indeed passed. When the evening came a eunuch called and took me into the palace. When I had gone there, I saw that the nobles, the learned men, and those eminent for their piety, and their knowledge of the law, were there. I, too, entered that assembly, and took my seat, when meanwhile the table-cloth was spread, and viands of various kinds, sweet

264 This might also be rendered, "which you are able to effect."

and salted, were arranged. They all began to eat, and civilly caused me also to partake. When the repast was finished, a nurse came from the inner apartments, and said, "Where is Bahrawar?[265] Call him." The pursuivants immediately brought him. His appearance was very gentleman-like, and many keys of silver and of gold were suspended at his girdle. Having said, "Peace be to thee!" he came and sate beside me. That same nurse began to say, "O Bahrawar! do thou make a detailed narration of all thou sawest."

Bahrawar began [then] to relate this story, and addressing me, said, "O dear friend! under the government of our Princess are thousands of slaves, who are deputed to carry on trade; of whom I, too, her humble and hereditary servant, am one. Committing to their charge merchandise to the value of hundreds of thousands of rupees, she despatches them to every country. On the return of each, she interrogates him in her own presence as to the affairs of that country, and listens to him. Once on a time it happened that this meanest of individuals had gone to traffic, and had arrived in the city of Nīmroz.[266] I observed that the dress of all the inhabitants of that city was black, and that lamentation and wailing went on incessantly; thus it was manifest that some great calamity had befallen them. It mattered not of whom I inquired the cause of this; none gave me any answer. Several days passed in this wonderment. One day, as soon as it was morning, all the people of the city, small and great, children and aged, poor and rich, went forth. They went and assembled in a plain, and the king of that country also, accompanied by all his nobles, mounted and proceeded thither, whereupon all formed a regular line, and remained standing.

---

[265] The meaning of this proper name is, "Fortunate," from بهر *bahr*, "fortune," with the affix ور *war*.

[266] Nīmroz, or "Half-day," was the name of a province, comprising the eastern parts of Persia and Mekrān, once governed by Sām Neriman, grandfather of Rustam. It was so called because the genii, at the command of Sulaimān, changed it from sea to land in half a day, or because the Emperor of China halted there half a day. Other derivations also are to be found in Eastern writers. Some think the city of Nīmroz to be Baghdād, as thought to be the centre of the earth, and hence of the sun's course.

"I too was standing among them, and was viewing this spectacle, but this was evident, that they were waiting for somebody. In the space of an hour a graceful and beautiful youth, fifteen or sixteen years old, uttering cries and vociferations, the foam issuing from his mouth, and mounted on a yellow bullock, advanced, holding the nose-string of the animal in his hand, towards the people; and, after dismounting from his bullock, knelt down, holding in one hand the nose-string, and in the other the naked sword. There was with him a rose-bodied, fairy-faced youth, to whom the youth gave the thing which he held in his hand. The slave took it and, beginning at one end, was going on shewing it to each, but such was the state of things that each who was looking at it could not refrain from weeping bitterly. In this same manner, he shewed it to all, and caused them to weep, and then, having passed in front of all of them, he went back to his master.

"On his going back, the youth arose, cut off the head of the slave with his scimitar, and, having mounted, departed in the direction whence he came. All stood and gazed. When he had disappeared from sight, the people returned to the city. I was inquiring of every one into the circumstances of this occurrence, and moreover was tempting their cupidity with money, and using flattery and entreaties, saying, 'Explain to me a little who this youth is, and what action[267] this is that he has done, and whence he came, and whither he has gone?' No one gave me any explanation, and I could not form any conception (of the truth). When, after seeing this wonderful occurrence, I came here and stated it before the Queen, from that time the Princess has continued in perplexity, and is embarrassed with regard to its investigation. Wherefore she has fixed this as her marriage portion, (declaring) that whatever person brings correct intelligence of this wondrous matter, the Queen will accept him, and he shall be master of all her territories and of herself.

"You have now heard all the story. Take thought with

---

267 حرکت *ḥarakat*, "action," is always used in a bad sense for a wrong or improper action.

yourself. If you are able to bring an account of that youth, then set out for the country of Nīmroz, and take your departure speedily. Otherwise decline it, and take the way to your own house." I replied, "If God will, I shall quickly discover the facts of the case from beginning to end, and return to the Princess, and enjoy the completion of my wishes. And if my destiny be bad, then that is irremediable, but let the Queen promise this—that she will not swerve from her agreement, and at the present moment an embarrassing thought remains, causing inquietude in my heart. If the Queen, from a feeling of condescension and kindness to me a traveller, will call me into her presence, and cause me to be seated without the curtain, and listen with her own ears to my representation, and favour me with an answer from her own lips [*lit.* 'tongue'], I shall then be satisfied and can do anything." This my request the matron represented in the presence of that fairy-faced (Princess). At length, by way of showing her appreciation of my merits, she gave orders, saying, "Summon him."

The nurse again came out and took me with her into the part of the palace where the Princess was. What do I behold? There, forming a line, facing either way, female servants and waiting women, and armed female attendants on the ḥaram, and Kilmāḳs, and Turkish, and Abyssinian, and Uzbak, and Kashmīrian women, adorned with jewels, stood filling their respective offices. Am I to call it the Court of Indra?[268] or the place where the fairies alight? A sigh of ecstacy involuntarily rose to my lips (*lit.* "tongue"), and my heart began to palpitate; but by a violent effort I supported myself. I advanced, gazing at them and surveying the spectacle, but my feet seemed to weigh each a hundred mans.[269] Whichever of them I looked upon, my heart wished to go no further. On one side a screen was let down, and a stool set with jewels was spread [with a silken or velvet coverlet], as well as a chair made of sandal-wood. The nurse made me a sign to sit down. I

---

[268] Indra, the Hindū Jove, holds a glittering court in Swarga, where gods, goddesses, and lovely dancing-nymphs are assembled.

[269] The من *man*, is a weight of 40 sīrs or 80 lbs.

seated myself on a stool, and she herself on the chair. She then began to say, "Well! now what you have to say, that say, relieving your mind fully."[270]

I commenced by extolling the good qualities, the justice and equity, the liberality and munificence, of the Queen. I then added, "From the time that I entered the confines of this country I have observed that at every stage, houses for travellers, and lofty edifices are erected, and men are appointed in every capacity who take care of travellers and of the indigent. I also passed three days at each halting place. On the fourth day, when I was about to take leave, even then no one willingly allowed my departure, and all the furniture that there was in the place, as chequered carpets, druggets, rugs, cool mats, carpets made at Mangal-koṭ,[271] tapestry, ceiling cloths, screens, canopies, awnings, bedsteads with curtains and covers, bags, quilts, counterpanes, bedcords,[272] sheets, pillows, little pillows, small pillows for the cheek,[273] cushions, bolsters, cooking pots large and small, pans, kneading vessels, plates,[274] bowls, salvers, spoons, ladles, skimming ladles, large spoons for serving out food, covers, trays, tray-lids, tray-covers, vessels for cooling water and others for hot water, flagons, basons, boxes for holding betel, perfume-boxes with four compartments, flower-pots, phials for sprinkling rose-water, censers for burning aloes, ewers, hand-basins,[275] all these they made over to me, saying, 'This is your property, if you wish, take it with you now, otherwise shut it up in a room

---

270 Literally, "having filled your mind."

271 This was a town, famous for its manufacture of carpets, in the Bengal Presidency, but its exact position I know not.

272 This is the cord laced between the frame of a bed, to support the bedding.

273 In Forbes' vocabulary, we find گل تکیه *gal takiyah*, rendered "a small pillow for the neck," which would make it come from گلا *galā*, "the neck." But as all pillows are for the neck, I would derive it from گال *gāl*, "the cheek," as Shakespear also gives it.

274 On the Bombay side, instead of رکابي *rikābī*, they use باسن *bāsan*, for "a plate."

275 Instead of چلمچي *chilamchī*, on the Bombay side, they use the word گهنڈي *ghinḍī*, which is not in the dictionaries.

and put your own seal on it. When it shall be your pleasure, as you return, carry it away.' I did just so; but this astonishes me, that since I, a solitary faḳīr, met with such attention, and thousands of indigent persons like myself are coming and going in your dominions, then if the same style of hospitality is maintained towards each, a sum which exceeds computation would be expended. Now whence comes the wealth to supply this expenditure? and of what nature is it? Were it the treasure of Ḳārūn,[276] even then it would not suffice. And if you look at the dominions of the Queen, as far as outward appearances go, the revenue of it would not be sufficient even for the disbursements of the kitchen—to say nothing of other expenses. If I may hear an explanation of this from the Queen's tongue, I shall then set out with a satisfied mind for the country of Nīmroz, and somehow or other manage to arrive there. Afterwards I shall discover all the circumstances, and, provided I live, present myself a second time in the service of the Queen, and obtain the wish of my heart."

Having heard this, the Queen said, with her own tongue, "O youth! if you have a thorough inclination to learn this matter, then tarry here to-day also. At evening I will send for you into my presence, and the circumstances of this unfailing wealth, such as they are, without diminution or keeping back anything, shall be related to you." I having obtained this comfort returned to the place where I was halting, and waited in expectation, saying, "When will it be evening, that my wish may be accomplished?" Meanwhile an eunuch, bringing on the heads of bearers[277] several four-cornered trays with coverings over them, came and presented himself and said, "Her Royal Highness has sent you what remains of her own repast—eat thereof." When he uncovered ⌊the dishes], in my presence, my brain was perfumed with the smell [of the food], and my spirit satisfied. I ate as much as I was able. What was left I took up and gave it to all of them, and sent my thanks for the delicate viands. At length, when the sun,

---

[276] As to Ḳārūn, *vide* Note 91.

[277] This word بهوئی *bhoī*, or bearer, is the word which, in the Anglo-Indian patois, is pronounced "boy," and is the usual word for summoning a servant.

traveller of the livelong day, wearied and labouring, entered his palace, and the moon, accompanied by her companions (the stars), came forth and seated herself in the public hall, then the nurse came and said to me, "Come! the Princess has called for you" [*lit.* "remembered you"]. I went along with her. She conducted me into the private apartment of the Queen. Such was the illumination that the Night of Grandeur[278] had no grandeur in comparison with it. A seat of cushions, embroidered with gold, was placed on a carpet of royal magnificence. A pillow covered with gold was laid there, and over it was supported, on jewelled pillars, a canopy with a fringe of pearls, and before the seat were trees of jewels,[279] with flowers and leaves (you would have said they were as natural as those produced by Omnipotence), and set[280] in beds of gold; and on both sides, on the right hand and on the left, servants and courtiers stood with their hands folded in respectful postures, and with their eyes turned down, and bands of dancing girls and female singers, keeping their instruments in harmony, were in waiting. Having beheld this state of things, and these magnificent preparations, my reason did not keep its place.[281] I said to the nurse, inquiringly, "By day there is this splendour, and by night this display, that one ought to call the day the festival of Ĭd, and the night the Night of Barāt.[282] Nay, in this world such a delightsome life is, I suppose, unattainable even by the king of tho seven regions.[283] Does this state of

---

278 The شب قدر *shab-i ḳadar*, or ليلة القدر *lailatu'l-ḳadar*, is the 27th night of Ramaẓān, the ninth month. On this night all vegetable creation adores the Deity, and the ocean becomes sweet. On this night the pious keep vigil, burning frankincense, pastiles, and other lights, and proclaiming, ever and anon, the aẕān, or call to prayer.

279 Such a tree was among the treasures of Shāh Jahān, and reminds us also of the golden plane-tree of the Persian kings.

280 This meaning is to be found in Shakespear's dictionary, but is omitted in Forbes' vocabulary.

281 Strange that the King of Persia should have found anything novel in regal state, but the book is full of these contradictions.

282 For an explanation of Ĭd and Barāt, *vide* Notes 48 and 195.

283 The Musalmān divide the earth into seven regions. Is this borrowed from the seven Dwīpas of the Hindūs? We might very well adopt it, keeping the old divisions of Europe, Asia and Africa, making Australia one, Polynesia another, and dividing the Americas.

things always continue?" The nurse replied, "All the departments under our Queen which you have seen are unceasingly conducted after this same fashion. Never does any cessation take place; nay, there is rather an increase. Do you sit here; the Queen has gone to another apartment. I will go and inform her."

The nurse, with these words, departed, and retraced her steps, saying, "Proceed into the presence." Immediately that I entered that apartment, I was struck with amazement. I could not perceive where the door was, or the wall, for this reason, that mirrors from Ḥalab [Aleppo], of the height of a man, were placed on all sides, and their frames[284] were studded with diamonds and pearls. The reflection of one was re-reflected by another, whence it appeared that the whole apartment was made of jewels. On one side a curtain was let down, behind which the Queen was seated. The nurse took her seat close to the curtain and told me also to sit down. Then, by command of the Queen, the nurse began to discourse in the following manner, saying, "Hearken! O wise youth! The sulṭān of this realm was a great king. In his house were born seven daughters. One day the King commanded a feast, and these seven girls having adorned themselves with sixteen ornaments and twelve other kinds of trinkets, and strung each separate hair of their heads with elephant pearls,[285] were standing in the presence of the King. Something passed through the mind of the King, whereupon he looked towards his daughters and said, 'Were your father not a king, and had you been born in the house of some poor man, who then would have called you princesses and queens? Thank God that you have the title of princesses. All this good-fortune of yours is owing to me' [*lit.*, 'to my breath'].

"Six of the girls said unanimously, 'What the Asylum of the

---

[284] In spite of this passage, the dictionaries have omitted to give the meaning "frame," under پرداز *pardāz*, though it is not only a book-meaning, but a conversational one also.

[285] The Hindūs have an idea that the finest pearls are found in the heads of elephants.

world says, is true, and our welfare is dependent entirely on Your Majesty's safety.' But this Queen of the world was younger than all her sisters, yet in understanding and quickness she was, even at that age, as you might say, older than all of them. She stood silent, and did not join in this speech of her sisters, because it was an avowal[286] of infidelity. The King looked towards her with an angry glance, and said, 'How now, lady? you have said nothing—what is the meaning of this?' Then the Queen, having bound her two hands with her handkerchief, made a humble petition, saying, 'If I shall obtain security for my life, and if my fault be pardoned, then this handmaid will represent the thought of her heart.' The command was pronounced, 'Speak! what dost thou say?' Then the Queen said, 'O point[287] to which the world turns in prayer! Your Majesty has heard that true words are bitter; wherefore I now wash my hands of my life in making the statement I do, and whatever the Writer has recorded in my destiny, of that there is no effacer—in nowise can it be altered. .

In worship vain with oft-repeated tread[288]
Go rub your feet, or meekly bow the head;
Engraven on your forehead is your fate—
Its writing none shall thence obliterate.

That Supreme Lord who made you a King, the same has also caused me to be called a Princess. In the laboratory of his omnipotence, the will of no creature has any influence. Your Majesty is my benefactor, and the object of my reverence and

---

[286] The كلمة *kalimah* is the Musalmān creed. It is, لا لله الا الله و محمد الرسول الله *lā ilāha illa'llāh wa Muḥammadu'r-rasūlu'llāh*, "There is no God but God, and Muḥammad is His prophet." It is here used by a catachresis for the confession of infidelity.

[287] The قبلة *ḳiblah* of the Arabs was formerly that of the Jews, viz. Jerusalem, and Muḥammad for some time continued to sanction the custom of turning thitherward in prayer, but finding it give rise to much scandal he changed his "ḳiblah" to Makkah. It is here used as a reverential title. *Vide* Note 88.

[288] The first line is inserted, and is not in the text. The fourth is freely given.

veneration.[289] Should I use the dust of the royal footsteps of Your Majesty as collyrium, it would be but right; but the destiny of each person goes along with him.' When the King heard this, he was enraged, and this answer was very displeasing to his mind. In his irritation he said, 'A little mouth and great words.[290] Now let this be her punishment. Take off all the ornaments which are on her arms and neck, and having placed her in a litter, cast her away in such a forest as that the name or vestige of man born of Adam does not exist there; thus let us see what is written in her destiny.'

"In accordance with the command of the King at that time of midnight (a night which was most dark), bearers carried away the royal lady (who had been reared in retirement,[291] and had seen no other place but her own palace) to a plain (where a *bird* even did not flap its wing, why speak of *man ?*), and, having left her, departed thence.[292] Wonderful were the emotions which passed through the heart of the Princess as she reflected what her state had been and what in an instant it had become! Then she was returning thanks to God and saying, 'Thou art so Omnipotent [*lit.* 'one so without wants'] that what Thou hast desired to do, that Thou hast done; and what Thou desirest to do, that Thou dost; and what Thou shalt desire to do, that Thou wilt perform. As long as breath remains in my nostrils I will not despair of Thy aid.' In this same troublous thought her eyes closed. As soon as it began to dawn, the eyes of the Princess opened. She cried out, 'Bring water for my ablutions.'[293] Then, all at once, she remembered the conversation

---

289 قبلہ و کعبہ *ḳiblah wa kābah.* The first has been explained before. کعبہ *kābah*, is the square temple of Makkah, supposed to have been built by Abraham, or restored by him and built by Adam. It is considered most holy, and contains the famous black stone, once white, and kissed black by adoring worshippers.

290 We have had this expression before, *vide* Note 153.

291 Literally, "in a cavern beneath the earth," from a Sanskṛit word which signifies "under ground."

292 One of the most clumsy sentences in the book, with no less than three parentheses.

293 For the manner of performing وضو *wuẓū*, or the washing of the faee, hands and feet before prayer, *vide* Ḳānūn-i Islām, p. 72.

of the preceding night, and said to herself, 'Where art thou, and where this speech!'[294] Having said this, she arose and performed her ablutions with sand,[295] and repeated a thanksgiving comprising two rakāts.[296] O my friend! from hearing of this state of the Queen my breast is rent. You must inquire of that simple and innocent soul, what she will say of it.

"In short, seated in that palanquīn, she remained in fervent prayer to God,[297] and at that moment was repeating this stanza:

> Thee, when thou hadst not teeth, with milk He fed;
> With teeth, then, also will He not give bread?
> He who on sea and land their food divides
> To bird and beast, for thee, too, well provides.
> Wherefore take thought? the fool, with all his pains,
> Still empty-handed, by his care nought gains.
> God gives support to all alike who live—
> The wise, the fool; to thee too, then, He'll give.

It is true, when nothing else succeeds, we then have recourse to God. Otherwise, each in his own devices thinks himself Luḳmān,[298] and Bū Ālī Sīnā.[299] Now, hear a marvel of the

---

[294] That is, "these words are quite unsuitable to your present position."

[295] When water cannot be procured, the face, hands and feet are to be rubbed with sand before prayer. This is called تيمم *tayammum.*

[296] The ركعت *rakāt* consists of a certain number of prayers and chapters of the Ḳu'rān, accompanied with a prescribed number of inclinations of the head, bendings of the body, or genuflexions.

[297] لو لگانا *lau lagānā*, is literally "to apply"—or "kindle—a flame." It is singular that the word لو *lau* should be found also in Scotch. Thus a burning house is said to be all in a *low.* So in German, *lauen*, "to be tepid," and hence our "lukewarm." The root is, perhaps, the Sanskṛit ली *lī*, to fuse, or melt.

[298] لقمان *Luḳmān*, surnamed الحكيم *all ḥakīm*, "The Sage," is by some reckoned amongst the Prophets and called the cousin of Job, and by others is said to have been the grand-nephew of Abraham, while others affirm that he was born in the time of David and lived to that of the prophet Jonah. The more common opinion is, that he was an Æthiopian slave, liberated by his master on account of his sagacity and fidelity. He was the author of many excellent maxims and proverbs, and is the Æsop of the East.

[299] Bū Ālī Sīnā, or Avicenna, as he is called by Europeans, was the Admirable Crichton of the East. He was born at السينا *A's-sīnā*, a village near Bukhārā.

operations of God. In this same manner three entire days and nights passed away and not even a single parched grain had flown into the mouth of the Princess. That flower-like form, being dried up, had become like a thorn, and that complexion, which used to beam like pure gold, became like turmeric. Her mouth was contracted with a spasm, through weakness. Her eyes were fixed like stone; but one breath remained, and that was coming and going. As long as there is breath so long is there hope.[300] On the morning of the fourth day a darwesh, with a form like that of Khiẓr,[301] of a luminous countenance and a clear heart, came and presented himself. Seeing the Princess in that state, he said, 'O daughter! though thy father is a King, still this was predestined in thy lot. Now, regard this aged faḳīr as thy servant, and fix thy thoughts night and day on thy Creator. God will bring things to a happy conclusion.' And the scraps of alms which he had with him in his faḳīr's wallet, these he placed before the Princess, and went about to seek for water. On looking, he perceived there was a well, but where [thought he] is a bucket and cord wherewith to draw water? He broke a few leaves from a tree, and made a cup of them, and, having loosed his sash, he tied the cup to it and drew water and gave the Princess something to eat and drink. At length she recovered her senses a little. That man of God, regarding her as friendless and helpless, gave her much consolation. He encouraged her, and himself began to weep. When the Princess saw that his sympathy and compassion was excessive, she recovered her strength of mind. From that day that old man made it his fixed custom to go forth in the morning to the city to solicit alms, and he brought

---

At ten he was master of the most difficult points in the Ḳu'rān. At sixteen he was an accomplished physician! and at twenty-one compiled an Encyclopædia of all the knowledge then extant in twenty volumes. He wrote many other works, and died at Hamadān, aged fifty-eight years, A.D. 1036.

300 This proverb has occurred before, *vide* Note 228.

301 Khiẓr is the Arabic name for Elijah. He is supposed to have discovered the water of life, and to be still living. Hence little rafts are launched on rivers with lighted lamps in honour of him, particularly on the Fridays of the month Shābān. The legend about him probably gave rise to the story of the Wandering Jew.

whatever morsels or scraps he obtained to the Princess, and gave her them to eat.

"In this manner some days passed. One day, the Princess had formed the design of anointing her head, and combing and knotting up her hair. As soon as she undid the string which tied her hair, a single pearl, round and lustrous, fell from her back locks. The Princess gave it to the darwesh, and said, 'Sell this in the city and bring the proceeds.' The faḳīr, having sold the jewel, brought the price of it to the Princess. She then desired him to cause a house, fit for her residence, to be erected in that place. The faḳīr said, 'O daughter! dig the foundation and collect a little clay. One day I will bring water, make the slime for the bricks, and complete the foundation of the house.' The Princess, by his direction, began to dig the earth. When she had dug the trench a yard deep, a door appeared beneath the ground. The Princess cleared away the dirt from it. A large house, filled with jewels and ashrafīs, then showed itself. The Princess took four or five handfuls of the ashrafīs and covered it up again, and having put the earth over it, made it level. In the mean time the faḳīr returned. The Princess said, 'Call masons and builders, expert and masters of their craft, and active labourers, who may quickly prepare, in this spot, a royal palace, which may be a match for that of Kisrạ,[302] and surpass that of Nīmān,[303] and a rampart, and fort, and garden, and well, and a house for travellers, which may be unrivalled; but first make a correct plan of them on paper, and bring it into my presence for approval.'

"The faḳīr brought and placed in readiness just such practised and clever superintendents. According to her commands the building of the edifice commenced; and, when she had selected intelligent and trustworthy servants for every department, they

---

302 كسري *Kisrạ*, Chosroes, a name common to several kings of Persia.

303 نعمان *Nīmān*, or, according to Johnson's Persian Dictionary, نُعمان *Nūmān*, a name common to the kings of حيرة *Ḥīrat*, in Arabia, but especially applied to the last.

began to wait upon her.[304] The intelligence of the construction of that magnificent building by degrees reached the King, the shadow of Omnipotence (who was the father of the Princess). When he heard of it he was much astonished, and inquired of every one, 'What person is this who has begun to erect these palaces?' No one was sufficiently acquainted with the circumstances to make any statement. All placed their hands on their ears, saying, 'None of your slaves know who is the builder of this edifice.' The King then sent a noble, and gave him a message, saying, 'I am desirous of coming to see those palaces, and I am also ignorant of what country you are Princess, and of what family you are sprung. To become acquainted with all these particulars is a thing I wish.'

"As soon as the Princess heard this pleasing news, she was much delighted in her heart, and wrote this representation, 'Asylum of the world, Health! Having heard the intelligence of Your Majesty's coming to my poor house, I have derived much happiness, and it is a cause of honour and exaltation to this the humblest of your servants. Worthy of praise is the fortune of this place! where the trace of your royal footstep will be left, and whose inhabitants will be overshadowed by your fortunate skirt, and who, both of them,[305] will be exalted by your glance of favour. This handmaid is in hope that since to-morrow is Thursday, and an auspicious day, and, in my estimation, a better day than that of the New Year,[306] Your Highness's person, which is like the sun, will condescend to visit me, and with your light bestow rank and dignity on this insignificant atom, and be pleased to partake of the food, such as it is, which this weak person

---

[304] An ungrammatical sentence. The nominative, which agrees with چن چنکر *chun chunkar*, ought to be, but is not, the nominative to هونے لگے *hone lage*.

[305] Alluding to herself and the faḳīr who waited on her.

[306] نو روز *Nau-roz*, or New-year's day, is a festival of much importance among the Musalmān. The exact period of the New Year's commencing is the moment when the Sun enters Aries, and according to the hour is the colour of the clothes worn on the festival. If it enters at night, dark clothes are worn; if in the day, bright crimson. Presents and congratulations are exchanged on this day by all classes.

can provide. This will be shewing extreme condescension to the poor, and encouragement to travellers. More would exceed the bounds of good manners.'[307] And, having shewn some civility to the noble [who brought the letter], she dismissed him.

"The King read the petition and sent to say, 'We have accepted your invitation. We will certainly come.' The Princess gave orders to her servants and all her officers that the requisite preparations for an entertainment should be made with such taste that the King, when he saw them, and partook of the repast, might be highly gratified, and all who came in the royal retinue, high and low, might be pleased with what they ate and drank. According to the commands and strict injunctions of the Princess, all kinds of viands, salt and sweet, were prepared, of such a flavour, that had the daughter of a Brāhman tasted them she would have repeated the creed of the Musalmān.[308] When evening came, the King, borne in an open palanquīn, approached the house of the Princess. She, accompanied by her body-servants and female attendants, went forth to meet him. As soon as her eyes fell upon the royal chair, she performed the obeisance due to royalty with such respect that the King was more astonished when he saw her decorous manners, and, with the same grace, coming forward,[309] she led the King to a seat worked with gold, and seated him there. The Princess had caused to be prepared a platform formed of a hundred and twenty-five thousand rupees, and had placed it there,[310] and had got ready and placed near them one hundred and twenty-five trays of jewels, and ashrafīs, and woollen stuffs, and fine cloths,[311] and silks, and

---

307 زيادهٔ حدِّ ادب *ziyādah ḥadd-i adab*, "It would be disrespectful to say more," is the usual termination of Persian letters from an inferior.

308 That is, "she would have forsworn her religion in order to procure always such delicious food, which is forbidden to her caste, who do not eat meat."

309 Thus I venture to translate جلوه کرکر *jalwah karkar*, taking the former word to mean the first appearance of a beauty as of a bride to her husband; her *début*, as it were.

310 The usual way of presenting these offerings, or Nazrs, is to make them the seat of the person to whom they are given, spreading cushions over them.

311 Literally, "woven light," the *Coa vestis* of the Romans.

stuffs embroidered with gold, and others of gold thread, and two elephants,[312] and ten horses of Ĭrāḳ[313] and Arabia, with golden housings. These she presented as offerings,[314] and herself, with both her arms folded,[315] stood before the King. The King said, with much kindness, 'Of what country are you a Princess, and in what way have you come hither?'

"The Princess, after making her obeisance, respectfully represented: 'This slave-girl is the same guilty person, who, by reason of the King's anger, came to this wilderness. And all these wondrous sights which Your Majesty surveys are from God.' On hearing this, the King's blood boiled. He rose and tenderly embraced her, and, having taken her hand, caused a seat to be spread for her beside his own throne, and ordered her to be seated. The King, however, was sitting in a state of amazement and wonder. He said, 'Tell the Queen to bring the princesses with her, and come quickly.' When they arrived, the mother and sisters recognized [the Princess], and falling on her neck, wept and offered thanks [to God]. The Princess placed before her mother and her six sisters so vast a treasure in money and jewels, that the treasures of the whole world could not enter the scale against it. Afterwards the King, having caused all to be seated with him, partook of a royal repast. As long as the Asylum of the world lived, his

---

312 The words زنجير *zanjīr*, and راس *rās*, are here used in a peculiar way, which almost renders them pleonastic. In enumerating a number of things a word peculiar to the class is added, which denotes their individuality. Thus, instead of saying only "ten men" (دس آدمي *das ādmī*), they say, دس نفر آدمي *das nafar ādmī* (ten persons men); and instead of "one pearl" (ايک موتي *ek motī*), they say, ايک دانه موتي *ek dānah motī* (one grain pearl). So here, "two chain elephants," "ten head horses."

313 There are two Ĭrāḳs. The عراقِ عرب *Ĭrāḳ-i Ârab*, "Arabian Ĭrāḳ," or Babylonia; and عراقِ عجم *Ĭrāḳ-i Âjam*, "Persian Ĭrāḳ," or Media.

314 The نذر *nazr*, and the پيشكش *peshkash*, are offerings from an inferior. بخشش *bakhshish*, and انعام *inâm*, gifts from a superior to an inferior.

315 The posture of servants.

life passed in this same manner. Sometimes he came himself, and sometimes he took the Princess with him to his own palace.

"When the King died, the sovereignty of this region descended to the Princess, since no other person was worthy of it. O Friend! this is the history which thou hast heard. Wherefore, to wealth bestowed by God, no decrease happens; all that is required is, that the disposition of a person be right. Moreover, just as much as you expend, just so much is there a blessing [of increase] upon it. To wonder at the accomplishment of anything by the power of God is not lawful in any religion." After these words the nurse said, "Now, if you have fixedly determined in your heart to set out for that place, and to bring that intelligence, then hasten your departure." I said, "I go this very moment, and, if God wills, I will speedily return." At length, having taken leave, and having fixed my eyes on the grace of God, I set out in that direction.

In the space of a complete year, after enduring toil and trouble, I arrived in the city of Nīmroz. All the persons I saw there, both military and civil, were clad in black. I beheld with my own eyes the very circumstances I had heard. After some days came the night of the new moon. On the first day of the month all the people of that city, small and great—children, nobles, king, women and men—assembled in a plain. I, too, in my then condition, amazed and distracted, along with that crowd, separated from my property and country, was standing and looking on in the garb of a faḳīr, saying to myself, "Let us see what will be disclosed from the future." Meanwhile, a young man, riding on a bullock, with his mouth covered with foam, uttering cries and exclamations, came forth from the forest. I, this weak person, who, enduring such toils, had gone to obtain information of his story, immediately on seeing him, lost my senses and stood in a state of amazement. That young man, after doing the things he was by former custom wont to do, went back again, and the people of the city turned thitherward. When I recovered my senses I felt regret, and said to myself, "What is this thou hast done? now thou wilt have to wait again a whole month." Having no alternative, I accompanied the rest, and passed that month as though it were the month of Ramaẓān,[316] counting each day. At length another night of the new moon arrived. To me it was like the festival of ʻĪd.[317] On the first day of the month the King and the people again went and assembled at the same spot. I then made a fixed resolve in my heart that this time, let happen what might, I would keep up my courage, and would get at the unravelling of that wondrous thing.

All at once the young man, according to his custom, having fastened his saddle on a yellow bullock, came riding on that animal, and, having dismounted, knelt down. In one hand he held a naked sword, and in one hand the nose-string of the bullock, and he gave the jar to the slave. The slave took it along, shewing it to each, and the people, when they saw it, began to weep. The youth broke the jar, and struck the slave such a blow with his sword that his head was severed from his body, and he himself mounted and turned back. I began to follow him with haste. The people of the city seized my hand, and said, "What is this thou art doing? why art thou intentionally throwing away thy life? If thy breath has thus risen to thy nostril,[318] then there are many ways of dying—pause and die." Although I besought them, and even struggled with them, that somehow or other I might escape from their hands, I could not release myself. Two or four men clung to me and led me in their grasp towards the town. Again, for a whole month, I endured anxiety to an excessive degree.

When that month also was finished, and the day of the new moon came, the whole population of that place assembled in the morning in the very same manner. I arose at the time

---

[316] رمضان المبارك *Ramaẓānu 'l-mubārik*, "The blessed Ramaẓān," is the ninth month of the Muḥammadans. It is the Musalmān Lent, and eating, drinking, and conjugal duty, are interdicted during this month, between sunrise and the appearance of the stars. On the 27th the Ḳu'rān began to descend.

[317] The رمضان كي عيد *Ramaẓān kī ʻĪd*, held on the first of the tenth month, Shauwāl, at the expiration of the Musalmān Lent.

[318] That is, "If thou art in such haste to commit suicide."

of prayer, and, apart from all the rest, entered the jungle, which lay exactly in the way of that young man, and concealed myself there, saying to myself, "Here, at least, no one will interfere with me." That person, according to the same rule, came, and after doing the same things, mounted and went his way. I pursued him, and, running and toiling, kept up with him. That dear person, by the sound of my steps, perceived that some one was coming after him. All at once, he turned rein, uttered a yell, and threatened me. Having drawn his sword, he came and stood near me. He was about to attack me; I bent most respectfully and saluted him, and, having folded my two arms, stood still. That person, well acquainted with propriety, addressed me, saying, "O Faḳīr! thou hadst nearly been innocently slain; but thou hast escaped. Some time is left thee to live. Go; whither art thou coming?" and, having drawn from his belt a jewelled dagger, with a tassel of pearls,[319] he threw it before me, and said, "At this time I have no money with me to give thee, take this to the King, and thou wilt get what thou askest for." Such terror and awe of him overpowered me, that I had neither power to speak nor strength to move. My voice was choked, and my feet became heavy.

Having said thus much, that valiant[320] man, uttering wild cries, proceeded on. I said, in my heart, "Let happen what may,[321] to stop now will mar thy design [*lit.* "is, in regard of thee, bad"]; such an occasion will not occur again." Washing my hands of my life, I, too, went on. Again he turned, and, in fierce wrath, threatened me, and fully purposed to slay me. I

---

[319] I would prefer to read the text thus, omitting اور *aur*, before آويزه *āwīzah*; but, if the conjunction be retained, the sentence must be rendered, "a jewelled dagger of pearls, with a tassel hanging from it."

[320] غازي *Ghāzī* properly signifies "an exterminator of infidels." Thus the great Maḥmūd was called Ghāzī; and, in our days, Akbar Khān was considered by the Faithful to have won the same glorious title.

[321] This sentence is pure Persian. We have had it in Urdū just before, جو هو سو هو *jo ho so ho.*

bowed my head and conjured him,[322] saying, "O Rustam[323] of the age! strike me such a blow that I may be cut in two pieces. Let not one strip of skin remain, and let me escape from this distressful and miserable life. I absolve you from my blood." He replied, "O form of Satan! why wilt thou load my neck with thy innocent blood,[324] and make me guilty? Go! take thine own way. What! is thy life grievous to thee?" I paid no attention to what he said, and went forward. Again, willingly and intentionally, he pretended not to observe me, and I followed him. Proceeding on, he crossed two kos of jungle and ground covered with thickets.

[At length] a square building appeared. The youth advanced to the door, and uttered a terrible shout. The door, of its own accord, opened. He entered: I remained standing, altogether shut out. "My God! [I said to myself], what shall I do now?" I was at my wits' ends. At length, after a short pause, a slave came and brought me a message, saying, "Come! he has summoned thee to his presence. I suppose the angel of death is hovering over thee. What calamity has come upon thee?" I exclaimed, "Bravo, fortune!"[325] and fearlessly entered the garden along with him.

At length he brought me to a room where that young man was sitting. Seeing him, I made a bow down to the carpet. He gave me a sign to seat myself. I knelt down respectfully.[326]

---

322 Literally, "gave oath," not like the *ὅρκον διδόναι* in Greek, which signifies "to give another an opportunity of clearing himself by oath;" but, "to stimulate a person by calling on him in the name of God to do a thing."

323 Rustam, son of Zāl, the most renowned of Persian heroes. He was general of the Persian forces under Kai Kāwus (Darius the Mede), and his successor Kai Khusrau (Cyrus); or, according to some, under Kishtasp (Darius Hystaspes). He defeated Afrāsiāb, King of Turkestān, and slew, in single combat, Asfandiyār, son of Kai Kāwus, but was at length treacherously slain by Bahman, or Adeshīr Dirūz-dast (Artaxerxes Longimanus), son of Asfandiyār.

324 So Forbes' edition, but I should prefer making نا حقّ *nā ḥaḳḳ* an adverb, and having no *zer* after خون *khūn*.

325 A rather unintelligible expression signifying disregard of danger, something like our "Hurrah for luck!"

326 Not that he really knelt, but we have no other word to translate the Oriental sitting on your heels, as it may be called; *i.e.* kneeling and resting the orbicular part of the body on the heels.

What do I [then] see? that that gallant youth[327] was seated alone on a cushion, and before him were placed a goldsmith's tools, and he had finished making a tree of emeralds. When the time came that he arose, all the slaves who were waiting around that balcony hid themselves in closets. I, too, through doubt of what was coming, pushed into a chamber. The youth got up and turned the keys of all the rooms, and went towards a corner of the garden, and began to beat the bullock on which he rode. The sound of its roaring reached my ears. My heart began to quake; but I had endured all this, in order to unravel this story. In trepidation I opened the door, and went and stood behind the trunk[328] of a tree, and began to look on. The young man threw down the club with which he was beating [the animal], and with a key opened the lock of one of the rooms, and went in. Presently he came forth again, stroked the back of the bullock, and kissed its mouth,[329] and having given it grain and water, came towards me [*lit.* "in this direction"]. On perceiving this, I ran with speed and went and concealed myself in the room.

The young man undid the chains which fastened all the doors, and all the slaves came out. They presented themselves, bringing a small carpet, a wash-hand basin, and an ewer. He, having performed his ablutions, stood up for prayer.[330] When he had done praying, he called out, "Where is that darwesh?" On hearing my own name, I ran and stood before him. He told me to sit. I made an obeisance and sate down.

---

327 I have so rendered مرد *mard*, which is always used like the Latin "vir," to signify "a man" emphatically, *i.e.* not a woman or a coward.

328 I cannot at all agree with the text of Forbes' edition here. He reads, تنے *tunne*, and renders it (as shewn by the vocabulary), "under shelter of a Tunn tree" (the *cedrela tunna*, तुन्न *tunn*, a tree resembling mahogany in its wood). But why specify the kind of tree? Would not any other tree have done as well? The story of Susannah warns one not to be too particular in specifying the tree. Certainly the collocation of the words shows that تنہ *tanah*, "stem," "trunk," is the word which Mīr Amman wrote.

329 The youth must have been mad indeed. Why should he have kissed the bullock, who was but an imp metamorphosed?

330 The Musalmān pray standing, with an occasional bow, genuflexion, or prostration.

Refreshments were brought. He ate, and presented me also with food, of which I partook. When the table-cloth was removed,[331] and we had washed our hands, he dismissed the slaves, saying, "Go and sleep." When no person remained in that apartment, he then entered into conversation with me and inquired, "O my friend! what such calamity has befallen thee that thou goest about seeking thy own death?" I circumstantially narrated to him all my adventures from beginning to end, just as they had befallen me, and I added, "I hope that by the favour of your Highness I shall attain my wish." On hearing this, he heaved a cold sigh, and became insensible,[332] and began to say, "O great God! excepting myself,[333] who is acquainted with the pain of love? 'He whose blister has not burst, how can he know the pain another suffers?'[334] The extent of this grief is known only to him who suffers from it.

Ask the lover, if love's sufferings you would know.
What knows the impostor of it?—of true lovers ask their woe."

After an instant he recovered his senses and drew a heart-consuming sigh—all the apartment echoed. I was then convinced that he too was overtaken in this same calamity of love, and was sick of the same disease. Then truly I took courage and said, "I have related all my story; let your Highness favour this slave by acquainting him with your own history. Then to the utmost of my ability I will exert myself for your sake first, and by my endeavours obtain for you the wish of your heart." In short, that true lover, regarding me as acquainted with his secret and suffering from the same distress of mind, began to relate his adventures in the following manner:— "Listen, friend! I am the sorrowful prince[335] of this country of Nīmroz. The King, that is to say, my father, after my

---

331 Literally: "advanced," according to the superstitious notion mentioned in Note 255, *q.v.*

332 These "love-swoons" with the Orientals are of short duration.

333 Literally: "thee," but he is soliloquizing.

334 A proverb.

335 Literally: "with burned liver;" the epithet جگر سوز *jigar-soz*, rhymes with Nīmroz, which is thought a beauty in composition.

birth, assembled the soothsayers and astrologers, and wise men, and ordered them to look into and examine the circumstances of my fortune, and to prepare my horoscope, and to detail circumstantially in the royal presence the true occurrences which were to befall me momentarily, hourly, during each watch, daily, monthly, and yearly. In obedience to the order of the King, all with one accord made a decision, each by the rules of his own science, and after determining the matter, respectfully represented that, 'by the grace of God, the prince has been begotten and born in so fortunate a moment, and during the rising of so auspicious a sign, that he will rule like Sikandar,[336] and in justice equal Naushīrwān,[337] and he will have a perfect acquaintance with all the arts and sciences that exist, and will easily master everything to which he turns his mind. For generosity and courage he will acquire such a name that people will forget Ḥātim and Rustam. But till he is fourteen years old, a great danger is apparent from his beholding the sun and moon. Moreover there is reason to fear that, becoming distraught and insane, he will put many persons to death, and will wander distractedly from the habitations of men, and go forth into the deserts, and pass his time with the beasts and birds. Let strict attention be paid to this point, that by night and day he should not see the sun or moon, nay, that he may not even have an opportunity of looking towards the sky. If this interval of time passes in safety, then after that he will reign the rest of his life in happiness and peace.'

"Having heard this, the King, for this same reason, laid the foundation of this garden, and caused many[338] apartments of every plan to be erected. He ordered that I should be brought up in a subterraneous room, and caused a tower of felt to be prepared above it, so that neither the heat of the sun nor the moonbeams could penetrate it. I, along with certain nurses

---

[336] Alexander the Great.

[337] The twentieth king of the fourth dynasty of Persia, viz. of the Sassanides, or Khusravians, who was cotemporary with Justin and Justinian, both of whom he defeated. Muḥammad was born in his reign, A.D. 578.

[338] I prefer this meaning to that given in Forbes' vocabulary, which seems quite inapplicable.

and attendants, began to be educated in that magnificent abode with the care against danger which I have described, and a wise tutor, a man of experience, was appointed to instruct me and to teach me every science and art, and practise me in the seven kinds of handwriting,[339] and the Asylum of the World continually superintended my education. A daily register of the occurrences of every moment of my life was read in the royal presence. I, regarding that place itself as the universe, was playing with various toys and flowers of different hues, and the dainties of the whole world were provided for me to eat. Whatever I desired that I ate. By the time I was ten years old I had acquired all crafts and accomplishments. One day, beneath that tower, from an aperture to admit light, a marvellous flower appeared to me, which, as I gazed, was increasing in size. I tried to grasp it with my hands. Just as I stretched out my hand towards it, so it rose higher and higher. I was amazed, and stood staring at it. Immediately a sound of hearty laughter struck my ears. I stretched my neck to see whence it came.[340] I saw then that, having rent the felt, a moon-like face was protruded [towards me]. On beholding it, my understanding and senses were unhinged. Again recovering myself, I beheld that a throne, covered with gold, was standing there, supported on the shoulders of fairy forms, and an occupant of the throne sat on it, wearing a crown of jewels on her head, and on her body a glittering robe, while she held in her hand a ruby cup of wine of which she had freely quaffed. That throne gradually descended from on high, and entered the tower. Then the fairy called me, and caused me to sit beside herself. She began to address me in tender language, and, joining her face to mine, gave me to drink a cup of wine, scented with the extract of rose, and said, 'The children of men are inconstant, yet my heart loves thee.' She spoke to me such ravishing words that in a moment all else was effaced from my heart, and such was

---

339 Penmanship is greatly esteemed among the Orientals. Some of the Kings of Persia, and many of the highest nobles in that country, and in Hindūstān, have been famous for their beautiful writing.

340 Literally, "to see it;" *i.e.* the آواز *āwāz*, or "sound."

my delight that [I seemed then first] to taste life, and thought to myself, 'To-day, indeed, I have been born into the world.'

"The sum of the story is this,—that why speak of *myself? no one* ever can have beheld such beauty, or heard of such.—We were both seated, contented in that bliss, when, in the midst of our security, the pellet of misfortune struck us.[341] Now hear the account of this sudden calamity. Just then four fairies descended from the sky and whispered something to that beautiful lady. As soon as she heard it, her countenance changed, and then she said to me, 'O my love! my heart indeed was wishing to sit with thee a short space and thus delight my soul, and in this same way always to come or take thee with me; but this heaven permits not two persons to remain together in repose and happiness. Well, my dearest life! thy God is thy protector.'[342] Having heard this, my senses completely left me, and the parrot escaped from my hand.[343] I said, 'O lady! now when shall we meet again? what cross words are these you have spoken? If you return quickly you will find me alive; otherwise, you will repent of it; or, tell me where you live, and your name and address, that I myself, searching for you according to that direction, may transport myself to you.' Having heard this, she replied, 'God forbid![344] be the ears of Satan deaf![345] may your life be one hundred and twenty years![346] If you survive we shall meet hereafter. I am the daughter of the king of the genii, and I dwell in the mountain Ḳāf.'[347] After she had said this, the throne was borne upward,[348] and in the same manner that it had descended it was forthwith raised on high.

---

[341] A proverbial expression.

[342] A form of bidding farewell.

[343] A proverb applied to those whose happiness has flown.

[344] That you should die.

[345] So as not to hear our ill-omened words and avail himself of them.

[346] The limit assigned to man's life, according to the Musalmān, and in *Genesis*, vi. 3, "Yet his days shall be a hundred and twenty years."

[347] A mountain, by some thought to be Caucasus, where the Sīmurgh, the Jins, and other fabulous beings, reside.

[348] With deference to Mīr Amman, this is bad grammar. The nominative to کہکر *kahkar* and اٹھایا *uṭhāyā* ought to be the same.

"As long as it was before me, my eyes and hers were fixed on one another [*lit.* 'my eyes and hers continued four']; when it disappeared from sight, my state became such as when the shadow of a fairy falls upon one.[349] My heart was overcast with an extraordinary dejection; my understanding and my senses took leave. The world became dark under my eyes. I was in a state of miserable bewilderment,[350] and my employment was to weep piteously, and throw dirt on my head, and tear my clothes. I thought not of food, nor distinguished between good and ill.

What mischiefs through this love arise!
What broken hearts and miseries!

The nurses and tutor became aware of this my sad state, and went trembling into the presence of the King, and stated that 'the condition of the Prince of the World is this.—We know not whence this spontaneous calamity has burst upon us, that he has ceased to rest, and to eat and drink.' Then the King, accompanied by the vazīr, the nobles, the counsellors, and the skilful physicians and truthful seers, the sagacious doctors, the good darweshes, the devotees, and those abstracted from worldly concerns, adorned that garden with their presence. Having seen my inquietude and my weeping and wailing, the King's condition also became one of distress. He wept and passionately embraced me, and commanded that a consultation should be made regarding my disease. The physicians wrote a prescription for the restoration of my spirits and the cure of my derangement, and the doctors gave drawings and charms which I was to drink,[351] or keep beside me,—they began to repeat prayers, and to blow [with their breath, to expel the devil], and the astrologers said that 'this his condition has arisen from the revolution of the stars,—give propitiatory offerings for it.' In short, every one was speaking in terms of his own science;

---

[349] This expression is applied to a deranged person; as we say "moon-struck."

[350] This sentence is wanting in connexion. After the infinitives, میرا کام تھا *merā kām thā*, or similar words, must be understood.

[351] For magic figures used in exorcisms, see Ḳānūn-i Islām, page 330, etc.

but my heart alone was experiencing what I suffered. No one's exertion or advice was of any use against my ill fate. Day by day my madness increased, and my body grew feeble from want of sustenance. All that was left to me was to shriek, and beat my head day and night. In that state three years passed away. In the fourth year, a merchant on his travels arrived, and brought curiosities from every country, strange and wonderful, to the royal palace. He obtained the honour of waiting on the King.[352] The King shewed him much favour, and having asked after his welfare, inquired whether, as he had seen many countries, his eyes had ever lighted on a perfect physician, or if he had heard any one mention such an one? He made representation, saying, 'Point of prayer of the World! Your slave has travelled much, but in Hindūstān there is a solitary mountain in the Great River [*i.e.* the Gangā]. There a Gusāīn,[353] with matted hair, has made a large temple to Mahādev, and a place of Hindū worship, and a garden of great beauty wherein he dwells. And he has his custom, that annually on the day of Shevrāt,[354] he comes from his cell, and swims in the river, and takes his diversion. When, after bathing, he begins to return to his seat,[355] then the sick and afflicted of every country and clime, who come from afar, assemble at his door. A great multitude is formed of them.

"'That saintly devotee[356] (who ought to be called the Plato[357] of the age) proceeds onwards, inspecting their urine and pulse, and writing prescriptions for each. God has given him such a healing hand, that instantly on drinking the medicine, an effect

352 The meanings of ملازمت *mulāzamat*, given in Forbes' vocabulary, are inapplicable here.

353 A kind of Hindū religious mendicant.

354 A night sacred to Shiva or Mahādev, on the 14th of the moon's wane, or dark fortnight in Māgha.

355 The آسن *āsan*, of the Hindū ascetic, is the place where he squats, absorbed in prayer or meditation.

356 The مہنت *mahant*, is, properly, the head of a religious house—an abbot.

357 Aflāṭūn, as the Orientals called Plato, is supposed by them to have been, not only a great philosopher, but also a skilful physician; for with them the two sciences of philosophy and medicine are almost inseparable.

is produced, and that disease altogether departs. I have seen these things with my own eyes, and the power of God was recalled to my mind, in that He has created such beings as His servants. If you command it, let us take the Prince of the World to him, and give him a sight of him. There is strong hope that he will perfectly recover, and that with speed. And, moreover, this plan is evidently a good one, since by trying the air of each country, and by the diversity of living in various places, the mind recovers its tone.' The King approved of his advice, and being pleased, said, 'Very good! perhaps his hand may be successful, and the horror may depart from the heart of my son.' He deputed to attend upon me a nobleman in whom he had confidence, who had seen the world, and was a man of experience, together with that merchant, and he sent along with me such equipment as I required. Having caused us to embark, along with our effects, on barges, travelling pinnaces,[358] native pleasure boats, with the cabin in the prow, cook-boats,[359] fly-boats, Khelnās,[360] and baggage-boats,[361] of various descriptions, he sent us away. Proceeding on, stage by stage, we arrived at that place. By the change of air and diet my constitution was somewhat strengthened; but I continued in the same state of silence, occupied with my tears. Never for an instant did my heart forget that fairy, and if I ever spoke, it was to repeat this couplet—

'What fairy face glanced on me? nought can I tell!
But till now my poor heart was all tranquil and well.'

"At length, when two or three months had passed, nearly four thousand persons, afflicted with diseases, assembled on that

---

358 The بجرا *bajrā*, or, in Anglo-Indian jargon, "budgerow," is a travelling pinnace, used by Europeans from Calcutta to Delhi.

359 The پلوار *palwār* is a travelling boat used by Europeans, as the cook-boat to the بجرا *bajrā*.

360 The کهیلنا *khelnā* is a kind of boat of which I have nowhere met with a description. The word is not in the dictionaries.

361 The اُلاق *ulāḳ* is the baggage-boat of the Huglī in Central Bengal. The پٹیلي *paṭelī* is the flat-bottomed cargo-boat of Hindūstān.

mountain. But all, however, were saying the same thing, 'Now, if God will, the Gusāīn will come forth from his temple, and, at his word, all will be restored to perfect convalescence.' In a word, when that day came, the Jogī[362] in the morning issued forth like the sun, and bathed and swam in the river.[363] He swam across and returned, and rubbed his whole body with ashes. He hid his fair body in the ashes, as a spark is hidden in them. On his forehead he made the sectarial mark with the finest sandal,[364] and having fastened his waist-cloth,[365] cast his bathing-towel over his shoulder. He fastened up his back hair in a knot, twisted his moustachios, and pulled up[366] his high shoes. From his countenance it was apparent that, in his opinion, the whole world was of no value. Taking a jewelled writing-case under his arm, and looking at each [sick person], and writing prescriptions, he approached me. When our eyes met, he stopped and reflected, and addressing me, said, 'Come with me.' I went with him.

"When all had had their turn, he led me into a garden, and taking me into a beautiful and richly-ornamented private apartment, said, 'Do you remain here;' and he himself went to his own place. After a period of forty days he came to me and found me better than I was before. He then smiled and said, 'Continue to walk about this little garden, and to eat any of the fruits you feel an inclination for.' And he gave me a small

---

362 The جوگی *jogī* is a Hindū ascetic, who gives himself up to meditation; and by abstracting his mind from earthly objects, attains supernatural powers.

363 The word دریا *daryā*, is applied to large rivers as well as to the sea. Thus the Indus is called the دریا سندہ *daryā-i Sindh*, the great river of Sindh.

364 The sandal (*santalum album*) brought from the मलयगिरि Malyagiri or Western Ghāṭs is reckoned the best. It has an exquisite scent, and is used by the Hindūs to make the ornamental mark on the forehead, by which their sect is known.

365 The لنگوٹ *langoṭ*, is a cloth about two feet long and six or eight inches broad, passed between the legs and tucked-in before and behind, to the *tasmah*, or *dū'ālī*. The انگوچھا *angochhā*, is tied by the Hindūs round the waist while bathing, and afterwards used as a towel.

366 The word اڑانا *iṛānā* is given by Forbes in his vocabulary, but is strangely enough omitted in his Dictionary; and also in that of Shakespear. It signifies "to pull up," "to fasten up."

china covered cup, filled with an electuary, saying, 'Always, without omitting a day, take six māshahs[367] from this.' With these words he departed, and I acted in accordance with his directions. Every day my bodily strength and mental ease increased, but no effect was produced on mighty love. The form of that fairy was ever before my eyes.

"One day I saw in a recess a book. I took it up, and on looking into it, found it contained all theological and natural sciences. It was as if you had poured the ocean into a pitcher. I perused it incessantly, and acquired uncommon power in the sciences of philosophy and magic. In the mean time a full year passed away; again that festal day arrived. The Jogī arose from his seat and went forth. I saluted him. He gave me his writing-case, and said, 'Come with me.' I went with him. When he had crossed the door, a multitude of people began to utter benedictions. The nobleman and the merchant, seeing me with him, fell at the feet of the Gusāīn, and began to pay their thanks to him, saying, 'By the favour of your Highness, at length thus much has been effected.' He, according to his custom, went to the steps descending to the river, and performed his ablutions and devotions, as he was wont annually to perform them. On his return he proceeded along, surveying the sick. It chanced that, among the crowd of deranged persons, he saw a beautiful and graceful youth, who was unable to stand from weakness. He said to me, 'Bring this youth along with you.' When, after distributing medicines and remedies to all, he entered his private apartment, he cut off a little of the skull of that youth, and was about to remove with a forceps the centipede which was sitting on his brain. The thought occurred to me, and I exclaimed, 'If you will be pleased to heat the tongs[368] in the fire, and place it on his back, it would be well, for [the centipede] will come forth of its own accord; and if you thus pull it out, it will not leave go its hold on the mar-

---

[367] A weight, used by apothecaries, of eight ratīs, each ratī being equal to fifteen grains.

[368] دست پناه *dast panāh*, is rendered in Forbes' vocabulary, "Your worship," "Your reverence," a most doubtful meaning, and one which certainly has nothing to do with this passage. Shakespear rightly translates it "tongs."

row of the brain, whereupon his life will be in danger.' Having heard this, he looked towards me, and got up in silence, and seizing a tree in his grasp,[369] tied a noose of his matted hair round his neck, and there hung. When I went, I then saw that, alas! alas! he was quite dead! I was much grieved at witnessing this wonderful spectacle, but as it was irremediable, it occurred to me to bury him. When I began to take him down from the tree, two keys fell out from his matted hair. I took them up, and buried that treasure of goodness in the earth. Then taking the keys, I began to apply them to all the locks. It happened that the locks of two closets were opened by those keys. I beheld, then, that from the floor to the ceiling, they were filled with jewels, and on one side was placed a box covered with velvet, clamped with gold, and locked. When I opened it, I saw a book, in which was contained the Great Name,[370] and spells to summon genii and fairies, and others for raising spirits, and for charming the sun.

"I was much pleased at acquiring such wealth, and began to take my measures accordingly. I opened the gate of the garden, and directed the nobleman and others of my retinue to send for vessels and load them with all those jewels, and cash, and goods, and books, and having myself embarked in a boat, I set sail thence into the sea. When, proceeding on, I drew near to my own country, the Asylum of the World was informed [of my approach]. He mounted and came forth to meet me, and in a state of violent emotion from his affection for me, he clasped me to his heart. I, having kissed his feet, said, 'Command this humble person to reside in the garden which was his former abode.' He replied, 'O my son! that place is an object of aversion to me, wherefore I have discontinued its repairs, and ceased to keep it ready. That place is now no longer fit to be the abode of man. In whatever other

---

369 کولا *kaulā* is rendered in Forbes' vocabulary, "a kind of orange," a meaning altogether inapplicable here, where it signifies "embrace," "grasp." An orange-tree would be a strange one to select for hanging oneself.

370 The Deity, according to the Musalmān, has ninety-nine names, among which is one of such power that he who knows it becomes endowed with supernatural gifts. The notion may perhaps be borrowed from the Jews, who think the name "Jehovah" too awful to be uttered.

abode you please, alight. It is more desirable that you should approve of some place in the royal fort, and stay there under my own eyes, and having prepared a garden at the foot of your palace, there walk about and enjoy yourself.' I resisted this arrangement with the utmost obstinacy, and caused that garden to be repaired anew, and having adorned it like Paradise, made my entrance into it. Afterwards, free from interruption, I sate fasting for forty days, in order to command the genii by my incantations, and having abandoned animal food, began to practise my spells. When forty days were accomplished, then at midnight such a tempest arose that the largest buildings fell down, and trees torn up by the roots were carried from one place to another, and the army of the fairies appeared. A throne descended from the air, on which sate a stately person, wearing a crown of pearls and a rich robe. On seeing him, I saluted him very respectfully. He returned my salute, and said, 'Friend! what disturbance is this that thou hast causelessly occasioned? what claim hast thou upon me?' I represented that this humble person had been for a long time in love with his daughter, and for this very reason had wandered over a far distance, wretched and miserable, and had been as dead while living. That I had now become weary of existence, and had sported[371] with my life in doing what I had done; that I was now in hopes that His Majesty would confer exaltation on me, distracted and wretched, and bestow on me life and repose by granting me a sight of her, which would be a very meritorious action.

"Having heard this my wish, he said, 'Man is earthly, and we igneous; for these two to assort is difficult.' I said, with an oath, 'I desire only to see her; I have no other purpose.' Then that sitter on the throne replied, 'Man abides not by his promise; in the time of his exigency he says anything, but he bears it not in mind. I have told thee this for thy good, for if thou ever formest any other purpose, then both thou and she will be ruined and brought to woe; nay, your lives will be in danger.' I reiterated my protestations, saying, 'I will never

---

[371] The كهيلنا *khelnā* is exactly the Greek word *κινδυνεύω* here.

do a thing which will occasion injury to both of us, but I will only gaze upon her.' This conversation was going on when, suddenly, that fairy (of whom we discoursed) arrived, adorned in the gayest manner, and the throne of the king departed. Then I rapturously clasped that fairy in my arms, as though she were my life, and repeated this poetry—

> For forty days I've kept the fast; then to my home,[372]
> Why should the fair with eye-brows arched not come?

"In that same happy state we began to live together in the garden. Through fear, I discarded any further designs. I did but skim the surface of bliss,[373] and contented myself with gazing upon her. The fairy was in her heart astonished at the constancy with which I adhered to my promise, and sometimes used to say, 'Dearest! you are truly very firm to your word, but I give you one piece of friendly advice. Take care of your book, for some day or other the Jins will find you off your guard, and steal it away.' I replied, 'I guard this as I would my life.'

"It happened one night that the devil tempted me. In the violence of my desire, I thought, 'Come what may—how long am I to restrain myself?" I clasped her to my breast, and attempted to gratify my wishes. Immediately there came a voice, 'Give this book to me, for in this there is the Great Name of God. Be not guilty of profanity!' In that intoxicating moment I was bereft of judgment; I took the book from under my arm, and gave it, without knowing or observing to whom, and proceeded with my purpose. The beautiful girl, perceiving this my mistaken act, exclaimed, 'O cruel! at last thou hast erred, and forgotten my advice!'

"With these words she became insensible, and I perceived, at the head of the bed on which she lay, an imp, who stood

---

372 The lines in the original, it is only fair to say, are pretty enough, but are almost incompressible into English verse.

373 The meanings given by Forbes and Shakespear are altogether inapplicable here. The latter renders بالائی مزے *bālāī maze*, "secret pleasures," which would include what is here evidently shut out. Forbes, by rendering the expression "superior," "extraordinary," reverses the true meaning, which is, that he stopped just short of consummating his nuptials.

there holding the book. I was about to seize him and beat him well, and snatch away the book, when, meanwhile, another took it from his hand and fled. I began to repeat the spells I had committed to memory. The Jin, who stood there, was transformed into a bull; but, alas! the fairy in no degree recovered her senses, but continued in the same state of stupor. Then my heart was confounded, and all my pleasure was embittered. From that day I have loathed the company of human beings. I remain dully [374] in a corner of this garden, and, to amuse myself, employ my time in making this jar [375] ornamented with trees of emerald, and every month I make a practice of mounting this same bull and going to that plain. I break the jar and kill the slave, in the hope that all will see this my state, and take pity on it, and perhaps some servant of God may so compassionate me as to pray for me, when I too may arrive at my desire. O comrade! these are the facts of my melancholy and insanity which I have related to thee."

I shed tears at the recital, and said, "O Prince! thou in truth hast undergone a great labour of love; but I swear by God that I put aside my own wishes. Now I will wander through forests and mountains for thy sake, and what I can do for thee that will I effect." Having made this promise, I took leave of the young man, and for five years wandered through the deserts like a madman, sifting dirt.[376] I found no trace of the lady.[377] At length, being disgusted [with life], I ascended a mountain, and was about to throw myself down, in order that neither bone nor rib might remain whole, when the same veiled horseman came up, and said, "Do not throw away thy life! after a few days thou shalt have thy wishes gratified." O men of God! I have, indeed, obtained an interview with you, and now I hope, through the divine grace, to obtain satisfaction and happiness, and that all of us, disappointed as we have been, will attain our objects.

---

[374] I have so translated پڑا *paṛā*, the exact force of which cannot be given in English.

[375] The word جھاڑ دار *jhāṛ dār*, has been omitted both by Forbes and Shakespear.

[376] That is, "in useless endeavours."

[377] By a blunder of the author we are not told that she ever disappeared.

THE ADVENTURES OF KING ĀZĀD-BAKHT.

When the second Darwesh had finished the relation of his travels, the night ended, and the time of morning approached. King Āzād-Bakht silently took his way to the palace, and, having arrived there, performed his prayers. Then, having entered the bath, he put on a splendid robe, and came forth, and seated himself on his throne in the public hall-of-audience, and gave command, saying, "Let a messenger go—four fakīrs have arrived in such and such a place—bring them along with you with all respect into the royal presence." According to the order, a mace-bearer went there and saw then that the four indigent persons having gone among the bushes,[378] and washed their hands and faces, were about to set out each on his own way. The servant said, "Princes![379] the King has sent for you four persons, come along with me!" The four Darweshes began to stare at each other, and said to the mace-bearer, "Son! we are kings of our own hearts, what have we to do with worldly monarchs?" He replied, "Men of God! it matters not, it is better that you come."

Meanwhile the four remembered that what Lord Ālī[380] had said had now come to pass. They were pleased, and accompanied the messenger. When they arrived in the royal castle, and entered the presence of the King, the four Kalandars uttered a benediction, saying, "Son! may it be well with thee!" The King went and took his seat in his private hall,

---

378 A polite mode of expressing the calls of nature.

379 Faḳīrs are addressed by the title of شاه *shāh*, or "king," out of respect.

380 In the text مرتضي *murtaẓa*, "chosen," "approved," a title of Ālī.

and summoned two or four of his chief nobles, and said, "Call in the four mendicants" (*lit.* the four clothed in rags). When they had come there, he ordered them to be seated, and inquired after their welfare, saying, "Whence have you come? and whither do you purpose going? where is the abode of the spiritual guides?" (*i.e.* of yourselves).

They replied, "May the life and fortune of the King increase! We are faḳīrs. For a long time we wander about, journeying and travelling in this same way. Our houses are on our shoulders, according to the proverb, 'the faḳīr's house is wherever evening overtakes him;' and to what length should we recount all that has befallen us in this transitory world!"

Āzād-Bakht gave them much consolation and encouragement, and having sent for food, caused them to take their breakfast in his presence. When they had finished he then said, "Relate to me your history, without omitting or withholding aught; and whatever I can do in your service that I will not fail to perform." The faḳīrs replied, "As to the various adventures which have befallen us, neither have we the power to relate them, nor would the King derive any gratification from hearing them—be pleased to excuse us." The King then smiled and said, "When you, seated on your couches during the night, were relating your several stories, then I too was present, and accordingly I have already heard the adventures of Two Darweshes, and I am now desirous that the remaining Two should recount theirs also, and that you should stop contentedly with me for a few days, 'for the footstep of the darweshes averteth ill.'" On hearing these words from the King, they began to tremble with fear, and holding down their heads, kept silence. They had no power left to speak.

When Āzād-Bakht saw that through consternation they had no sense left in them to say anything, he said, "In this world there is, perhaps, no one to whom some wonderful adventure or other has not occurred. Notwithstanding that I am a king, yet I, too, have seen such strange things that I myself will first relate them. Do you listen at your ease." The Darweshes said, "King! Peace be to thee! since your condescending kindness to us in our condition as poor faḳīrs is such—be pleased to say on." Āzād-Bakht began his story in the following manner, and said—

O kings! to a king's story now attend!
To all I have heard or seen give ear,
Now from the first I'll tell it to the end,
Then fix your best attention here.

When my father died and I ascended the throne, I was in the very prime of my youth, and all this empire of Rūm was subject to me. It happened that one year a merchant came from the country of Badakhshān,[381] and brought with him much merchandize. The reporters[382] brought information to me that up to that day so great a merchant had never entered the city. I ordered him to be summoned.

He came, bringing with him curiosities from every country, fit to be presented to me, as offerings. Of a verity every article appeared to me inestimable, and moreover there was in a casket a ruby of an exceedingly beautiful colour, and of a good water, and in shape and size perfect, and which weighed five miṣkāls.[383] Though a king, I had never seen such a jewel, and had never heard of such a one from anybody. I accepted it with satisfaction, and bestowed on the merchant many rewards and honours, and gave him a writing of immunity from tolls, to the effect that throughout my dominions none should interfère with him by demanding a tax, and that wheresoever he went his comfort should be attended to; that the people [of the place where he stopped] should guard and escort him, and look upon his loss as their own. That merchant attended in the royal presence during the time I held my court, and was well acquainted with the etiquette of courts, and his manner

---

381 Badakhshān is a country to the north of Kābul, bordering on the Oxus, the capital of which is Balkh. The finest rubies are found there in a mountainous range. which forms its eastern boundary.

382 Every Asiatic prince maintains these emissaries, who keep him informed of every new event, discharging the functions of a worthier class of reporters in this country.

383 The Miṣkāl is equal to four māshahs and three-and-a-half ratīs. Our ounce contains twenty-four māshahs, consequently the jewel weighed about five-eighths of an ounce.

of discourse, and pleasing conversation, was worth hearing. Every day I sent for that ruby from the jewel-office, and inspected it in full court.

One day I had taken my seat and was holding a public court, and the nobles and pillars of state were standing each in his proper place, and the ambassadors of the kings of all countries who had come on complimentary missions, they[384] too were all present. At that time I, as was my wont, sent for the ruby. The superintendent of the jewel-office brought it. I took it in my hand and began to praise it, and gave it to the ambassador of the Franks.[385] When he saw it he smiled, and in a time-serving way extolled it. In the same manner each passed it on from hand to hand, and looked at it, and all said unanimously, "By reason of the auspicious fortune of the Point to which the world turns in prayer, this has been obtained, otherwise up to this day no king has got possession of so inestimable a gem." At that time the vazīr of my father, who was a wise man, and had been dignified with the same post [under my reign], was standing at the chair of his office. He made obeisance, and represented that he wished to say something, if I would grant him his life.

I commanded him to speak. He said, "Point to which the world turns in prayer! Your Highness is a king,[386] and it is very inconsistent with the position of kings to laud so highly a stone. Though in colour, quality, and weight it is peerless, still it is but a stone,[387] and at this moment the ambassadors

---

[384] Here we find وُہ *wuh*, with the singular pronoun instead of the plural وے *we*. This disregard of grammar occurs so often that it amounts almost to a rule.

[385] فرنگ کے *Farang-ke*, of Europe, for the word Frank, is now applied to all Europeans, who are called by the general name of Faringī, a name which carries something disrespectful with it, and for which صاحب لوگ *Ṣāḥib log*, "the master-people," is a courteous substitute.

[386] پادشاہ *pādshāh*, is the very highest title of royalty, and is nearer our Emperor. To the English and French kings alone this title used to be given by the Sublime Porte.

[387] A play here on the word سنگ *sang*, which signifies both "weight," and "stone." The equivoque cannot be preserved in English.

of all countries are present in court. When they return to their own respective cities, they will assuredly tell this story, and say, 'He is a strange king who has got a ruby from somewhere or other, and has made such a curiosity of it, that every day he sends for it into his presence, and, after praising it himself, exhibits it to all.' Then whatever king or rājā hears this account will make it a subject of ridicule in his court. My lord! there is in Naishāpūr [388] a merchant of no eminence, who has set in a collar twelve rubies, each of which weighs seven misḳāls, and has hung them on the neck of a dog." On hearing this my wrath arose, and I said, in my displeasure, "Strike the neck of this vazīr." [389]

The executioners immediately seized his hands, and were about to take him out, when the ambassador of the King of the Franks came before me, with his hands respectfully joined. I asked him what he wanted. He respectfully stated, "I hope that I may be made acquainted with the crime of the vazīr." [390] I replied, "What other crime is greater than that of speaking falsely, especially in the presence of kings?" He answered, "His falsehood has not been proved. Perhaps what he has represented may be true. At present to put him to death while innocent is not right." To this I responded, "The reason can never admit that a person who, for the sake of gain, wanders from city to city, and country to country, suffering hardships, and collects his money kauṛī by kauṛī, would set in the collar of a dog twelve rubies, which would weigh seven misḳāls each!" He said, "It is no marvel for God's Omnipotence; perhaps it may be so; and rare things often fall into the hands of merchants or faḳīrs:

---

[388] Naishāpūr, once the capital of Persian Khurāsān, and two stages from Mashhad, the present capital, is in E. long. 58° 5′, N. lat. 36° 15′. The word is said to mean "City of Shāpur." It still carries on a brisk trade with Shikārpur, and other towns, especially in turquoises, which are brought in stuck on straws.

[389] The usual phrase for commanding decapitation.

[390] The sagacious ambassador of the Franks in this story is, probably, a copy from the Frankish ambassador who was slain by Yazīd, according to the legend, for upbraiding him with the murder of Alī's sons. The head of the said ambassador, when struck off, repeated the Muḥammadan creed, so that all true believers may comfort themselves with the assurance of the salvation of so remarkable a convert.

for this reason, that both these people go into every country, and bring away whatever they can get. Your Majesty's best course is, if the vazīr is indeed so criminal, to order him to be imprisoned, because vazīrs are the understanding [as it were] of kings; and this is an action unbecoming monarchs, to give an order for executing [any one] for a speech, the truth or falsehood of which has not yet been established; and thus to forget the services and loyalty of his whole life. Peace be to the king! former sovereigns invented prisons for this very reason, that, if the monarch or chief were angry with any one, they might imprison him, and that when, after some days, his wrath had departed, and the innocence [of the prisoner] was clearly shown, the king might thus remain free from innocent blood, and to-morrow,[391] in the day of resurrection, might not be called to account." However much I tried to prove him in the wrong, he spoke so reasonably that he left me without the power of replying. I then said, "Well! I assent to what you say. I abstain from putting him to death, but let him be incarcerated. If, in the space of a year, his words are proved true, that such rubies are on the neck of the dog, then he shall be released: if not, he shall be put to death with extreme torture." I commanded them to lead the vazīr to prison. Having heard this mandate, the ambassador kissed the ground of service, and made his obeisance.

When this intelligence reached the house of the vazīr, wailing and lamentations were raised, and it became the house of mourning. The vazīr had a daughter of fourteen or fifteen years of age, very beautiful and clever, and well skilled in writing and reading. The vazīr lavished much tenderness upon her, and held her very dear. Accordingly he had caused to be built for her in the rear of his public hall a pleasure-house, and the daughters of nobles were with her as companions and graceful female attendants waited upon her, with whom she indulged in laughter and merriment and sportive

---

[391] The Musalmān constantly use this expression, as if the day of resurrection was so nearly impending, that the intervening time was but a day.

amusements. It happened that, on the day I sent the vazīr to prison, that girl was sitting among her play-fellows, and for amusement was celebrating the marriage of a doll, and with drums,[392] and timbrels,[393] was making preparations for the ceremony of the vigils,[394] and having put on a frying-pan, was frying and making sweet-cakes,[395] and comfits,[396] when, all at once, her mother, weeping and beating her breast, and with her head uncovered and bare feet, entered her daughter's house, and struck a blow with the palms of both her hands[397] on the girl's head, and began to say, "Would that God had, instead of thee, given me a blind son, then my heart would have been comforted, and thy father would have had one to help him." The daughter of the vazīr asked, "Of what use would a blind son have been to thee? whatever a son could have done, I, too, am able to do." The mother answered, "Dirt on thy head![398] This calamity has befallen thy father, that, in the presence of the King, he has made a speech of such a nature that he has been confined in the prison." She asked, "What speech was that? let me just hear." Then the wife of the vazīr said, "Thy father perhaps said that there is a merchant in Naishāpūr who has fastened to the collar of a dog twelve rubies of inestimable value. The King did not believe him. He thought him

---

[392] The ڈھولک *ḍholak* is a drum smaller than the ڈھول *ḍhol*, and with only one side covered with leather.

[393] The پکھاوج *pakhāwaj* sometimes means a timbrel, sometimes a drum, of what kind I know not.

[394] The رتجگا *ratjagā*, "nocturnal vigils," is a ceremony observed by women on the ninth month after the birth of a child, and at a marriage. *Vide* Ḳānūn-i Islām, pp. 2, 271.

[395] The گلگلا *gulgulā* is a sweet cake fried in butter; or wheat-flour, sugar, and curds, with anise and cardamom seeds, made into dumplings, and fried in clarified butter.

[396] The رحم *raḥm* is a sort of sweet cake of a white colour.

[397] دو ہتڑ *do haṭṭar* (द्वौ *dwau* two, हस्त *hast* a hand), is omitted in Forbes' vocabulary. It is the corresponding word to دلتّي *dulattī*, which signifies a "kick with both feet."

[398] That is, "Confusion to thee!" "Be ashamed of thyself!"

a liar, and has made him a prisoner. If I had this day a son, then he would use every kind of exertion, and ascertain the truth of this statement, and assist his father, and, by representation to the King, cause him to release my husband from the prison."

The vazīr's daughter said, "Dear mother! it is not possible to contend against fate. In an unexpected calamity men must have patience, and rest in hope of God's mercy. He is gracious! He will not suffer any one's difficulties to be abiding; and to weep and wail is wrong. God forbid that our enemies should represent it to the King in a different light, and that the calumniators should speak insidiously against us, which might be the cause of more displeasure. Rather let us offer benedictory prayers for the Asylum of the World. We are his hereditary slaves, he is our lord. Just as he has been wroth[399] with us, so will he become kind." The girl exhorted her mother with so much good sense, that she recovered, to some extent, her patience and fortitude, whereupon she went to her own palace and held her peace. When the night came, the vazīr's daughter sent for her nurse's husband,[400] fell at his feet, besought him much, and began to weep, and said, "In order that I may be quit of my mother's curse, and that my father may obtain his release, I hold this intention, if thou wilt be my companion—I will go to Naishāpūr, and, having seen that merchant, (on the neck of whose dog these rubies are), will effect whatever it is possible to do, and release my father."

At first, indeed, that man refused; at length, after much discussion, he consented. The vazīr's daughter then desired him to make ready their travelling equipment with all secresy, and to purchase merchandize fit for offerings to kings, and to

---

399 غضب *Ghaẓib* is the reading I should prefer, not غضب *ghaẓab*, which is a substantive, and in spite of the dictionaries, never, I believe, means "angry," which is expressed by غضب ناک *ghaẓab-nāk*.

400 دادا *dādā*, also signifies "paternal grandfather," either of the old gentlemen will answer the present purpose—eligat lector.

bring with him the requisite slaves and servants, but not to reveal the matter to any one. The husband of her nurse agreed, and busied himself with the preparations. When all the things were ready, he placed them on camels and mules, and set out,—and the vazīr's daughter also, having dressed herself in man's apparel, went with him. No one in the house had the slightest information of what was going on. When the morning came, there was a talk in the vazīr's house that his daughter had disappeared, and no one knew where she had gone.

At length, through fear of disgrace, the mother concealed her daughter's loss, and there the vazīr's daughter assumed the name of "the merchant's son."[401] Proceeding on, stage by stage, she arrived in Naishāpūr. She alighted merrily at the inn for travellers, and unloaded all her effects, and stopped there the night. In the morning she went to the warm baths,[402] and put on a fair robe, such as the inhabitants of Rūm wear, and went forth to look at the city. When, as she was coming along, she arrived in the market-place, she stopped in the centre where the four roads met. On one side she saw a jeweller's shop, where there was a great heap of jewels, and slaves clothed in rich robes, were standing with their hands crossed respectfully, and where there was a person[403] who was the chief, whose age was about fifty years, dressed in rich apparel, such as is worn by the wealthy, and a jacket with short sleeves, and some friends of his sate near him, in a dignified manner on chairs, and continued conversing among themselves.

The vazīr's daughter (who had made herself known as the merchant's son) having seen this, was astonished, and was glad, making these reflections in her heart, "God grant that it may not be false! it is probable that this may be the merchant of

---

401 An awkward name to assume in point of distinction. She had much better have called herself ابراهيم *Ibrāhīm*, or اسحاق *Isḥāḳ*.

402 And here her incognito must have been discovered, going with a man's dress to the women's baths. But these difficulties are nothing to an Oriental writer.

403 تها *thā*, "was," must be understood here, otherwise the nominative شخص *shakhṣ* has no verb.

whom my father spoke. Great God! make known to me his history." It happened that, when she turned her eyes on one side, she saw a shop, in which two iron cages were suspended, and two men were imprisoned in them, whose appearance was like that of Majnūn,[404] for only skin and bone were left, and the hair of their heads and their nails had grown long.[405] They sate with their hands down, and two armed Abyssinians, of hideous aspect, stood on each side of them. The merchant's son was astonished. He recited the deprecatory formula called 'lā ḥaul,'[406] and looking on the other side, beheld a shop in which carpets were spread, and on them was set an ivory chair, in which was a cushion of velvet, whereon sat a dog with a collar of jewels round his neck, and fastened with a chain of gold; and two beardless and beautiful slaves attended on it; the one holding a fan of peacock's feathers, with a jewelled handle, was fanning it, and the other holding in his hand a handkerchief of gold thread, was wiping its mouth and feet. When the merchant's son looked attentively, [he then saw] that twelve rubies, just as he had heard, were actually there, in the collar of the dog. He offered thanks to God, and began to reflect in what manner he could convey those rubies to the King, and by shewing them, release his father. He indeed was in this state of bewilderment, and all the people of the market, and of the road, beholding his beauty and comeliness, were amazed, and continued absolutely confounded. All the people were discoursing thus among themselves, "Till to-day a person of such a shape and beauty never met our sight." The merchant also observed him, and sent a slave, saying, "Go thou and with entreaty invite and bring that merchant's son to me."

The slave came and brought the message of the merchant, saying, "If you will have the kindness, then my lord is desirous of seeing your honour, be pleased to come and see him." This was the very thing the merchant's son wished. He replied, "Certainly." As soon as he came near the merchant, and the

---

404 That is, they were emaciated like that unhappy lover, *vide* Note 141.

405 No imaginary picture this. I have seen a murderer so confined in India, from whose wasted and naked frame reason had long since fled.

406 *Vide* Note 258.

merchant's eye fell upon him, a dart of love was plunged in his breast.[407] To do him honour, however, he rose quite up, but his senses were bewildered. The merchant's son perceived that he had now entered the net.[408] They mutually embraced. The merchant kissed the forehead of the merchant's son, and seated him beside himself. With much courtesy he inquired of him, saying, "Inform me of your name and family? whence have you come, and whither do you purpose going?" The merchant's son replied, "The country of this, your most humble servant, is Rūm, and Istambol is from of old the birth-place of my family—my father is a merchant. Now, by reason of his old age, he has no strength left for journeying. Wherefore he has given me leave to go, in order that I may learn the business of a merchant. To this day I had never set foot outside the house, this is the first journey which I have undertaken. I had not courage to travel by sea. I had set out by land, but such is the fame of your honour's character and good qualities, in this country of Persia, that I have come hither solely in the desire of meeting with you. At length, by God's grace, I have been ennobled by waiting upon you, and have found your virtues greater than the report. The wish of my heart has come to pass. May God keep you in safety! I shall now depart hence."

On hearing this the understanding and senses of the merchant quite left him. He said, "O my son! cause me not to hear such a thing—kindly abide in my poor house some days. Come, now! at least tell me this, where your goods and servants are." The merchant's son said, "The house of the traveller is the inn, after leaving them there I came to your honour." The merchant said, "It is not well to remain in a tavern. I have good credit and reputation in this city. Quickly send for them. I will māke vacant, and give you a room for your goods. I will look at whatever things you have brought, and will take such measures that, in this very place, you will obtain a rich profit. You, too, will be comfortable, and will escape from the fatigues of travel, and, by staying a few days, you will oblige me also."

---

407 Forbes has no stop here. I think a full point necessary.
408 That is, "That he had fallen in love with him."

The merchant's son made pretended excuses,[409] but the merchant would not admit them, and directed his agents to send porters quickly, and having caused the goods [of the merchant's son] to be brought, to deposit them in such and such a place.

The merchant's son sent with them a negro slave, telling him to load all the goods and bring them, and he himself remained sitting with the merchant till evening. When the market time was over, and the shops were closed, the merchant went home. Then, one of the two slaves took the dog under his arm—the other lifted the chair and carpet, and those two Abyssinian slaves placed the cage on the heads of labourers, and themselves, fully armed, accompanied them. The merchant, holding the hand of the merchant's son in his own, and conversing, came to his house.

The merchant's son beheld that it was a magnificent abode, fit for kings or chiefs. On the edge of a stream a bright carpet was spread, and in front of an ottoman, preparations for an entertainment were arranged. The dog's chair also was spread with a cushion in the same place, and the merchant brought the merchant's son with him and sate down. Without ceremony he presented him with wine. Both began to drink. When they were merry, the merchant called for food. The cloth was spread, and all the delicacies the world could supply were set out. In the first place, they brought some food in a large shallow platter, covered with a golden cover, which they took to the dog, and after spreading a cloth of brocade, they set it before the dog, which came down from his seat and eat as much as it wanted, and drank water out of a golden bowl. It then went back and sate on the chair. The slaves wiped clean its paws and mouth with a towel. Afterwards the slaves carried the platter and bowl to the cage, and having asked the merchant for the key, opened the lock of the cage. They took those two men out, gave them some blows with a club, and fed them with the leavings of the dog, and made them to drink of the water of which the dog had drunk. Then, having fastened the lock of the cage, they delivered the key to the merchant. When all

[409] Lit.: "From the surface of his heart," *i.e.* which he did not really intend.

this was ended, the merchant himself began to eat. The merchant's son was displeased with this action. He was disgusted, and did not put his hand to the food.[410] Although the merchant besought him, he nevertheless persisted in refusing. The merchant then inquired the reason why he did not eat. The merchant's son replied, "This action of yours appears to me unseemly, because man is the noblest of created beings, and the dog essentially filthy. Wherefore to feed two creatures of God with the leavings of a dog, in what religion or sect is this allowable? Do you not regard this—that they are your prisoners—as simply arising from your good fortune? otherwise you and they are equal. I now feel a suspicion that you are not a Musalmān. How can I tell who you are that worship a dog? To eat your food is an abomination to me until this doubt is removed from my heart." The merchant said, "My son! I know all this that thou sayest, and on this very account I have a bad name, so that the people of this city have given me the name of the dog-worshipping merchant. In that same manner they are calling after me, and have made me notorious. But, may the curse of God rest on infidels and idolators!" He recited the creed, and satisfied the merchant's son. Then the latter inquired, "If you are in truth a Musalmān, then what is the reason of this? By this action you have given yourself a bad name." The merchant said, "O son! my name is defamed, and I pay in this city a double tax on this very account, that this secret should not be known to any one. The history is such a strange one that whoever hears it would gain nothing but sorrow and indignation. Do thou also excuse me, for I have neither the power to tell thee, nor wilt thou have the patience to listen to it." The merchant's son reflected in his heart, "My business is with my own concerns. What necessity is there for me to press him unjustly?" He said, "Well! if it is not fit to be told, then do not tell it." He put his hand to the food, and having taken a morsel, began to eat. With such prudence and discretion did the merchant's son, for two

[410] The Orientals, as is well known, eat with their hands, and do not use forks or knives.

months, live with the merchant, that no one had the slightest idea that she was a woman. All thought but this, that she was a man, and her friendship with the merchant increased day by day to such a degree that the latter would not suffer her out of his sight for a moment.

One day, in the midst of a convivial party, the merchant's son began to weep. The merchant, on seeing this, comforted him, and began to wipe away his tears with his handkerchief, and asked the cause of his weeping. The merchant's son said, "O my father! what shall I say? Would that I had never obtained admittance into your service, and that you had not shewn that kindness towards me which you have shewn. Now two difficulties present themselves to me. Neither does my heart wish to be separated from your service, nor is the contingency of my remaining here possible. My departure has now become necessary, but in separating from you, I see no hope of surviving."

Having heard these words, the merchant began to weep with such vehemence that he was stopped by the hiccough, and he said, "O light of my eyes! have you so soon become weary of this old servant, that you depart, having plunged him in woe? Put away from your mind the intention of departure; as long as my life lasts, remain. I shall not survive my separation from you an instant. I shall die before my appointed time. The climate of this country of Persia is very good, and agrees well with you. It is better thus, that you should send a confidential person, and invite to this place your parents, with their property. Whatever equipage[411] or carriage you require, I will supply. When your mother, and father, and family are come, carry on the business of a merchant at your ease. I, too, during my life have endured many reverses of fortune, and have wandered from country to country. Now I have become old, and have no son, I look upon you as dearer than my own son, and I make you my heir and absolute manager. Do you exer-

[411] سواري *sawārī*, is "carriage for *persons*." برداري *bardārī*, "carriage for *goods*."

cise prudence and vigilance in superintending my business also. As long as I live, give me with your own hand a morsel to eat; when I die, be pleased to bury me, and take all my property and effects."

Then the merchant's son replied, "In truth you have sympathized with me, and taken more care of me than a father [could have done], so that I have forgotten my own parents; but the father of this guilty person gave me leave of absence for one year, if I tarry longer, he, in his old age, incessantly weeping, will die. Now a father's approbation is one way to God's favour, and should he be dissatisfied with me, I fear that he might utter a curse upon me, so that I should remain excluded from the mercy of God in both worlds. Your kindness to me then will be in this, that you direct your slave to fulfil the will of his sire, and discharge his filial duty. And to my latest breath it will be incumbent on me to be thankful for your honour's kindness. Though I go to my own country, I shall still every moment remember you with my heart and soul. God is the causer of causes, it may be that some such cause may again arise, that I may obtain the opportunity of kissing your feet." In short, the merchant's son addressed the merchant in words of so much taste [*lit.* such and such words, having mixed them with salt and pepper] and feeling, that that poor man, having no alternative, began to lick his lips [*i.e.* to yield, to be captivated]. Inasmuch as he was charmed and fascinated with him, he began to say, "Well! if you will not stop, then I myself will accompany you. I prize you as my own life, wherefore when the life departs, of what use will be the empty body? If thou art to be pleased in this way only, then proceed and take me with thee." Having said this to the merchant's son, he began to make his own preparations also, and gave orders to his agents to busy themselves with all speed in preparing carriage.

When the news of the merchant's departure had been spread abroad, the merchants of the place, when they heard it, all began to prepare for the journey. The dog-worshipping merchant, taking with him treasures and jewels incalculable, servants and attendants without number, and rarities and goods in great quantities, worthy of royalty, pitched outside the city tents and screens, and tents without poles, and pavilions, and kundlās,[412] and took up his quarters in them. All the merchants bringing with them their merchandize, each according to his own capital, went along with him. Of itself[413] an army was formed.

One day, having turned their backs on the inauspicious quarter,[414] they departed thence. They loaded thousands of camels with sacks of goods, and placed chests of cash and of jewels on mules, and five hundred slaves, Tartars from the plain of Ḳibchāḳ, and Abyssinians and Turkish slaves, fully armed, and masters of the sword, went in advance, mounted on steeds of Arabian descent, born in other countries,[415] and Turkaman, and ʻIrāḳian and ʻArab horses. In rear of all came the merchant and the merchant's son, clothed in rich robes, and borne on easy litters; and a Baghdād seat[416] fastened on a camel, on which was the dog sleeping on a cushion, and the cages of those two prisoners suspended on a camel, were borne along. As they arrived at each stage, all the merchants came and presented themselves at the levée of the merchant, and sate and drank wine at his board [*lit.* table-cloth]. The merchant, in the delight of having the merchant's son as his companion, was returning thanks to God, and proceeding on stage by stage. At length they arrived in safety and health in the environs of Constantinople, and halted outside the city. The merchant's son said, "O my father! if you will give me permission I will go and see my parents, and clear out a place for you; when your exalted mind thinks fit, be pleased to enter the city."

The merchant said, "It is for your sake, indeed, that I have come hither. Well! quickly finish the meeting [with your friends] and return to me quickly, and give me a place to

---

412 I have not been able to find a description of the tent called a كندلا *kundlā.*

413 I have never met with this sense of براي *barāe* before.

414 Literally, on Yoginī, an evil sprite attendant on Durgā, and supposed by astrologers to denote an unlucky quarter. The meaning given in Forbes' vocabulary is inapplicable here.

415 This is the only distinction that can be made between تازي *tāzī*, and عربي *ʻArabī*, and if there be no distinction, Mīr Amman has written nonsense.

416 Some kind of easy chair, but the exact description I know not.

alight near to yourself." The merchant's son took leave and came to his own house. All the people in the vazīr's palace were amazed, saying, "Who is this man who has intruded here?" The merchant's son, that is, the vazīr's daughter, went and fell at the feet of her mother, and wept, and said, "I am your daughter." On hearing this, the vazīr's lady began to abuse her, saying, "O wanton girl! thou hast turned out very unchaste. Thou hast blackened thine own face, and disgraced thy family. We truly, having lamented thy death [*lit.* life], had calmed ourselves, and were at peace, having washed our hands of thee. Away! remove thyself!"

Then the vazīr's daughter took her turban from off her head, and flinging it away, said, "O my dear mother! I have not been to a bad place, I have done no wrong thing—in obedience to your orders I have undertaken all this scheme in order to free my father from prison. Praise be to God! by the blessing of your prayers, and by the grace of God, I have returned, having accomplished the whole business, since I have brought with me from Naishāpūr the merchant with the dog (on whose neck those rubies are hanging), and have not dealt unfaithfully with what you intrusted to me [in other words, "my chastity"]. With a view to my journey I adopted male attire. Now, the affair of one day remains, having concluded which, I will release my father from his dungeon, and will return to my own home. If you command me I will return, and having stayed abroad one day, will come and wait upon you." The mother, when she had well ascertained that her daughter had performed an action worthy of a brave man, and yet had in every way preserved herself free from injury, prostrated herself [*lit.* rubbed her nose] in the temple of God, and delightedly embraced her daughter, and kissed her lips. She took her calamities[417] upon her, and offered up benedictions, and allowed her to depart with these words, "Do as seems good to thee—me thou hast satisfied."

The vazīr's daughter, having again become the merchant's son, returned to the dog-worshipping merchant. There, inas-

---

417 *Vide* Note 97.

much as her absence was unendurable to the merchant, he had been compelled to come on. It happened that close to the city the merchant's son was going from this quarter, and from that the merchant was coming. In the middle of the way they met. The merchant, on sight of her, said, "Son, whither hast thou gone, leaving me, the old man, alone?" The merchant's son said, "I went home, having received permission from yourself. At length my desire to wait upon you suffered me not to remain there. I have come and am present." Seeing, at the gate of the city, a shady garden on the edge of the sea, they pitched their tents and alighted there. The merchant and the merchant's son, seated together, began to drink wine and eat roasted meat. When the time of evening prayer arrived, they came forth from the tent to look about them, and sat on chairs. By chance a huntsman in the service of the King came out in that direction. Having observed their retinue and their behaviour, he was astonished, and said in his heart, "Perhaps the ambassador of some king has arrived." He stood and was looking at the sight.

A messenger of the merchant called him forward and asked him who he was? He replied that he was the chief huntsman of the King. The messenger gave an account of him to the merchant. The merchant told a negro slave[418] to go and say to the falconer, "We are travellers; if you please, come and sit down. Coffee and pipes are here."[419] When the chief huntsman heard the word "merchant," he was the more astonished, and accompanied the slave to the merchant's party, and beheld their furniture, and magnificence, and soldiers, and slaves. He saluted the merchant and the merchant's son, and observed the exalted position which was given to the dog. His senses utterly departed, and he became like one dazed. The merchant having caused him to be seated, entertained him with coffee. The huntsman inquired the name and designation of the merchant. When he asked leave to depart, the merchant allowed him to go, after presenting him with some pieces of cloth and several

---

[418] Literally, "an infidel slave," or what is vulgarly called "a coffree."
[419] The usual civility offered to a stranger in Turkey, Arabia, and Persia.

rarities. In the morning, when he attended the King's court, he began to speak to the courtiers of the merchant, and of his company. By degrees the news spread to me. I called the chief huntsman before me, and inquired as to the circumstances of the merchant. He made a statement of all he had seen. At hearing of the dog's exaltation and of the two men's imprisonment, I was enraged. I said, "That reprobate merchant is worthy of being put to death." I commanded the executioners,[420] saying, "Go quickly! cut off the head of that impious person, and bring it." It providentially[421] happened that the same ambassador of the Franks was present in the court. He smiled. I was the more incensed, and said, "O disrespectful person! It is far removed from good manners to shew the teeth[422] in the presence of kings; it is better to cry than to laugh unseasonably." He respectfully said, "Asylum of the World! some thoughts passed through my mind. On that account your devoted servant smiled. In the first place [I thought] this, that the vazīr is truthful; now he will obtain deliverance from his prison. Secondly, that the King will escape from the innocent blood of that vazīr. Thirdly, this, that the Point to which the world turns in prayer has, without cause and without offence, ordered the execution of the merchant. I was astonished at these doings, that Your Majesty, without inquiry, on the word of a silly fellow, sits ordering the execution of everybody. God knows what the circumstances of that merchant really are! Be pleased to send for him into your royal presence, and inquire into his affairs. If he is

---

[420] This meaning is most unaccountably omitted by both Forbes and Shakespear.

[421] I must object to the meaning given in the dictionaries to قضاكار *ḳaẓākār*, "by chance." The Musalmān do not admit of "chance," nor should we, if we gave any heed to philosophy or religion.

[422] Unless دانت كهولنے *dānt kholne* is taken as a plural substantive, this sentence is ungrammatical. Forbes, in his vocabulary, makes it a substantive, and translates it "laughter," which may be regarded as plural (like *ἀνήριθμον γέλασμα*) though that is strange enough. But Forbes in his "Dictionary" (Shakespear omits it) makes دانت كهولنے *dānt kholne* an infinitive, in which case it ought to be دانت كهولنا *dānt kholnā*, with the singular verb هي *hai*, not هين *hain*.

proved to be guilty, then you are at liberty to do as you please. Treat him as you think fit."

When the ambassador had in this manner admonished me, I too bethought myself of the speech of the vazīr. I commanded, saying, "Bring quickly [*lit.*, "make present"] the merchant with his son and the dog, and the cage." The attendants[423] ran to summon him, and in an instant brought the whole party into the presence. I called them before me. First came the merchant and his son, both of them clothed in sumptuous apparel. At sight of the beauty of the merchant's son, all, both low and high, were amazed and confounded.[424] The merchant's son brought in his hand a golden tray filled with jewels (the lustre of each individual stone of which lit up the whole apartment), and offered[425] it before my throne. He made his bow respectfully, and stood still. The merchant also kissed the ground, and began to utter a benediction. He was discoursing in such a style that you would have said it was [*lit.*, "you would say it is"] the nightingale with its thousand songs. I approved of his abilities much, but said to him with a countenance of rebuke, "O fiend in human shape! what net is this that thou hast spread, and what well that thou hast dug, in thy own path? What is thy faith, and what custom is this? Of what Prophet is this a sect? If thou art an infidel, even then what turn of mind is this? and what is thy name that this is thy deed?"[426]

He said, "May the life and fortune of the Point to which the world turns in prayer remain increasing! The faith of thy slave is this, that God is one, He has no partner, and I recite the creed of Muḥammad Muṣṭafā (may God bless and preserve him and his posterity!), and after him I regard the twelve

---

[423] قورچي *ḳorchī* has but one meaning in Forbes' vocabulary, "keeper of a wardrobe," a signification which here is simply ridiculous.

[424] With deference to Mīr Amman بهيچك *bhaichak* is an execrably ill-chosen word here, as it signifies "aghast at some horrible and portentous sight."

[425] The meanings given for نچهاور *nichhāwar* in Forbes' vocabulary do not apply here.

[426] Observe in the Hindūstānī text the rhyme in these sentences, which is thought a grace in composition.

Imāms[427] as my guides;[428] and my rule of life is this, I repeat the prayers at the five times,[429] and observe the fast,[430] and I have also returned from performing the pilgrimage to Makkah,[431] and I bestow the fifth of my property in alms,[432] and I am called[433] a Musalmān. But [with regard to] all these faults which are to outward view existing in me, on account of which Your Majesty is displeased, and I continue in ill-repute among all God's creatures; for this there is a reason which I am unable to disclose. Although I am notorious as the dog-worshipper, and pay double taxes, [yet] I have consented to all this, but have not told the secret of my heart to any one."

At this excuse my anger increased, and I said, "Dost thou cajole me with thy words? I will never listen to thee until thou givest, for thy perversity, a reasonable ground, which may be satisfactory to my mind. Then thou shalt escape with thy life; else, in retribution for it, I will cause thy belly to be ripped up, as a warning to all, that none may infringe the religion of Muḥammad." The merchant said, "O King! refrain from the blood of me unhappy, and confiscate [instead] all my property, which exceeds computation and reckoning, and release me and my son, making us a votive offering[434] for your throne, and bestow on us our lives." I smiled, and said,

---

[427] *Vide* Note 8.

[428] With Muḥammadans it is customary for the principal person to stand in front of the rest in prayer, and the others follow his motions. Thus the Khalīfah would stand first of all in an assembly of the faithful. There is an allusion perhaps to this in the word پیشوا *peshwā*.

[429] *Vide* Note 51.

[430] That is, during the 9th month or Ramaẓān, from dawn to sunset. For a full description of this fast, *vide* Ḳānūn-i Islām, p. 56.

[431] *Vide* Ḳānūn-i Islām, p. 60.

[432] It is a فرض *farẓ*, or divine command, to give alms annually of five things, viz. money, cattle, grain, fruit, and merchandize. The per-centage varies, but the highest is a fifth, which is for treasure derived from mines. *Vide* Ḳānūn-i Islām, p. 58.

[433] This word کہانا *kahānā* is omitted in Forbes' vocabulary. It is the causal of کہنا *kahnā*, "to say," and from its first meaning "cause to say," gets a second, "to be called," "to call oneself."

[434] Thus the scape-goat was set free to bear the sins and curses of the people away with it.

"O thou without understanding! dost thou hold out to me the lure of thy wealth? There is now no escape for thee except in speaking the truth." On hearing this, the tears began to drop involuntarily from the merchant's eyes, and having looked towards his son, he heaved a sigh, and said, "I indeed have been pronounced guilty before the King; I shall be put to death; now what shall I do? to whose care shall I commit thee?" I said to him menacingly, "O deceiver! enough! now thou hast made too many excuses; say quickly what thou hast to say."

Then, indeed, that man, stepping forward, came near the throne, kissed the foot of it, and commencing with a eulogy of me, said, "O king of kings! had not you issued an order for my execution, I would have endured all punishments, and not told my history. But life is dearer than all. No one of his own accord falls into a well. Self-preservation, then, is a duty, and to abandon duty is contrary to the command of God. Well, since your imperial will is so, be pleased then to hear the history of this weak old man. First, let an order be given to bring and place in your presence those two cages in which the two men are imprisoned. I will relate my story; if I anywhere speak falsely, then, by interrogating them, be pleased to convict me and do as justice requires." I approved of these words of his, and having sent for the cages, and caused those two to be taken out, made them stand near the merchant.

The merchant said, "O king! this man who is on the right hand is your slave's eldest brother, and the one on the left is my second brother (*lit.*, "middle brother"). I am younger than both of them. My father was a merchant in the country of Fārs. When I was fourteen years old my father died. When the interment and shrouding[435] were finished, and the flowers had been removed,[436] these two brothers said to me one day, 'Now

---

[435] For a description of the funeral rites observed by Muḥammadans, *vide* Ḳānūn-i Islām, chap. xxxviii. The winding-sheet is of calico, inscribed with chapters of the Ḳur'ān. The kafan or shroud must be white, and consists of three pieces for a man, and five for a woman.

[436] Before the corpse is carried forth for interment, wreaths of flowers are laid on it, or a sheet ornamented with flowers. These are removed when the corpse is lifted to be carried to the grave.

let us divide whatever property our father left; let each do [with his share] what his heart desires.' When I heard [this] I said, 'O brothers! what words are these? I am your slave, I lay no claim to the rights of a brother. I have lost a father; you two will be over my head in his place. I want but a dry crust, with which I may support myself as long as I have to live, and remain present in your service. What business have I with shares or portions? I will fill my stomach with your leavings, and remain with you. I am a boy; I have, too, neither read nor written; what can I do? Do you now instruct me.'

"Having heard this, they replied, 'Thou wishest to ruin us and reduce us to want along with yourself.' I went silently into a corner and began to weep. Again I admonished my own heart thus: 'After all, my brothers are my elders. They reprove me with a view to my instruction, that I may learn something.' In this same meditation I fell asleep. In the morning a footman of the Ḳāẓī came and took me into the Court of Justice. There I saw that these two brothers were present. The Ḳāẓī said, 'Wherefore dost thou not divide and portion out the inheritance of thy father?' I gave them the same answer which I had given in the house. My brothers said, 'If thou sayest this from thy heart, then write out and give to us a bill of discharge, to the effect that thou hast nothing to do with the property or goods of thy father.' Even then I thought that those two were my elders, and spoke for my instruction, in order that when I received my paternal inheritance, I might not expend it improperly. In accordance with their wish, I wrote an acquittance with the seal of the Ḳāẓī. They were satisfied, and I returned home.

"Next day they began to say to me, 'O brother! we require this room in which thou livest; do thou take some other place, and go and live there.' I then perceived that they were not even willing that I should stop in my father's house. Having no alternative, I resolved to get up and go away. Asylum of the world! when my father was living, then whenever he returned from his travels, he used to bring rarities from each country [he visited], by way of present and give them to me, because every one is fondest of his youngest son. I sold them, and had got together a small stock of my own, with which I was carrying on a little traffic. On one occasion my father brought for me from Turkistān a slave-girl, and once he brought horses, amongst which there was a young colt which promised well; that also he gave me. I provided it with grain and grass at my own expense.

"At length, seeing their unkindness, I purchased a house, whither I went and stayed. This dog also went with me. I collected household furniture for necessary purposes, and purchased two slaves to wait on me, and with my remaining stock I set up a mercer's shop, and sate down in reliance on God. I was content with my fate. Though my brothers had displayed malice to me, still, as God was kind, in the space of three years I collected such a shop that I became a man of credit. All the costly things that were required in the high families went from my shop alone. Thereby I amassed much money, and began to live in great comfort. Every moment I was offering up thanksgivings to the Divine Majesty, and dwelt at my ease. I frequently recited this stanza with reference to my own condition,

Why should not the king be wrathful? Nought have I to do with him,
Thou alone art my great Sovereign, and Thy praise alone I hymn.
Let my brother, too, be angry; thence I've nought to hope or fear.
Thou alone art my Deliverer,—to whom else should I draw near?
Wrathful be they, friend or foeman, only be Thy favour sure.
Night and day from hour to hour, let that love alone endure.
The world is wrathful, but Thou only art incomparably great,
All shall kiss the thumb submissive,—Thou alone be not irate.

It happened that on a Friday[437] I was seated in my house, when a slave of mine, who had gone to the bāzār to make purchases, came back after a short interval weeping. I asked the reason, saying, 'What is the matter with thee?' He replied in a vexed way, 'What matters it to you? do you enjoy yourself; but at the day of resurrection what answer will you give?' I said, 'O Abyssinian! what such calamity has befallen thee?' He said, 'The exasperating thing is this, that in the centre of

437 جمعه *Jumâ*, Friday, is the Sabbath of the Muḥammadans.

the bāzār, a Jew has pinioned the arms of thine elder brothers, and is striking them with a whip, and derides them, saying, "If you will not pay my money, then I will continue beating you until I beat you to death. Marry, I shall at least receive the recompense of a meritorious act, [even if I should lose my money by killing you]." Well! this is the condition of your brothers, and you are unconcerned. This is a pretty thing! what will people say?' On hearing these words from the slave, my blood boiled. With bare feet I ran towards the bāzār, and said to my slaves, 'Bring money quickly.' As soon as I arrived there, I saw then that whatever the slave had said was true. On them blows were descending. I said to the footmen of the Governor, 'For God's sake! stop a little. Let me ask of the Jew what such offence they have committed in return for which he has inflicted on them this chastisement.'

"Having said this, I went up to the Jew, and said, 'To-day is Friday; wherefore hast thou continued inflicting stripes upon them?' He replied, 'If you mean to aid them, do it effectually; instead of them do you pay me my money, otherwise take your way home.' I said, 'What sum? produce your bond; I will count over the money to you.' He said, 'I left the bond with the magistrate when I came here.' Meanwhile my two slaves came up, bringing two bags of money. I gave a thousand rupees to the Jew, and released my brothers. Their condition had become and was such that I brought them home along with me, naked, and hungry, and thirsty. I forthwith caused them to bathe in the warm bath, dressed them in new clothes, and gave them food to eat. I never at any time said to them, 'What have you done with the large property of my father?' [I thought] that perhaps they would be ashamed.

"O King! these two are present. Be pleased to ask whether I speak the truth, or whether there is any admixture of falsehood also in what I say? Well! when after some days they had recovered from the bruises of their beating, I said to them one day, 'O brothers! you have now lost your credit in this city. It is better for you to travel for a time.' When they heard this, they remained silent. I perceived that they were willing. I began to make preparations for their journey. I provided them with tents, baggage, and conveyance for their things and for themselves, and purchased goods to the amount of twenty thousand rupees. A caravan of merchants was going to Bukhārā.[438] I sent them along with it.

"After a year that caravan came back. I got no good news of them. At length I, with many adjurations, inquired of an acquaintance [respecting them]. He said, 'When we arrived in Bukhārā, one lost all he possessed in a gambling-house. He now performs the part of sweeper there, and smears and plasters the floor of the gambling-house. He waits on the gamblers who assemble there, and they,[439] by way of charity, give him something. He has become the low drudge there, and so abides. And the other, having fallen in love with the daughter of a vendor of the drink called bozah,[440] has expended all his property; now he does the dirty work in the boozing-ken. The people of the caravan did not tell you, lest you should be ashamed.'

"When I heard these things from that person, my condition became a strange one; through anxiety sleep and hunger left me. I took with me provisions for the journey, and set out for Bukhārā. When I arrived there, I sought them both out and brought them to my house. I caused them to bathe, and to put on new garments, and through fear of their being put to shame, I did not utter a word. I again bought for them merchandize, and set out home. When I drew near to Naishāpūr, I left them and their baggage in a village, and returned home, in order that my arrival might not be known to any one. Two days after I made it known that my brothers were returned

---

438 بخارا *Bukhārā*, called شریف *sharīf*, "the noble," is the capital of Transoxiana, and is in N. lat. 40°, E. long. 62°. It has been repeatedly taken and re-taken by various conquerors, as by Tīmūr Lang and Jangīz Khān, but has been now for 300 years in the possession of the Uẓbak Tartars. Of late it has obtained an infamous notoriety from the murders of Captain Conolly and Colonel Stodhart, perpetrated by its ruler.

439 Here we have (in the text) وہ *wuh* for "they," instead of وے *we*, yet no munshī would suffer such an error to pass without notice.

440 Forbes, in his vocabulary, renders بوزہ *bozah*, "a kind of ale or beer," but it is rather the fermented liquor of the Palmyra-tree, mixed with opium, decoction of hemp, and other intoxicating ingredients. The similarity of "bozah," and our word "booze," is remarkable; and still more "bozah-khānah" and "boozing-ken."

from a journey, and that I should go out the next day to meet them. In the morning I was about to go [when] a householder of that very village came to me and began to utter cries of complaint.[441] Hearing his voice I came out, and seeing him weeping, I inquired, 'Why art thou uttering lamentations?' He said, 'By reason of your brothers, our houses have been plundered, would that you had not left them there!' I asked, 'What calamity has happened?' He said, 'At night there came an attack of robbers. They plundered their property, and carried off the plunder of our houses also.' I expressed my regret, and asked, 'Where are the two now?' He replied, 'They are sitting outside the city, quite naked, in a wretched and forlorn state.' I immediately took with me two suits of clothes, dressed them in them, and brought them home. People hearing of it were coming to see them, and they, from shame, were refraining from going out. Three months passed in this same way. I then reflected in my heart, saying, 'How long will these[442] remain crouching in a corner? If it can be done, I will take them with me on a journey.' I said to my brothers, 'If you say the word, this devoted servant will travel with you.' They remained silent. I again made ready the things necessary for a journey, and articles of merchandize, and set out and took them with me.

"At the time when—after bestowing part of my effects as alms,[443] and embarking my goods in the ship—the anchor was raised and the vessel went on,[444] the dog had remained sleeping on the shore. When it suddenly awoke, and saw the ship in the mid-stream, it was surprised, and barked, and sprang into

---

[441] فریاد کرنے لگا *faryād karne lagā*, does not mean simply "to complain," but to cry out, "faryād! faryād!" until the wrong-doer or the judge is thoroughly roused to investigate the matter.

[442] Here یہہ *yih* is used as plural for یے *ye*, as a few lines before وہ *wuh* occurs for وے *we*. *Vide* Note 439.

[443] This is done at the commencement of a journey, to secure a prosperous issue.

[444] The text is here wrongly punctuated. There should be a comma only at چلی *chalī*, a full stop at تہا *thā*. The sentence which ends with تہا *thā*, is the relative to the antecedent introduced by جس وقت *jis waḳt*, and should not be separated from it.

the river, and began to swim. I hastily despatched a skiff. At length they brought the dog and placed it on board the ship. A month passed happily and safely away on the water,[445] [when] somehow or other my second brother fell in love with my slave-girl. One day he addressed my eldest brother as follows, 'The benefits which we have received from our youngest brother cause us much shame. What remedy shall we take for this?' The eldest brother replied, 'I have fixed on an expedient in my heart; it will be an excellent thing if it succeeds.' At length the two, after taking counsel, determined that they would slay me, and possess themselves of all my property.

"One day I was sleeping in the cabin of the ship, and my slave-girl was manipulating my feet,[446] when my second brother came and awoke me in a hurry. I started up in confusion, and came out. This dog also came with me. I beheld then that my eldest brother was leaning with his hands on the side of the vessel, and stooping over, continued looking at some sight in the water, and was calling to me. I went to him and said, 'Is all well?' He said, 'There is a marvellous sight going on, for mermen, holding in their hands pearl oyster-shells and trees of coral, are dancing.' If any one else had said such a thing so repugnant to reason, I would not have believed him. I deemed what my eldest brother said truth, and bent my head to look. Notwithstanding I gazed I saw nothing, and he continued saying the same thing, 'Now, have you seen it?' But had there been anything, I should have seen it. Meanwhile, my second brother, catching me off my guard, came unawares behind me and gave me such a push that I had no power to help myself, and fell into the water, and they began to weep and lament, saying, 'Pray run, our brother has gone down in the sea.'

---

[445] The expression مانجھ دھار *mānjh dhār*, would only apply to a river, but دریا *daryā* here would seem to be "the sea," from the coral and oysters the brother talks of, and from the merchant floating eight days before reaching land.

[446] One of the luxuries of the Orientals is to employ a female to press and shampoo their feet while they are sleeping, which operation is supposed to cause and prolong slumber. Kṛishṇ, however, in the 53rd chapter of the "Prem Sāgar," wakes a Brāhman in this way.

"In the mean time the vessel passed on, and the roll of the sea tossed me far away. I suffered immersion after immersion, and was drifting on with the waves. At length I was exhausted, and called to God for assistance.[447] My efforts were quite useless. All at once my hand touched something. I opened my eyes and saw that it was this very dog. Perhaps at the moment they threw me into the sea, this dog too leapt in with me, and by swimming was keeping up with me, and clinging to me. I seized hold of its tail. God made it the means of my preservation. Seven days and nights the same state of things continued. On the eighth day we touched the shore. I was altogether powerless; stretched out and rolling over, I somehow or other threw myself on dry land. One day I remained senseless, the next the voice of the dog penetrated my ears. I recovered my senses, and returned thanks to God. I began to look about me. At a distance the environs of a city appeared, but where had I the strength to make for it? Having no resource I went on two steps and then sat down. In this same way I got over a full *kos* before evening.

"In the mid-way I came to a mountain, there I passed the night. In the morning I entered the city, and saw the shops of the bakers and confectioners. My heart began to quake. I neither had the money to purchase, nor was my mind willing to beg. I was encouraging my heart by saying, 'I will get some from the next shop,' and so passed on. At length I had no strength left, and the fire [of starvation] kindled in my stomach. My spirit was on the point of departing from my body. All of a sudden I saw two young men who were coming along, dressed in the Persian garb, and holding one another's hands.[448] Seeing them I was glad, and said to myself, 'These are men of my own country, perhaps they may be persons I know—to them I will tell my story.' When they came near, they turned out to be my own two brothers! I was highly delighted at seeing them, and returned thanks to God, saying, 'God has preserved my

---

[447] Literally: "Remembered God;" but it is here used for "supplicated the Divine aid."

[448] Orientals do not walk arm in arm, but hand in hand.

honour—I have not held out my hand [to beg] of a stranger.' I went up to them and saluted them, and kissed the hand of my eldest brother. They, on seeing me, raised an outcry. My second brother struck me a blow with his open hand, so that I staggered and fell. I caught hold of the skirt of my eldest brother [thinking] that, perhaps, he would protect me. He gave me a kick. In short both of them pounded and bruised me well, and acted like the brethren of the holy Yūsuf.[449] Although I besought them in God's name, and supplicated piteously, they had no mercy on me. A crowd assembled. All inquired, 'What is his offence?' Then my brothers said, 'This rascal was the servant of our brother, whom he threw into the sea, and took all his property. We were a long time in search of him—to-day we found him in this state.' And they were asking me, 'O cruel wretch! what is this which entered thy heart, that thou hast slain and made away with our brother? How had he injured thee? Was that treating thee badly when he made thee his factotum?' Then both of them rent their collars and gave loose to hypocritical tears for the [pretended] loss of their brother, and heaped kicks and buffets[450] upon me.

"Meanwhile the footmen[451] of the magistrate came up and threatened them, saying, 'Why do ye beat him?' and taking me by the hand, led me to the chief officer of police. These two[452] also went along with me, and told the same story to the magistrate, and having given him something by way of bribe, demanded that justice should be done them, and required my innocent blood. The magistrate interrogated me. My state was such that, through hunger and blows, I had not the power to speak. I stood with my head hanging down, and uttered not a word in reply. The magistrate, too, was con-

---

[449] Joseph, who is by Muḥammadans included among the Prophets.

[450] مکّی *mukkī* is a blow with the clenched fist; طمانچه *ṭamānchah*, a slap with the open hand.

[451] I have translated پیاده *piyādah* literally, but it means, not what "footman" signifies with us, but "police;" and corresponds to our former "Bow-street *runners*."

[452] Pointing to his brothers.

vinced that I was certainly a murderer. He commanded, saying, 'Take this man into the plain and impale him.' Asylum of the world! I had given money and released them from the bondage of the Jew, in return for which these two expended their money in attempting my life. Both of them are present; be pleased to ask them whether, in saying this, I deviate one hair's breadth from the truth. Well! they led me away! when I saw the stake I washed my hands of life.

"Save this dog I had none to bewail me; its state was such that it was rolling at every one's feet, and howling. One struck it with a stick, another with a stone; but it would not quit the place, and I, standing with my face towards Makkah, was addressing myself to the Deity in these words, 'At this moment there is none save Thyself to interpose and save me, innocent as I am. Now, if Thou wilt deliver me, then I shall be delivered.' Having said this, I repeated the Martyr's Creed,[453] and fell down in a swoon. By the providential contrivance of God, the king of that city was sick of the colic.[454] The nobles and the physicians assembled, but no remedy which they adopted was of any use. A venerable person said, 'The best of all medicines is this, to bestow some alms on the necessitous, and to set free the prisoners. Blessing has much greater effect than leeching.'[455] Immediately the servants of the King hurried towards the prisons.

"It happened that one came out into that plain [where I was]. Seeing the crowd he found that they were impaling some one. On learning this,[456] he brought his horse near the stake, and

---

453 "I bear witness that there is no God but God, who is one and has no co-equal; and I bear witness that Muḥammad is his servant and was sent from Him." This creed is repeated at the initiation of faḳīrs; over a dying person, or by the person himself if he has the power of utterance; and during the purification of a corpse. *Vide* Ḳānūn-i Islām, pp. 285, 408, 411.

454 A slight instance of the exquisitely bad taste of Orientals. Could not the King's malady have been left an open question without turning the whole affair into a burlesque by afflicting him with the colic!

455 I have made an attempt to preserve the play on words in the original, where دوا *dawā*, "medicine," and دعا *duā*, "prayer" or "benediction," have much the same sound.

456 It is implied in the معلوم کیا *malūm kiyā*, that he asked some one what was going on.

with his sword cut the ropes. He threatened and reproved the magistrate's footmen, saying, 'At such a time when this is the King's state, are you slaying one of God's servants?' and he caused me to be released. Then these two brothers of mine went again to the magistrate, and asked him to put me to death. The [King's] deputy had, indeed, received a bribe, whatever they were saying, that he was doing. He[457] [therefore] said to them, 'Rest content. I will now imprison him in such wise that, destitute of water and of food, he will, of his own accord, perish of hunger; no one will know of it.' They seized me and put me aside. At about a *kos* distance from the city there was a mountain, where, in the time of King Sulaimān, the Devs[458] had dug a pit narrow and dark, to which people gave the name of the prison of Sulaimān. There they confined any one who had incurred the grave displeasure of the King, and there he perished from natural causes. In a word, these two brothers of mine and the magistrate's staff took me to that mountain, and after throwing me into that pit, and satisfying their minds, went away. O King! this dog went with me. When they threw me down into the pit, then it lay itself on the brink. I had fallen within in a state of insensibility. When I recovered my consciousness a little, I imagined myself dead, and fancied that place my grave. Meanwhile the voices of two persons reached my ears, who were saying something to one another. I was fully persuaded that they were Nakīr and Munkir,[459] and that they had come to question me. I heard the rustling of a rope, as though some one let it down there. I

---

457 Here the words كوتوال *kotwāl*, حاكم *ḥākim*, شحنه *shaḥnah*, are used indiscriminately of one and the same functionary, though properly speaking the first is a police magistrate, the second a governor, and the third a viceroy.

458 Devs are evil and malignant spirits, who, with fairies and jins, acknowledged the universal sway of Sulaimān, the son of David.

459 Munkir and Nakīr, or "Unbelieving" and "Hateful," are two angels who examine the dead. They make the corpse sit up, and inquire of it what God and what Prophet it acknowledges. Bad men stammer or are mute, on which they are forthwith knocked down with an iron mace or *gurz* armed with spikes, and then assisted to rise with an iron rake, and beaten to an intolerable pitch. These preliminaries are a prægustation of future torments.

was amazed; when I groped with my hands on the ground, they were filled with bones.

"After a short time the sound of munching and crunching in mastication reached my ears, as though some one was eating something. I said, inquiringly, 'O servants of God! who are you? Tell me for the sake of God!' They laughed and said, 'This is the prison of Prince Sulaimān, and we are prisoners.' I inquired of them, 'What! am I living?' They laughed again obstreperously, and said, 'Up to now thou art indeed alive, but thou wilt die presently.' I said, 'You are eating—how would it be if you were to give me a very little?' Then in a rage they gave me a flat refusal, and gave me nothing else,[460] and after eating and drinking went to sleep. I, fainting with weakness and debility, was weeping, and calling on God. Point to which the world turns in prayer! for seven days in the deep, and for so many days after, through the false accusation of my brothers, I had suffered blows and beating, and was held fast in such a prison, that the idea of escape did not so much as enter my imagination.

"At length, the moment of my dissolution approached. Sometimes my breath came, sometimes it left me. From time to time, however, at midnight, a person was coming and letting down bread and a vessel of water, which he had tied up in a handkerchief, and was calling out. Those two persons who were imprisoned near me, were taking it and eating and drinking. From above, the dog, always observing these circumstances, reflected as follows, 'Just as this person lets down water and bread into the pit, do thou also contrive that some food reach that friendless one, who is thy[461] master.' With this idea it went into the city, [where] round loaves were set out in order on the counters of the bakers' shops. Making a spring it carried off a cake in its mouth, and ran away. The

---

[460] A play on words, جواب *jawāb*, meaning "answer" and "refusal." Thus in Anglo-Indian parlance a rejected lover is said to be "jawābed."

[461] In the text we have میرا خاوند *merā khāwind*, "my master," which is incorrect with تو *tū*, "thou," preceding it; but an intricate sentence soon obscures Mīr Amman's ideas of grammar.

people pursued it, and were pelting it with clods, but it did not drop the loaf. The people grew tired and turned back, the dogs of the city continued the pursuit; with them it fought and struggled, and preserved the bread. It reached the pit and threw down the loaf into it. It was clear daylight. I saw the bread lying near me, and heard the dog's bark. I took up the cake, and this dog having thrown down the bread, went in search of water.

"At the edge of a village was the hut of an old woman, where were set jars and pots filled with water, and the old dame was spinning. The dog went up to the jar and was about to take up a small metal pot used for drinking water from the larger jar.[462] The woman made a threatening gesture, the metal pot slipped from its mouth and fell on the large earthenware jar, which broke, and the other jars rolling over,[463] the water flowed out. The old woman took a stick and rose to beat [the dog], which caught hold of her skirt, and began to rub its face on her feet and wag its tail, and then ran off towards the mountain. Then coming back to her, sometimes it took up the cord, at other times seized the bucket in its mouth, and shewed it, and rubbed its face on her feet, and catching hold of the corner of her dress, pulled her along. God inspired the heart of that woman with pity, so that she took the bucket and cord and went with the dog, which, holding her by the corner of her dress, came forth from the house and went on and on before her.

"At last the dog conducted her up that very mountain. The actions of the dog revealed to that woman's mind that, without doubt, its master was imprisoned in that pit, and that probably

---

[462] This periphrasis of twelve words is requisite here to explain what لوٹا *loṭā* is. It would seem as though Mīr Amman in this passage designed to instruct us in the nomenclature of pots of all classes, for he has used no less than seven terms for those useful articles. The ٹھلیا *ṭhiliyā*, کوزہ *kūzah*, گھڑا *ghaṛā*, and مٹکا *maṭkā*, I take to be here identical, though the "kūzah" is properly tall and thin with a narrow neck, the others short and swagbellied.

[463] In India a number of porous earthenware jars are set one above the other, so that the water percolates from the highest to the lowest, and is thus deliciously cooled and purified.

it wanted the water for him. In short it conducted the old woman to the mouth of the pit. The woman filled a brass pot with water, and let it down. I took the vessel and eat a morsel of bread. I then drank two or three gulps of water, and satisfied the ravenous craving[464] of my stomach. After returning thanks to God, I sat on one side, and awaited the merciful intervention of the Deity, saying, 'Let us see what will happen next.' This dumb animal, in the very same way, continued to bring bread, and give me water to drink by the hands of the old woman. When the tavern-keepers[465] saw that the dog was always carrying off the bread, they took pity on it, and made it a rule when they saw it to fling a loaf down before it, and if the woman did not bring water, then the dog broke her jars. Having no alternative, she too came daily and gave me a cup of water. That friendly animal satisfied me with water and bread, and itself lay couched at the mouth of the prison. In this manner six months passed; but when a man is confined in such a prison that the breath of heaven [*lit.* "of the world"] cannot reach him, what will be his condition? Only skin and bone was left to me. Life became a torment to me. It used to come into my mind that, 'O God! if this breath departed, it would be better.'

"One night those two prisoners were sleeping; my heart overflowed, and I involuntarily began to weep, and prostrated myself before God [*lit.* "in the court or shrine of God"]. At the last watch [*i.e.* "from three to six A.M."] what did I see? that, by the powerful interposition of God, a rope was let down into the pit, and I plainly overheard a voice, saying, 'O ill-fated and unfortunate one! Bind the end of the cord fast round thy hand, and come forth.' When I heard this, I imagined in my heart that at length my brothers had softened towards me, and from natural affection [*lit.* "from ebullition of their blood"] had themselves come to take me out. With excessive joy I

---

464 Literally, "the dog of this stomach," or "this dog of the stomach."

465 بهٹهيارا *bhaṭhiyārā* may perhaps be here considered equivalent to نان باي *nān bāī*, and be rendered "baker," but its usual meaning is the one given above. It is wrongly spelt in Forbes' vocabulary.

fastened that cord well round my wrist, and some one drew me up. The night was so dark that I did not recognize who it was that pulled me out. When I had come out, he said, 'Come quickly! this is not the place for standing still.' I had indeed no strength in me, but, urged by fear, I managed, rolling and tumbling, to descend the mountain. I saw then that two horses were standing there, saddled. That person seated me on one, and himself mounted the other, and went before me. Proceeding on, we arrived at the edge of the river.

"The morning broke, and we had come ten or twelve *kos* from that city. I surveyed the young man, and saw that he was clad in complete mail, and wore both ring and plate armour, and had on a cuirass, and back and side pieces burnished like four mirrors.[466] His horse also was provided with armour, and he was looking fiercely and frowningly at me, and biting his hand with his teeth. [Presently] he drew his sword from its scabbard, and making his horse bound, aimed a blow at me. I threw myself from my horse, and began to supplicate, saying, 'I have committed no offence, why dost thou slay me? O kind sir! thou hast liberated me from such a dungeon—now what unkindness is this!' He replied, 'Speak the truth—who art thou?' I answered, 'I am a traveller; I was overtaken in a calamity, by your bounty I am now come forth alive.' I added many flattering words. God infused pity into his heart; he sheathed his sword, and said, 'Well! let God's will be done! There, I have spared thy life. Mount quickly, this is not the place for tarrying.' We urged on our steeds, and proceeded. On the road, as he went forward, he shewed signs of sorrow and regret. By noon we arrived in an island. Then he dismounted from his horse, and assisted me also to alight. He undid the saddles and valises from the horses' backs, and let them loose to graze. He also laid aside the weapons from his own belt and sate down. He then said to me, 'O unfortunate! now relate thy story, that I may know

---

[466] I have here indulged in a periphrasis in order to explain the expression, چار آینہ *chār āinah*.

who thou art.' I acquainted him with my name and residence, and detailed to the end all the calamities that had befallen me.

"The youth, when he had heard all my narrative, began to weep, and addressing me, said, 'O young man! now hear my history. I am the daughter of the king of the country of Zerbād,[467] and that stripling who is confined in Sulaimān's prison is named Bahrahmand [or 'Fortunate']. He is the son of the chief minister of my father.[468] One day the King commanded that all his dependent princes and their sons should issue forth into the plain under the lattices [of the palace], and exercise themselves in archery and playing with the ball,[469] so as to exhibit the skill and horsemanship of each. I took my seat in an upper room, concealed from view, near[470] the Queen who was my mother, and nurses and handmaids were in attendance. I was viewing the spectacle.[471] This son of the minister was the handsomest of all, and he was lunging[472] his horse, and exhibiting his skill. He pleased me, and in my heart I felt a liking for him. For a long time I kept this concealed.

"'At length, when my emotion became uncontrollable, I told it to a nurse, and bestowed on her a profusion of presents. She, by some means or other, brought that youth secretly to my apartment.[473] Then he too began to love me. Many days

---

467 The countries below Bengāl, *i.e.* to the south-east of it, are so called. Amongst these are Āva and Pegu.

468 Observe the succession of Hindī words, showing it to be a Hindū kingdom. Thus we have راجا *rājā*, پتا *pitā*, منتري *mantrī*, مهاراج *mahārāj*, اگيا *agyā*, كنور *kunwar*; in the Urdū they would be پادشاه *pādshāh*, باپ *bāp*, or قبله گاه *ḳiblah gāh*, وزير *vazīr*, حكم *ḥukm*, شاهزاده *shāhzādah*.

469 The چوگان *chaugān* is played on horseback. The riders are provided with bats, and keep the ball flying by striking it when it comes within reach.

470 We shall probably hardly escape the censure of the facetious writer of Art. 1, No. XCII., in the "Edinburgh Review," if we venture to derive the English "near" from the Hindī نيڙے *neṛe* (the word in the text), and نير *niyar*. At least one may be permitted to hint at the resemblance.

471 I should prefer a full stop after تهين *thīn*.

472 كاوے دينا *kāwe denā*, "to lunge," has been omitted in Forbes' vocabulary.

473 Vocabularies and dictionaries are all silent as to the word دهراهر *dhirāhar*. The meaning given above is evidently the one required in this passage.

passed in this amour. One day the guards having seen him armed, and entering the palace at midnight, seized him and informed the King. He ordered him to be put to death. All the pillars of the state, by their expostulations [*lit.* 'having said and heard'], obtained that his life should be spared. The King then ordered him to be cast into Sulaimān's prison, and the other youth, who is confined with him, is his brother.[474] On that night he, too, was with him. They left them both in that pit. It is three years to-day since they were first imprisoned, but no one has discovered why the young man entered the King's palace. God has preserved my honour,[475] and to shew my gratitude for that, I have imposed on myself [the task] of supplying him with food and water. Since then I come once in eight days, and bring eight days' food put together.

"'Yesternight I saw in a dream that some man said to me, "Arise with speed and take a horse, a suit of clothes, and a rope-ladder, and some money for your expenses, and go to that pit, and draw that unfortunate one out from it."[476] When I heard this, I started up, and joyfully put on man's attire, and took a casket filled with jewels and gold coins, and went there with this horse and suit of clothes, to draw him up with the ladder. It was in thy destiny that thou shouldst escape from such a prison, and no one is privy to this deed[477] of mine. Perhaps it was some divinity who sent me for thy deliverance. Well! what was in my destiny that has happened!' Having related this story, she undid from a towel a cake fried in clarified butter, some wheaten bread and pulse, and a meat

---

[474] Forbes, strangely enough, omits this word بهگنا *bhagnā*, in his Dictionary, though he gives it in his vocabulary. Shakespear omits it altogether. The word is Sanskṛit, and signifies "brother," though here, like the German "bruder," it probably means only "a sworn friend." It is the Bengālī form (*bohinī*) of the feminine of this word which Bopp has twisted into the Latin "soror" and our "sister"!!

[475] This word پت *pat*, the Sanskṛit पद् *pada*, is omitted in Forbes' vocabulary.

[476] The author does not tell us why, during the space of three years, the princess never thought of this before. She had surely been dreaming all that time.

[477] Forbes has omitted this word کرتب *kartab*, the Sanskṛit कर्त्तव्य *karttavya*, in his vocabulary.

curry.[478] First, however, she took out a piece of sugar-candy,[479] which she dissolved in a metal cup, and having poured into it some extract of the musk-willow, gave it to me. I took it from her hand and drank it, and then ate a little breakfast. After a short interval she caused me to tie a cloth[480] round my waist, and took me into the river. She cut my hair with scissors, and pared my nails, and having caused me to bathe and wash, dressed me and made a new man of me. I turned to Makkah, and repeated a thanksgiving of two Rakâts.[481] That beautiful girl continued to watch my motions. When I had finished my prayers she began to ask, 'What is this that thou hast done?' I said, 'I have performed the worship of the Creator, whose Person has no partner; who made all things, and caused such a lovely lady as thyself to do me service, and softened thy heart towards me, and released me from such a prison. To Him I offered my devotions, and paid my thanksgivings.' When she heard this, she said, 'Are you a Musalmān?' I said, 'Thanks, Praise be to God [I am].' She said, 'My heart is pleased with your words; teach me also, and make me recite the Creed.' I said in my heart, 'Praise be to God that she has joined our religion!' In short, I repeated, 'There is no God but God, and Muḥammad is the Prophet of God:'[482] and caused her to repeat it. We then mounted our horses and departed from that place. When we stopped for the night, she introduced

---

[478] The word پوري *pūrī* is omitted in Forbes' vocabulary, as is also كچوري *kachaurī*, and سالن *sālan*, and ماس *mās*. The first is a cake made either of fruit, meat, or pulse; the second may be taken with it, and express the kind of pūrī, or separately as above. For a full account of Sālan, *vide* Ḳānūn-i Islām, Cookery, Appendix, pp. 35–37.

[479] قند *ḳand*, whence our word "candy," is omitted in Forbes' vocabulary.

[480] The word لنگی *lungī* is omitted by Forbes in his vocabulary, and erroneously explained by him in his Dictionary, as it is also by Shakespear. Though it here seems to be used instead of لنگوٹی *langoṭī*, it is in point of fact a scarf worn like a sash round the waist or over the shoulders. Sindh is famous for its "lungīs," which are there given as presents.

[481] The "Rakât" consists of certain chapters of the Ḳur'ān, with a prescribed number of genuflexions, etc.

[482] The Muḥammadan creed.

the subject of religion, and listened, and was pleased. In this same manner for two months continually we travelled on day and night.

"At length we arrived in a country lying between the confines of the kingdoms of Zerbād and Sarāndīp.[483] A city appeared, more populous than Istambol, and with a very pleasant and agreeable climate. Finding that the King of that city was more just and munificent to his subjects than Kisra,[484] our hearts rejoiced. We purchased a house, and took up our abode there. When, after some days, we had recovered from the fatigues of our journey, I prepared the necessary articles, and married that lady according to the Maḥammadan law, and began to live there. In three years' intercourse with the high and low of that place, I acquired a reputation, and opened an extensive trade. At last I outstripped all the merchants of that place. One day I went to pay my respects to the chief vazīr, when I saw a great multitude in the plain. I inquired of some one what was the reason of so great a crowd? and learned that they had caught two persons in the act of theft and adultery, and that, as they had probably also committed murder, they had brought them out to stone them.

"On hearing this, I remembered my own adventures, how that one day they had led me too to imprisonment, and that God had delivered me, and I said with a sigh,[485] 'I know not whether it is true, or whether, like me, they have been involved in a false accusation.' I pushed aside the crowd and went in. Then I saw that they were these my two brothers, whom they

---

[483] سرانديپ *Sarāndīp*, سرانديب *Sarāndīb*, or سرانديل *Sarāndīl*, is the Persian word for लङ्का *Lankā*, or Ceylon. The etymology of the word is doubtful. Perhaps the termination may be the Sanskṛit द्वीप *dwīp*, "an island," and سران *sarān*, may be "angels," who are called سرانِ چرخ *sarān-i charkh*. It is curious that Madagascar is called سرانده *Sarāndah*. Shakespear and Forbes both omit the word in their Dictionaries.

[484] Cyrus.

[485] Forbes has omitted this word, آيا *āyā*, in his vocabulary. It is an interjection, equal to—O! *or* heigh! *or* heigho!

were leading along, with their hands tied behind their backs, and with naked heads and feet. On seeing their forms my blood boiled, and my heart was on fire. I gave the officer a handful of gold coins, and said, 'Stop for a short time;' and putting my horse to a gallop,[486] went to the house of the magistrate. I presented him with a ruby of inestimable value,[487] and interceded for them. The magistrate said, 'A person has appeared against them, and their crime has been proved, and the King's order has passed; I have no alternative.' At length, after much supplication and entreaty, the magistrate sent for the accuser, and obtained his consent for five thousand rupees not to press the charge of murder. I counted out the money, and obtained a writing of acquittance, and delivered them from this great calamity. Asylum of the world! inquire of them whether I speak the truth, or am telling idle falsehoods? Then my two brothers were standing there with downcast faces, like persons covered with shame. Well! having obtained their release, I brought them to my house. I caused them to take the warm bath, and to be dressed, and gave them a place to live in in the public apartments. At that time I did not bring my wife into their presence, but waited on them myself, and ate with them, and at bedtime entered my own part of the house. Three years passed in this kindly treatment of them, nor were they guilty of any misdeed, to occasion my displeasure. Whenever I rode out anywhere, they remained in the house. It happened that that good lady [my wife] had gone to the warm bath. When she entered the public hall, no one of the male sex was visible. She took off her veil. Perhaps my second brother, as he lay there, was awake. As soon as he saw her, he became enamoured of her. He spoke to my eldest brother. Together they formed a scheme for murdering me. I had not the slightest information of their bad intention; nay, I was saying in my heart, 'Praise be to God! that this time

---

[486] Forbes has omitted the word سرپٹ *sarpaṭ*, in his vocabulary. سرپٹ پھینکنا *sarpaṭ phenknā*, is "to gallop."

[487] The routine way in which bribery is always referred to as a matter of course is a pretty good index of the then state of Indian society. Is it better now?

they have as yet done nothing of the kind. Their conduct has become what it ought to be. Perhaps they are at length ashamed of themselves.' One day after dinner my eldest brother began to shed tears, and to dilate on the praises of his native country, and the delights of Īrān. When he heard this, the other, too, began to sob. I said, 'If you purpose returning, very good then—I am obedient to your wishes. I, too, have the self-same desire. Now, if it please God Most High, I, too, will accompany you.' I related to that lady the circumstances of my brothers' dejection, and told her of my intention also. That acute woman said, 'You know best; but they wish again to do some treacherous act. They are your deadly enemies. You have fostered snakes in your sleeve, and do you place reliance on their friendship! Do as you please; but beware of these noxious creatures.'

"Prepared for any fate,[488] I made preparations for the journey in a short space of time, and set up my tents in the plain. A large caravan assembled, and they agreed upon me as their leader, and the director of the caravan. Having watched a favourable moment, I set forward; but on every side I was on my guard against my brothers, and I, in everything, observed their wishes, and sought to please them.

"One day, at one of our halting-places, my second brother stated that at the distance of a league[489] from that place, there was a perennial spring, like that of Salsabīl,[490] and that tulips,

---

488 I must confess I think تقدیر *taḳdīr* is here a slip of Mīr Amman's for تدبیر *tadbīr*, "counsel," which latter would refer to the hurried departure of the merchant. بہر تدبیر *bahar tadbīr*, "by every means I could devise."

489 A فرسخ *farsakh*, فرسنگ *farsang*, or *parasang*, is a measure of distance equal to about 18,000 feet, and may therefore be rendered "league."

490 "As plenty of water is one of the greatest additions to the pleasantness of any place, the Ḳur'ān often speaks of the rivers of Paradise as a principal ornament. Some of these rivers, they say, flow with water, some with milk, some with wine, and others with honey, all taking their rise from the root of the tree Tūba. And lest they should not be sufficient, we are told that this garden is also watered by a great number of lesser springs and fountains, whose pebbles are rubies and emeralds, their earth of camphire, their beds of musk, and their sides of saffron; the most remarkable among them being Salsabīl and Tasnīm."—Sale's Preliminary Discourse to the Ḳur'ān, p. 691. The word Salsabīl signifies "waving like a chain."

and hyacinths, and narcissuses, and roses, grew spontaneously in the [adjacent] plain for miles. That it was, in point of fact, a wonderful place for walking about in, and that if I chose we would go there the next day, and amuse ourselves, and shake off the weariness of travel. I said, 'Your honours' decision is absolute; if you command it, we will halt to-morrow, go there, and, after walking about, return.' They said, 'What is better than this?'[491] I gave orders to publish throughout the caravan that to-morrow we should halt, and I told the cook to prepare a breakfast of various dishes, as we should go for a walk next day. When the morning came, these two brothers of mine dressed themselves, tightened their belts, and reminded me, saying, 'Be pleased to come quickly, just in the cool [of the morning] and take our walk.' I called for my horse, but they remarked that the pleasure which arose from walking on foot was not[492] observable in riding, and desired me to tell the servants to lead the horses after us. Two slaves[493] carried pipes and coffee-pots, and went with us. We went on practising archery by the way. When we had got to a distance from the caravan, they sent one of the slaves for something. When they had gone a little further, they sent off the other also to call him back. As misfortune was to befall me, it was as if some one had sealed up my mouth—they did just as they liked, and having engaged me in conversation, were leading me on. This dog, however, remained with me. We had come a very long distance, but neither fountain nor garden appeared, but a plain full of thorns. There I wanted to make water, and sate down for that purpose.[494] I saw behind me a gleam like that of a sword, and as I turned

---

[491] This sentence is pure Persian, but Mīr Amman is, perhaps, not more to be blamed for introducing it than our learned novelists are for introducing the scraps of French and Italian by which they display their erudition.

[492] There is a slight slip here in Forbes' edition, as well as in the Calcutta one. The word نہیں *nahīṅ*, "not," is omitted, which destroys the whole sense.

[493] The word دونوں *donoṅ* has been thought to refer to the two slaves then present before Āzād-Bakht, and guarding the cage, but this is an error. The دونوں *donoṅ* is used emphatically, instead of دو *do*, to shew that there were only two.

[494] *Vide* Herodotus, book ii. chapter xxxv. for a similar custom among the Egyptians.

to look, that gentleman, my second brother, gave me such a swòrd-cut that my head was severed in two pieces.[495] While I said, 'O cruel! why strikest thou me?' my eldest brother cut me on the shoulder. Both wounds were deep.[496] I swooned and fell. Then those two merciless ones mangled me to their hearts' content, and left me weltering in blood. This dog, seeing my condition, rushed furiously upon them; [497] they wounded it also. After that they made the marks of wounds on their own bodies with their own hands, and went to the caravan with hands and feet bare, and gave out, saying, 'Our brother has fallen a martyr to robbers in that plain, and we, too, fighting hand to hand with them, have been wounded. Quickly depart, or they will presently fall on the caravan, and take and strip all of you.' As soon as the people of the caravan heard the name of the Badūīns,[498] their hearts immediately failed them, and they took their departure in alarm, and went off.

"My wife had heard and kept in mind the conduct and virtues of these [brothers of mine], and all the treacherous acts they had committed against me. When she heard of this occurrence from these liars, she straightway slew herself with her poignard, and rendered up her spirit to God!"

O Darweshes! [499] when the dog-worshipping merchant had in this manner, and thus far, related his history and sufferings, I was seized with an involuntary fit of weeping on hearing it. The merchant, observing this, said, "Point to which the world

---

[495] Pardon, reader! a trifling hyperbole.

[496] The former undoubtedly! Forbes has omitted, in his vocabulary, the Persian word كاري *kārī*, which signifies "effectual," and hence "deep," "dangerous," "mortal."

[497] Shakespear has omitted this meaning of بهپکنا *bhapaknā* in his Dictionary. The word, in its first sense, means "to break out like a flame."

[498] The word in the text is that which we write in our jargon, Bedouin. Forbes, in his vocabulary, has given بدوا *badūā* as the nominative, but neither he nor Shakespear exhibit this nominative in their Dictionaries, nor is there any occasion for supposing it. The word بدوون *badū'on*, which occurs here, is from بدو *badū*, "dwelling in the desert."

[499] Here King Āzād-Ba<u>kh</u>t addresses the darweshes in his own person.

turns in prayer! were it not disrespectful I would, indeed, strip naked, uncover my body, and shew it." And then, in order to prove his veracity, he tore his collar to the shoulder, and shewed me. In very truth there was not four fingers' breadth of his body which was whole, and free from wounds. In my presence he took off the turban from his head. There was so deep a dint in his skull that an entire pomegranate would have gone into it. All the nobles who were present shut their eyes, they could not endure to look upon it.

Again the merchant said, "Health to the King! when my brothers, after settling my business—as they supposed—had gone away, I was lying on one side, and the dog near me on the other, both wounded. So much blood went from me that I had not the slightest strength or sense left. I cannot tell where my spirit stopped, that I still survived. The place where I had fallen was within the confines of the country of Sarāndīp,[500] and there was a very populous city near that spot. In that city there was a vast idol-temple, and the king of that place had a daughter, extremely well-shaped and beautiful. Many kings and princes were miserable through love for her. The custom of concealing women did not exist there. Hence that girl used to roam about with her companions the whole day, for amusement and sport.[501] There was a royal garden near where I was, and on that day, after obtaining leave from the King, she had come to that very garden. As she went about for amusement, she came out into that plain on horseback, accompanied by several mounted female attendants. They came where I lay. Hearing my groans they stopped near me. Seeing me in this state, they fled, and told the Princess, saying, 'A poor fellow and a dog are lying there drenched in blood.' Hearing this from them, the Princess herself came to my head. Distressed at the sight, she said, 'Just see if he has any life left?' Two or four of her attendants dismounted and looked, and respectfully replied, 'Till now, indeed, he is still living.'

---

500 Ceylon being an island seems to occasion the author no difficulty.

501 Sport in the sense of "hunting." A Cingalese Diana.

The Princess immediately commanded them to take me up carefully[502] on a carpet, and carry me into the garden.

"After they had taken me there, she sent for the royal surgeon, and gave many injunctions with reference to the cure of myself and the dog, and held out to him hopes of rewards and presents. The doctor wiped my whole body, and cleaned it from dirt and blood, and washed the wounds with spirits, and stitched them up, and covered them with plaster, and, instead of water, dropped the extract of the musk-willow into my throat. The Princess herself remained sitting at my pillow, and was seeing that I was attended to, and during the whole day and night was giving me to drink, with her own hands, some broth or sharbat, two or four times. At length consciousness returned to me, when I beheld the Princess saying, in much distress, 'What sanguinary monster perpetrated this cruelty upon thee? Did he not fear even the Great Idol?' After ten days, by the invigorating stimulus of the extract of the musk-willow wine,[503] and electuaries, I opened my eyes. I beheld then that the court of Indra[504] was assembled around me, and the Princess was standing at the head of my bed. I heaved a sigh, and tried to move. I found I had no strength. The Princess kindly said, 'O Persian! keep your mind easy, and do not grieve. Although some cruel person has brought you to this state, still the Great Idol has made me kind to you—thou wilt now recover.'

"I make oath by that God who is One, and has no partner, that on seeing her I again lost my senses! The Princess also perceived [the effect the sight of her had on me] and with her own hand sprinkled some rose-water over me from a rose-water bottle used for sprinkling. In the space of twenty days the

---

502 A rather unusual sense of امانت *amānat*, which signifies "something deposited in one's care," and therefore untouched.

503 عرق *ārak*, may mean any spirit, but as that made from the musk-willow has been mentioned before, we may translate it as above. It is the word whence comes our "arrack."

504 This expression has occurred before, *vide* Note 268. It is here more in place, as the merchant is speaking of a Hindū court, which might be supposed to resemble that of a Hindū deity.

wounds filled up and healed over [*lit.* "formed granulations over themselves"]. At night, when all went to sleep, the Princess used to come to me, and, after giving me food and drink, to go away. In short, in the space of forty days I took the bath [of convalescence]. The Princess was much delighted. She gave the surgeon great rewards, and caused me to be dressed. By the favour of God and the careful attention and efforts of the Princess, I became well and sound,[505] and my bodily condition became exceedingly robust, and the dog also grew fat. Every day she gave me wine to drink, and listened to my conversation and was pleased. I also amused her by narrating some short tale or narrative [*lit.* "half-story"].

"One day she began to ask me, saying, 'Narrate, indeed, thy story, as to who you are, and how these adventures befell thee.' I narrated to her all that had happened to me, from the beginning to the end. When she heard it, she wept, and said, 'I will now treat thee in such a way that thou shalt forget all thy sufferings.' I said, 'God keep you in safety. You have bestowed on me life anew. Now I have become and continue yours; for God's sake always regard me with the same kindness!' In short, she was remaining seated alone with me during the whole night, and keeping company with me. Some days one of her female attendants also accompanied her. She was listening to and entering into all kinds of conversation. When the Princess got up and went away, and I was alone, I used to perform my ablutions, and, concealing myself in a corner, repeat my prayers.

"Once on a time it so happened that the Princess had gone to her father. I, having performed my ablutions, was continuing at my ease to repeat my prayers, when all of a sudden the Princess, conversing with a female attendant, entered, saying, 'Let us see what the Persian is doing at this time —whether he is asleep or awake?' When she did not see me in the apartment, she was amazed, and said, 'How! where is he gone? he surely has not formed an attachment to some

---

505 چوبند *chauband*, has been omitted in the dictionaries. It has the same meaning as چوبر *chaubar*, that is, "stout," "robust."

one!' She began to look and search in every hole[506] and corner. At length she came to where I was performing my devotions. That girl had never seen [the Musalmān] prayers.[507] She stood silently and looked on. When, after finishing my prayers, I raised my hands to bless God, and prostrated myself, she was seized with a violent and involuntary fit of laughter, and said, 'What! has this man become deranged? What strange motions are these he continues making!'

"Hearing the sound of laughter, I feared in my heart. The Princess advanced and began to ask, 'O Persian! what is this thou art doing?' I was unable to give her an answer; thereupon her attendant said, 'May I take thy calamities! I am thy sacrifice. The case is, I fancy, that this is a Musalmān, and the enemy of Lāt Manāt.[508] He worships an unseen God.' The Princess, on hearing this, struck her hands together, and said, in much anger, 'I knew not that he was a Turk[509] and an unbeliever in our gods,[510] [and thus] he had then[511] fallen under the displeasure of our idol. I was wrong in taking care of him and keeping him in my house.' With these words she departed. I, on hearing this, was in dismay, saying to myself, 'Let us see how she will treat me now.' Through fear my sleep was disturbed.[512] I could not refrain from weeping till the morning, and I bathed my face with tears.

"I passed three days and nights in weeping in this fear and

---

506 It should be كونا كتھرا *konā kuthrā*, and not كونا كٹھرا *konā kuṭhrō*.

507 A negative is here expressed by a question, as is frequently the case.

508 لات *Lāt* or الآت *Allāt*, منات *Manāt*, and عزىٰ *Ūzzạ*, were three idols of the pagan Arabians, and are therefore marvellously out of place in Sarāndīp and among Hindūs. There was, however, an idol at Somnāth, called Lāt, which was a large stone fifty fathoms in height, placed in a temple, supported by fifty-six columns of massive gold. The author might mean this, but we have then a difficulty in "Manāt."

509 All Muḥammadans are called Turks in the south of India, to this day.

510 The word خدا *khudā* is here ill-chosen. It should be ديوتاون *devtāoṅ*, which is more applicable to the gods of idolators.

511 At the time when I found him wounded.

512 Forbes has omitted اچاٹ *uchāṭ* in his vocabulary. Shakespear gives as its meanings, "displeased, discontented, uneasy," etc.

hope;[513] nor did I ever close an eye.[514] On the third night the Princess, accompanied by a nurse, came to my apartment, much inebriated with wine. She was filled with anger, and holding in her hands a bow and arrows, sate down outside on the border of the parterre [in front of my room]. She asked her female attendant for a cup of wine, and after drinking it, said, 'Mother![515] is that Persian who has been overtaken by the wrath of our Great Idol dead, or does he yet live?' The woman said, 'May I take thy calamities! he has still a little breath left.' She said, 'He has now fallen from our regard, but bid him come forth.' The nurse called to me. I ran out and beheld then that the face of the Princess was glowing[515] with anger and had become red. My spirit forsook my body. I saluted her, and crossing my hands reverentially, stood still. Having looked at me with an angry glance, she said to the nurse, 'If I were to slay this enemy of our faith with an arrow, will the Great Idol pardon me or not? In this I have been guilty of a great crime, that I have kept him in my house and attended to him.'

"The nurse said, 'What fault has the Princess committed? She did not know at all that he was an enemy when she took care of him. You had pity upon him; to you, in return for your goodness, good will happen, and he will remain receiving the fruit of his wickedness from the Great Idol.' Having heard this, she said, 'Nurse! tell him to be seated.' The nurse beckoned me to sit down, which I did. The Princess drank another cup of wine, and said to the nurse, 'Give this unfortunate also a cup; then he will perish easily.' The nurse gave me a cup. I drank it without excuse, and saluted her. She never looked straight towards me, but ever and anon cast furtive

---

513 رجا Forbes, in his vocabulary, makes this word "*rijā*," and in his Dictionary, "*raja*," as does also Shakespear. The proper way of writing it is, رجا *rajā-a*, and the pronunciation in Hindūstān has been corrupted to "*rijā*."

514 Forbes, in his vocabulary, has omitted the word جھپکنا *jhapaknā*, which signifies "to watch," and also "to wink."

515 Forbes has omitted in his vocabulary the word دیّا *daiyā*, "mother," as also تمتمانا *tamtamānā*, "to sparkle or glow."

side-long glances at me. When I became merry, I began to repeat some poetry, among which I recited this couplet also—

In thy power am I: say, I now live!—well! what then?
If one breathes awhile under the steel, well! what then?[516]

When she heard this, she smiled, and looking towards the nurse, said, 'What! art thou sleepy?' The nurse, having found out what she wished, said, 'Yes! sleep has overpowered me!' She truly, having taken leave, went to hell.[517] After a moment the Princess asked me for a cup of wine. I filled one quickly, and presented it to her. She took it from my hand with tender grace, and drank it off. I then fell at her feet. The Princess stroked me with her hand, and said, 'O unwise! what harm hast thou found in our Great Idol, that thou hast begun to worship an invisible God?' I said, 'You ought to be just. Be pleased to reflect a little, [and you will see] that that God is worthy of adoration, who, from a drop of water, has formed a beautiful lady like you, and has bestowed on you such loveliness that in a moment you can madden the hearts of thousands of men. Of what account is an idol that any one should worship it? The stone-cutters, by fashioning a stone, make it into shape, and spread it out as a net for fools. Those whom the devil has seduced regard the created thing as the creator, and bow down their heads before that which they have fashioned with their own hands. We are Musalmān, and venerate Him who has created us. For them He has created hell—for us, paradise. If the Princess would direct her faith towards God, then she will find the joy of it, and will distinguish between right and wrong, and will perceive her [present] belief to be erroneous.'

"At length, from hearing such admonitions as these, the heart of that stony-hearted one became soft. Through the Divine favour and mercy she began to weep, and said, 'Well! teach

---

516 The meaning of these somewhat obscure verses is, that though she were to forbear from slaying him with her bow, as she threatened, he would still be ever living in misery as a despairing lover; like one who is permitted a short respite, while the dagger is held over him.

517 In other words, "she went away,"—fye! fye! Mīr Amman! this is not civil even of an unbeliever.

me also your religion.' I instructed her in the creed, which she, with sincerity of heart, recited; and having expressed her penitence and prayed for pardon, she became a Muslim. I then threw myself at her feet. She continued till morning repeating the creed and praying for pardon. She then said, 'Well! I indeed have embraced your faith; but my parents are infidels; what remedy is there for them?' I said, 'You are clear;[518] each shall receive according to his deserts.' She said, 'They have betrothed me to the son of my paternal uncle, and he is an idolator. If to-morrow (which God avert!) that infidel should have connexion with me, and I should conceive, it would be a very evil thing. We must from this moment take thought for this, so that I may obtain deliverance from this calamity.' I said, 'What you say is indeed reasonable; what occurs to your own mind, that do.' She replied, 'Now I will not stay here, but will depart somewhither.' I asked, 'In what manner will you be able to fly, and whither will you go?' She replied, 'Do you first leave me. Go and stop with the Musalmān [travellers] in the caravanserah; then all will hear of it and will not suspect you. Do you continue then to look out for vessels, and inform me when a ship sails for Persia. For this purpose I will continually send the nurse to you; when you send me word, I will come out, embark in the vessel, and go away [with you], and obtain a release from the hands of these wretched infidels.'

"I said, 'I am ready to sacrifice myself for your life and welfare, [but] what will you do with the nurse?' She said, 'It is easy to devise what shall be done with her. I will give her a cup of deadly[519] poison to drink.'[520] We decided on this

---

518 تمهاري بلا سے *tumhārī balā se.* Literally "from your calamity" sub aud., دورهي *dūr hai*, "it is far," or similar words.

519 Forbes, in his vocabulary, has given the word هلاهل *halāhal* as Sanskṛit, and rendered it "poison." Strangely enough, however, the word is both Arabic and Sanskṛit, and in the latter language means "poison," but in the former "poisonous," or "deadly." In this passage it is evidently the Arabic word, and should be rendered "deadly," and in all cases when joined to the Persian زهر *zahr*, "poison," it ought to be so translated. On the other hand, in Hindī it is doubtless Sanskṛit.

520 With Muḥammadans it is no crime, but rather a meritorious act, to slay an infidel or an idolator. With these Eastern Jesuits, too, the end sanctifies the means.

plan. When it became day, I went to the caravanserah, hired a small room, and took up my abode there. I was living during that separation simply upon the hope of meeting. In two months,[521] when the merchants of Turkey, Syria, and Iṣfahān[522] had assembled, they fixed to depart, by way of the sea, and began to embark their goods on board ship. From living in the same place, I had formed many acquaintances. They said to me, 'Why, sir! will you not go too? How long will you stop in this land of unbelievers?' I replied, 'What do I possess that I should go to my own country? All the stock I have is this one female slave,[523] a dog, and a box. If you will give me but a very little room, [just enough] to sit in, and will fix the passage-money, I shall be satisfied—I, too, will embark.'

"The merchants gave me possession of a cabin,[524] for which I paid the passage-money. Having set my mind at ease [on this head] I went, on some pretext, to the house of the nurse, and said, 'O mother! I have come to take leave of thee; I am now going to my own country. If, by your kindness, I could obtain one interview with the Princess, then it would be a great matter.' At length the nurse consented. I said, 'I will come at night and wait in such a place.' She said, 'Very well!' After I had spoken to her, I returned to the inn. I took up my box and my bedding, and carried them to the ship, and entrusted

---

[521] Mīr Amman here sins against grammar. It should be دو مہینوں میں *do mahīnoṅ meṅ.* We may, however, rescue the author from this charge, by considering دو مہینے *do mahīne* as one word, in the sense of "space of two months."

[522] *Vide* Note 233. Iṣfahān, the capital of Ǐrāḳ-i Ǎjamī, lies in N. lat. 32° 25′, and E. long. 86° 40′. It stands on the ruins of the ancieut Hecatompylos, or of the Aspa of Ptolemy. The present city is of no great antiquity. Shāh Ǎbbās the Great made it his capital, and greatly enlarged it between A.D. 1620 and 1628. Chardin, in his time, reckoned the population as equal to that of London, *i.e.* about 600,000. It suffered terribly in the rebellion of 1721, and under Nādir Shāh, but is still a large city.

[523] This is a slip of Mīr Amman's. The slave-girl was the Princess, who had not yet joined the merchant. He could not then speak of her as "this very girl," since she was absent, and those he addressed had never seen her.

[524] Forbes, in his vocabulary, wrongly translates تخت *taḥt,* "lower part," or "beneath," which meaning is wholly inapplicable here.

them to the captain, and said, 'To-morrow morning I will bring my slave-girl.' The captain replied, 'Be pleased to come soon. In the morning we shall take up the anchor.' I said, 'Very well!' When it was night, I went to that same place which I had agreed upon with the nurse, and having gone there, waited. When a watch of the night was past, the door of the palace opened, and the Princess, dressed in soiled and dirty garments, came out, bringing a box of jewels. She delivered that little box to my care, and accompanied me. As it dawned we arrived at the sea-side, and having embarked in a small boat,[525] we went and got on board the ship. This faithful dog also accompanied us. When it was clear day-light, the anchor was raised and we set sail. We[526] were proceeding happily on when the sound of the discharge of cannon reached us from the port. All were filled with astonishment and anxiety. We anchored the vessel and began to talk with one another, saying, 'What! is the superintendent of the port about to commit some treachery? what is the reason of their discharging cannon?'

"It happened that all the merchants had beautiful slave-girls, and all of them, through fear of the superintendent of the port, shut up these girls in boxes, lest he should take them away from them. I, too, had done the same thing; for having made my Princess sit down in a chest, I had padlocked her in. Meanwhile, the superintendent of the port, seated with his servants and attendants in a vessel called a Ghurāb,[527] came in sight. By degrees he arrived at the ship and boarded us. The reason of his coming was perhaps this, that when the King received intelligence of the death of the nurse and the disappearance of the Princess, he, without mentioning her name, for fear of the disgrace, commanded the superintendent of the

---

525 The astonished reader will find that even in so common a book as the "Bāgh o Bahār" there are vocables which are not to be found in any dictionary. Such is the word لنبوت *lambot*, "a skiff," which occurs neither in Forbes' vocabulary, nor in his Dictionary, nor in that of Shakespear.

526 The punctuation of the text might be improved here. There should be a full stop after هوئے *hūe*, and a comma after چلے جاتے تھے *chale jāte the*.

527 Anglo-Indicè "grab," a sort of Arab vessel.

port, saying, 'I have heard that the Persian merchants have some very nice female slaves, which I wish to take for the Princess. You will stop them and bring into my presence all the slave-girls that there are in the ship. After I have seen them, the price of those I approve shall be paid, otherwise they shall be returned.'

"In accordance with the King's order, this superintendent of the port had himself boarded the ship. Now near me there was another person who also had a pretty slave shut up in a box. The superintendent came and sate on that box, and began to cause the slave-girls to be produced. I returned thanks to God, saying, 'Well! there is no mention of the Princess.' In short, the superintendent's people put all the slave-girls they could find in the boat, and the superintendent himself laughingly asked the owner of the box on which he was sitting, the question, 'Thou too hadst a slave-girl?' The block-head said, 'I swear by your honour's feet, I am not the only one who has done this. All, through fear of you, have concealed their slave-girls in boxes?' When the superintendent heard this, he began to search all the boxes. He opened my box also, and having taken out the Princess, led her away with all the rest. My despair was excessive, so that I said to myself,[528] 'Such is the character of this unlucky accident, that thou hast lost thy life for nothing, and let us see how he will treat the Princess!' In anxiety on her account, I forgot my fear for my own life also, and remained the whole day and night praying to God for her. When the first dawn appeared, they put all the slave-girls on board a boat, and brought them back. The merchants were pleased, and took each his own slave. All came, but the Princess was not among them. I inquired, 'Has not my slave come? what is the cause of this?' They replied, 'We know not; perhaps the King has chosen her.' All the merchants began to console and cheer me, saying, 'Well! what has happened has happened! do not thou distress thyself; we will all make a subscription and pay you the value of her.' My senses were lost. I replied, 'Now I will not go to Persia.' I

---

[528] This periphrasis of six words is used to render كه *kih*, "that."

said to the boatmen, 'My friends! take me also with you, and be pleased to put me on shore.' They consented. I left the ship, and came and took my seat in the ghurāb, and this dog also accompanied me.

"When I reached the port, I kept only the casket of jewels, which the Princess had brought with her. All my other goods I distributed to the servants of the superintendent of the port, and I began to spy out everywhere to see if perchance I could get intelligence of the Princess; but I neither got any trace of her, nor could I find anything to guide me as to the affair. One night I got, by a stratagem, even into the King's seraglio and searched, but met with no information. For nearly a month I hunted the streets and quarters of the city, and in that grief almost brought myself to death's door, and I began to wander about like one distraught. At length I reflected in my heart thus, 'It is probable that my Princess, if she is anywhere, is in the house of the superintendent of the port. I was going round the residence of the superintendent, and looking if I could anywhere find a way of access that I might enter. A drain appeared, which admitted of a man's passing by it, but an iron grating was fixed at its mouth.[529] I resolved to enter by that drain. I took off my clothes from my body, and went down into that filthy slime. After a thousand efforts I broke that grating, and by way of the sewer entered the secret seraglio.[530] Having dressed myself like a woman, I began to look about me on all sides. In one apartment, a voice reached my ear as if some one was praying. When I advanced, I beheld then that it was the Princess herself, who was weeping excessively, and continued grovelling on the ground, and praying to God, saying, 'For the sake of Thy Prophet and his pure progeny, give me deliverance from this land of unbelievers, and grant me once a happy meeting with that person who showed me the path of

---

[529] Forbes, in his vocabulary, has rendered دهانه *dahānah*, "that which covers the mouth of a pit or well;" but it should rather be the mouth itself.

[530] The چور محل *chor maḥall* is the apartment or apartments devoted to the secret amours of the master of the family, where he may carry on intrigues unknown to his lawful wives.

the true religion.' I, as soon as I saw her, ran and fell at her feet. The Princess clung to my neck. For a moment we were both in a state of insensibility. When we recovered our senses, I inquired of the Princess what had happened. She said, 'When the superintendent of the port took all the slave-girls on shore, I was only praying to God that my secret might not be disclosed, and that I might not be recognized, and that thy life might not be perilled. He is such a concealer[531] that no one recognized me in the least degree as the Princess. The superintendent of the port was surveying each with an eye to purchase. When my turn came, he approved of me and sent me secretly to his house; the rest he presented before the King.

"'My father, when he did not see me among them, dismissed them all. It was on my account that he practised all this artifice.[532] He has now given out that the Princess is very ill. If I should not be found, then some day or other the news of my death will fly through the whole country, in order that the King may not be dishonoured. But I am now suffering this annoyance, that the superintendent of the port has in his heart sinister views with regard to me, and always invites me to sleep with him. I am continuing to refuse. Although he is enamoured of me, he, as yet, seeks my compliance, and therefore holds his peace. But I am terrified [when I think] how long can this last? Wherefore I too have determined this in my heart, that when he seeks to gratify his wishes, I will yield up my life and die. But from meeting you, another scheme has occurred to my mind. If it please God, no other way of deliverance appears but this.'[533]

"I said, 'Speak then! what sort of plan is that?' She said, 'If thou wilt use exertion and labour, it may then succeed.' I replied, 'I am obedient to your order. If you command, I will

---

531 The meaning for ستّار *sattār*, given in Forbes' vocabulary, viz. "concealed," "hidden," is obviously inapplicable here, and is not substantiated by any dictionary.

532 Forbes, in his vocabulary, has omitted the word پرپنچ *parpanch* (s. प्रपञ्च : प्र and पचि "to spread"), which signifies "deceit," "artifice."

533 The sentence is literally translated, but Mīr Amman means, "No other way of safety appears but this, yet, God willing, this will succeed."

leap into burning fire, and could I get a ladder I would, for your sake, ascend to heaven. I will perform whatever you enjoin.' The Princess said, 'Do thou go into the temple of the Great Idol, and in the place where they take off their shoes, there lies a piece of black canvàs. It is the custom of this country that whoever becomes poor and indigent puts on that canvas and sits down in that place. The people of this place who go on pilgrimage[534] bestow alms on him, each according to his ability. After two or four days, when he has collected money, the priests of the idol-temple give him a rich dress at the expense of the Great Idol, and send him away. He goes away a rich man, and nobody knows who he was. Do thou also go and sit down under the sackcloth, and carefully envelope thy hands and face, and speak to none.

"'When, after three days, the Brāhmans and idolators give thee a rich robe and try to send thee away, do thou, notwithstanding, on no account depart thence. When they beseech thee excessively, then do thou say that thou hast no need of rupees or money, that thou art not hungering after wealth, but that thou hast met with oppression, that thou hast come to complain; that if the mother of the Brāhmans will do thee justice, so much the better, otherwise the Great Idol will see that thou dost have what is just, and will hear [*lit.* 'come to'] thy complaints against the oppressor. Until that mother of the Brāhmans comes to you herself, however much any one may beseech thee, be not thou inclined to assent. At length, having no resource, she herself will come to thee. She is very old, her age being two hundred and forty years; and thirty-six sons, which have been born to her, are the governors of the idol-temple, and bear a very exalted rank with the Great Idol. From which cause her commands are of such weight that all the people of that country, small and great, look upon their happiness as depending on what she says; what she commands, that they implicitly obey. Take hold of the skirt of her dress and say, "O mother! if thou wilt not obtain justice for me, an

---

[534] جاترا *jātrā*, would be a more appropriate phrase here, as زيارت *ziyārat* is the Muḥammadan term.

oppressed traveller, from the tyrant, I will dash my head in the service of the Great Idol. At length he will take pity, and intercede for me with thee." When she asks thy story, say that thou art an inhabitant of Persia. "In order to perform a pilgrimage to the Great Idol, and hearing of your justice, I have come hither from a great distance.[535] I abode here some days at my ease. My wife also had accompanied me. She is very young, and of good shape and figure also, and well featured (*lit.* "correct as to her nose and eyes"). I know not how the superintendent of the port saw her, but he took her from me by force, and has put her in his own house. And we Musalmān have this custom, that whoever see our[536] women or takes them away when it is unlawful for them to enter his ḥaram, then we slay him how we can, and take back our wives; else we give up eating and drinking, because, as long as he remains alive, that woman is forbidden to her husband. Now, having no resource, I have come here; let us see what justice you enact."' When the Princess had taught and instructed me in all this, I took leave and came forth by the same aperture,[537] and fixed that grating again.

"As soon as it was morning, I went to the idol-temple and put on that black canvas, and sate down. In three days so many rupees and gold coins and clothes were collected about me, that a magazine was formed of them. On the fourth day the priests, performing their worship and singing and playing, came to me, bringing a rich dress, and began to send me away. I did not consent [to go], and appealed for justice to the Great Idol, saying, I did not come to beg, but I have come to the Great Idol and the Mother of the Brāhmans for justice; until I get justice done me, I will not depart hence.' When they heard this, they went to that old woman,[538] and related my case.

---

535 کالے کوسوں سے *kāle kosoṅ se*, "from black kos." Is this akin to the expression, کالا پاني *kālā pānī*, literally "black water," for "banishment"? I know not, but the epithet here appears to imply distance rather than colour.

536 I so translate the words ان كي *in kī*, which would be much better omitted.

537 The word تابدان *tābdān*, is properly "an aperture to admit light."

538 Forbes, in his vocabulary, has omitted the word زال *zāl*, "an old woman," a Persian word, but which occurs in the Bilūchī language also, with the same meaning.

After that, a Brāhman, learned in the four Vedas, came and began to say to me, 'Come! the Mother calls thee.' I immediately went into the temple, covered from head to foot with the black canvas. I beheld then that on a jewelled throne in which were set rubies, diamonds and pearls, and coral, was seated the Great Idol, and a rich cover was spread on a golden chair, on which, in a stately and dignified manner, sate an old woman clad in black, propped up on cushions and pillows, with two boys of ten or twelve years of age, one on her right hand, and the other on her left. She called me forward. I went respectfully forward and kissed the foot of her throne, and then took hold of the skirt of her dress. She asked my story. I made it known to her after the same fashion as the Princess had instructed me.

"When she heard it, she said, 'What! do the Musalmān keep their wives concealed?' I replied, 'Yes; may it fare well with your children![539] this is our custom from of old.' She said, 'Thy sect is a good one. I will instantly give command for the superintendent of the port to come and present himself with thy wife, and will inflict such a punishment on the dolt that he will not commit such an improper action a second time, and that all shall prick up their ears and fear.' She began [then] to ask her children as to who the superintendent of the port was? who had the hardihood [*lit.* "power"] to take away by force the wife of another man. The people [about her] said, 'He is such a person.' When she heard this, she commanded those two boys (who sate near her), saying, 'Go quickly to the King, taking that person with you, and say that the Mother says it is the order of the Great Idol that since the superintendent of the port practises violence and oppression on people, and, for example, has taken away the wife of this poor person, and his guilt has been fully proved to have been great, that you quickly take an inventory of that offender's goods, and deliver them over to this Turk (who has found favour in our sight), otherwise this night thou shalt perish, and fall under our wrath.' The two young lads went forth from the temple,

---

[539] This benediction is introduced simply as a compliment, and has nothing to do with the rest of the sentence.

12

and mounted. All the priests, blowing horns, singing, and encompassing them, followed in their retinue.

"In short, the people of that place, great and small, regarding the earth of that spot where the foot[540] of the boys fell as sacred, took it up, and applied it to their eyes. In this same manner they proceeded to the castle of the King. The King received intelligence [of their coming], and came out to receive them with bare feet,[541] and having brought them in with great honour and respect, seated them near himself on the throne, and asked, 'Wherefore have you honoured me by coming to-day?' Those two Brāhman boys told him what they had heard from their mother before they came there, and menaced him with the anger of the Great Idol.

"On hearing this the King said, 'Very well!' and ordered his servants, saying, 'Let the officers of justice go and bring quickly into my presence the superintendent of the port, together with that woman, when I will inquire into his crime and punish him.' When I heard this, I was confounded in my heart, and said to myself, 'This affair has taken a bad turn. If along with the superintendent of the port they bring the Princess also, the secret will be revealed, and what will be my position?' I was stricken with dismay in my heart, and had recourse to [prayer to] God, but my countenance changed,[542] and my frame began to shake. The boys, seeing me thus change, perceived perhaps that this order was not agreeable to me. They immediately arose, displeased and angry, and

---

[540] In Forbes' edition we have پانون *pānon*, which is a mistake for پانو *pāṅw*, as I find by referring to the copy written by Mīr Amman himself, which invaluable MS. the owner (Mr. Romer) has kindly lent me. It is hardly necessary to remark the inconsistency of saying that the boys were mounted, and immediately after talking of the spot where their feet touched the ground. Oriental writers swallow these camels easily, though they often strain at a gnat.

[541] It is too well known to require mention, that the Orientals uncover their feet, as we do our heads, to show respect. Sometimes, however, it is a sign of consternation and grief. *Vide* p. 125, l. 8; p. 143, l. 9. The reverse has a different meaning: Judges iii. 24.

[542] *Literally*, "sky-rockets went up in my face," alluding to the shooting up and receding of the blood, causing an alternate redness and pallor, and, to pursue the metaphor in Eastern style, like the above-named fireworks, more conspicuous in the night of the Oriental's sable countenance, than in the twilight of the European face.

said, threateningly, to the King, 'O little man! hast thou become distraught, that thou hast stepped aside from obedience to the Great Idol, and imagined our word false, that thou wishest to summon both and make inquiry? Now, take care! thou hast fallen under the wrath of the Great Idol; we have transmitted his command to thee—now do thou look to it,[543] and let the Great Idol look to it.'

"The King experienced an extraordinary sensation at these words, insomuch that he joined his hands and stood up, and trembled from head to foot. He began to appease them with humble entreaties, but those two would on no account sit down, but remained standing. On this all the nobles that were standing there began with one voice to speak against the superintendent of the port, saying, 'He is such a wicked villain, and guilty wretch, and does such evil things, that we are unable to make mention of them in the presence of the King. That which the mother of the Brāhmans has sent to tell you is correct, because it is the order of the Great Idol, and how can that be false?' When the King heard from the tongues of all the same thing, he was ashamed and abashed at what he had said. He quickly bestowed on me a neat dress, and having written a mandate with his own hand, he signed[544] and sealed it, and delivered it to me. He also wrote a letter to the mother of the Brāhmans, and having placed a tray of jewels and gold coins before the boys as an offering, he sent them away. I returned highly pleased to the idol-temple, and went to that old woman.

"The contents of the King's letter which had come was this: After compliments, and the expression of his humble devotion, he wrote that, in accordance with her highness's order, he had conferred on me the post of superintendent of the port, and had given me the robe of honour [which denoted my installation], and that now I had the power to put the former

543 That is, "Settle it between you, and you will be finely punished."

544 I take دستی *dastī* here for دست خط *dast khaṭṭ*, "signature," but if this sense be objected to, it will mean "private," "own," and refer to مہر *muhr*. Forbes, in his vocabulary, has omitted the word altogether.

superintendent to death, and that all his wealth and property had been assigned to me, to do with it as I pleased, and that he was now in hopes that his life would be pardoned. The mother of the Brāhmans, being pleased at this, commanded that the music[515] should sound in the music-room of the temple. And she sent along with me five hundred matchlock-men fully armed, who could hit a little shell tied with a hair,[516] and gave orders, saying, 'Go to the port, and having made the superintendent prisoner, deliver him over to this Musalmān, that he may put him to death by any tortures he pleases. Take care too that, except this dear person, no other finds access to the female apartments, and that you hand over to him the superintendent's property and treasure. When this person of his own free will dismisses you, return, bringing with you a receipt and certificate from him.' Then, having presented me with a complete dress from the Great Idol, she caused me to mount, and bade me farewell.

"When I arrived at the port, a man went forward and informed the superintendent of the port. He was seated like one dazed when I arrived. My heart indeed was still filled with anger. As soon as I beheld the superintendent of the port, I drew my sword and struck him such a blow on the neck that his head was separated, and flew off like a head of Indian corn,[517] and having caused the agents, treasurers, examiners, and factors of that place to be apprehended, I seized all the papers, and myself entered the seraglio. There I met the Princess. We embraced and wept and returned thanks to God. I wiped away her tears, and she mine. I then took my seat outside on an ottoman, and gave dresses to the officials, and reinstated all in their several appointments. I promoted the servants and the slaves. To each of those persons who had been sent with me

---

[515] Forbes, in his vocabulary, has omitted this sense of نوبت *naubat*, yet I believe that it is from this that the guard-room has its name of نوبت خانه *naubat khānah*, and not from نوبت *naubat*, "turn," "time," "relief," as the dictionaries would imply.

[516] This is a proverbial expression for a good marksman.

[517] Forbes in his vocabulary has omitted the word بھتّا *bhuṭṭā*, "a head of corn."

from the temple I gave presents and largess, dressed their Jamādārs and Risālahdārs[548] [in robes of honour], and dismissed them; and taking with me jewels of great price, and pieces of the finest cotton, and shawls, and brocade, and goods and rarities of every realm, and a large sum of ready money as an offering to the King, and suitable presents for each one of the nobles, according to their rank, and for all the priestesses, and for distribution among the priests, I returned, after a week, to the idol-temple, and laid them before the mother of the Brāhmans, by way of offering.

"She bestowed on me another robe of honour, and gave me a title. I then went to the King's court, and presented my offerings, and made a statement [of what was requisite] for putting a stop to the various oppressive and mischievous practices which the superintendent of the port had devised. On this account the King, and the nobles, and the merchants were all pleased with me. [The King] lavished many favours upon me, and having presented me with a robe of honour and a horse, bestowed on me a dignity and a grant of land in free tenure, and conferred honours upon me. When I came forth from the presence of the King, I satisfied the servants and the officials, by giving them so much that all began to recite my creed.[549] In short, I became very affluent, and having married the Princess, began to live in that country in much ease and comfort, and to serve God. By reason of my justice all classes of the King's subjects were content. Once a month I visited the idol-temple and the King's presence, and returned. The King daily conferred on me higher promotion.

"At length he admitted me into the number of his confidential advisers, and did nothing without my advice. My life began to pass in perfect tranquillity, but God Himself knows that the anxious recollection of those two brothers of mine often returned to my heart, and the thought of where and how they were. After the space of two years a caravan of merchants

---

548 The جمعدار *jamādār* answers to our lieutenant. The رسالهدار *risālahdār* is rightly explained by Forbes as "a captain of a troop."

549 "Jurare in verba mea," or, as we say, "to swear by me," that is, "they were all won over to my side, and became my partizans."

came from the country of Zerbād[550] to that port, all of whom were journeying towards Persia, and they wished to go by sea to their own country. The custom of that place was, that whatever caravan arrived, its chief used to bring me presents and curiosities of every country and present them to me as offerings. The next day I used to go to his house, and take a tithe of his goods by way of tax, and give him a passport for departure. In the same way those merchants of Zerbād also came to visit me, and brought inestimable presents. The next day I went to their tents. Then I saw two men dressed in torn and old clothes, who, carrying on their heads packages and bundles, brought them before me. After I had looked at them they again took them up and carried them away, and continued performing much toilsome service. On looking at them attentively, I saw that these very men were my two brothers. At that time my sense of shame and feeling of honourable pride would not allow me to see them in this kind of servitude. When I went home I said to the people, 'Bring those two persons.' They brought them. Again I caused apparel and clothes to be made and given to them, and I took charge of them. Those two villains again laid a plan to murder me, and one day, at midnight,[551] finding all off their guard, came like thieves to the head of my bed. I, through fear of my life, had placed a guard at the door, and this faithful dog was sleeping by the side of my bedstead. When they drew their swords from the scabbards, the dog first of all barked and attacked them, and at the noise it made all awoke. I too started up in alarm. The people seized them and found it was their honours themselves. All began to heap execrations upon them, since, in spite of this fostering care of them, they had perpetrated such an ill-deed! Peace to the King!—Then, indeed, I too feared. It is a well-known proverb, 'One fault, two faults, if a third fault [be committed], the mother is to blame.'[552] I determined on this plan in my heart,

---

550 *Vide* note 467.

551 This expression sounds strangely to European ears, but Musalmān reckon their day from sunset to sunset. It is with them, therefore, quite admissible.

552 The meaning of this is, that the best of us may offend once or twice, but he who commits a third offence is, as we say, "a born villain." He has got his evil nature from his mother, and is incorrigible.

that I would confine them; but if I had placed them in a prison, then who would have taken charge of them? they would have died of hunger and thirst, or would have practised some other deceit. I have, therefore, placed them in a cage, that they may always remain under my eyes, and thus I may be satisfied, lest, being concealed from my sight, they may contrive some other artifice; and the honour and respect shown to this dog is because of its loyalty and fidelity.[553] Great God! a faithless man is worse than a faithful brute. This is my history which I have related in your presence. Now either be pleased to order my execution, or bestow on me my life. It is the order of the King."

Having heard it,[554] I applauded that honest man,[555] and said, "There has been no interruption in thy kindness, nor in their shameless and villainous conduct has there been any diminution. It is true, 'If you bury a dog's tail twelve years, even then it will remain as crooked as ever.'"[556] After that I inquired into the story of those twelve rubies (which were in the collar of that dog). The merchant said, "May the age of the King be one hundred and twenty years![557] In that same part where I was governor, after three or four years, one day I had taken my seat in a balcony[558] of the female apartments for the purpose of enjoying the look-out over the sea and the waste around, and I was gazing in every direction. All of a sudden, in a part of the jungle, where there was no high road, somewhat that looked like the forms of two men appeared, who were coming along. I took my telescope[559] and looked, when the shapes that shewed

---

553 This sentence is so badly managed in the Urdū as to express exactly the reverse of what is intended. Thus, the honour shewn to the dog is said to be the cause of its fidelity.

554 Here king Āzād-Bakht addresses the Darweshes again in his own person.

555 جوان "young man" seems an ill-chosen word here, as the khwājah represents himself as old and infirm.

556 A proverb corresponding to our "What is bred in the bone will never come out of the flesh." A similar sentiment is to be found in the "Hitopadeśa" (Suhṛidbheda, Sloke 136), whence it originally sprung.

557 *Vide* note 346.

558 The resemblance between بالا خانه *bālā khānah* and "balcony" is so strong, that we may imagine the latter word derived from the former.

559 دوربين *dūr-bīn*: دور *dūr*, "far," بين *bīn*, from ديدن *dīdan*, "to see," exactly translates "telescope."

themselves were marvellous ones for human beings. I sent off mace-bearers to summon them.

"When they came, I found that one was a man and one a woman. The woman truly I sent into the seraglio to the Princess, and called the man before me. I saw then that he was a young man of twenty or twenty-two years old, whose beard and moustachios had commenced growing. But, from the fierceness of the sun's rays, the complexion of his face was like that of a black iron plate for baking bread, and the hair of his head and the nails of his hands had grown long, so that his form had become scarce human, and there was a boy of three or four years old on his shoulder, and the two sleeves of his coat, which were filled with something, were thrown like a chain round his neck. I beheld that his form and appearance were of a strange description. I was much astonished, and asked, 'O Friend! who art thou, and of what country art thou a native, and what is this thy state?' The young man involuntarily began to weep, and having undone that purse, placed it before me on the ground, and said, 'Hunger! hunger! for God's sake give me something to eat. It is a long time since I have been feeding on grass and forest-leaves,[560] as I journey on. Not the smallest particle of strength is left in me.' I immediately sent for bread and meat and wine, and gave to him. He began to eat. Meanwhile an eunuch came from the seraglio, bringing some more purses from his wife. I caused all of them to be opened. I beheld jewels of every kind, each one of which deserved to be called the revenue of an empire. Each was more priceless than the other in shape, weight, and lustre, and from the rays they emitted the whole apartment was coloured with different hues. After he had eaten a morsel and drunk a cup of wine, and rested, his senses returned. I then asked, 'Whence did you procure these stones?' He replied, 'My native land is the country of Āzurbāijān.[561] In my childhood I was parted from my home and my parents, and endured great

[560] Forbes has omitted this word, بناسپتی *banās-pattī*, in his vocabulary. It signifies "leaves of the forest," and is from the Sanskṛit वनस्य पत्र *vanasya patra*.

[561] A province of Persia, corresponding with the ancient Media.

hardships, and for a long time was buried alive, and several times escaped from under the very grasp of the Angel of Death.' I said, 'My good Sir! give me a circumstantial narrative, that I may understand [how these things were].' He then began to relate his adventures, saying, 'My father was by profession a merchant. He was continually travelling to Hindūstān, and Turkey, and China, and Cathay,[562] and Europe. When I reached my tenth year, my father went to Hindūstān, and wished to take me with him. Although my mother, and my mother's sister, and my mother's brother's wife, and my father's sister, said that I was still a boy and unfit to travel, my father did not listen to them, and said, "I have grown old, and if this [boy] is not brought up under my eye, I should carry this regret to the grave. He is a man-child, and if he does not learn now, when will he learn?" Having said this, he took me with him, *nolens volens*, and departed. The journey passed in peace and safety. When we arrived in Hindūstān, we sold some goods there, and taking with us rarities for that place, went to the country of Zerbād.[563] This journey also was happily accomplished. Thence also, having finished our purchases and sales, we embarked on board ship, in order that we might speedily arrive at our native country. After a month, one day a storm and typhoon arose, and it began to rain in torrents without intermission.[564] All the earth and sky became murky,

---

[562] Northern China—

"the seat
Of mightiest empire, from the distant walls
Of Cambalu, seat of Cathaian Can."
Milton's "*Paradise Lost*," Book XI.

[563] *Vide* note 467.

[564] In Shakespear's Dictionary we find both موسلا دهار *mūslā dhār*, and موسل دهار *mūsal dhār*. In that of Forbes only the former is given. دهار *dhār* is a Sanskrit word, signifying "stream," but the explanation of موسلا *mūslā*, or موسل *mūsal*, is more difficult, the former meaning a "tap-root," and the latter "a wooden club or pestle." The expression would appear to signify, "continuous," "lasting," or "fixed," as it were "rooted;" or descending heavily like a club. In either case it is far-fetched.

as though involved in smoke,[565] and the rudder of the ship was broken. The pilot and the captain began to smite their heads [in despair]. For ten days the wind and the waves were carrying us where they listed. On the eleventh day the ship struck on a rock and went to pieces. I know not where my father, and his servants, and goods went.

"'I found myself on a plank, and for three days and nights that board was carried along at random. On the fourth day I reached the shore, when life was just left in me. Having got off the plank, crawling on my knees, I somehow or other reached the dry land. At a distance fields appeared and many persons were assembled there, but all of them were black and naked as they were born. They said something to me, but I did not understand a syllable of their language. The field was one of the pulse called chanā,[566] and those people had kindled a large fire, and were parching the ears[567] of grain and eating them, and I saw there some houses also. [I thought] "Perhaps their food is no other than this, and there they dwell." They began to make signs to me also, that I should eat. I too plucked up a handful of the pulse, parched it, and began to toss the peas one after another into my mouth,[568] and having drunk a little water I went to sleep in a corner.

"'After a considerable time I awoke, when one of them came near me,[569] and began to point out my road. I pulled up a little pulse, and proceeded by that road. It was a plain, level as the palm of the hand; you might, as it were, call it a model

---

[565] Forbes has omitted the word دھوؤاں دھار *dhūāṅ dhār*, which is compounded of the Sanskṛit words धूम *dhūm*, "smoke," धार *dhār*, "holding." Shakespear has a misprint under this word, giving घूमाधार *ghūmādhār*, instead of धूमाधार *dhūmādhār*. The expression is a fine one, and in poetical beauty surpasses the Virgilian "ponto nox incubat atra," etc.

[566] *Cicer arietinum*, on which horses and sheep are fed. It is by Europeans in India called "gram." Forbes, in his vocabulary, erroneously renders it "vetches."

[567] Forbes has omitted the word بوٹ *būṭ*, m., a Hindī word which has the same meaning as چنا *chanā*. *Vide* the preceding note.

[568] This periphrasis of ten words expresses the meaning of پھانکنا *phānknā*.

[569] In Forbes' edition a comma is wrongly inserted after نزدیک *nazdīk*.

of the plain of the resurrection.[570] There I journeyed along, eating the pulse as I went. After four days a castle appeared. When I got near it, I beheld a very high fort built all of stone, every side of which was two *kos* in length, and the door was cut out of a single stone, with a large padlock attached, but no trace of man was visible there. Proceeding thence I saw a hillock, the earth of which was in colour as black as antimony.[571] When I had passed that hill, a very large city appeared, round which was a rampart with bastions at intervals. On one side of the city was a river of great breadth. Proceeding on I reached the gate, and after saying, "In the name of God!"[572] I set foot within. I saw a person dressed in the garments of Europeans, sitting on a chair. When he saw me, a stranger and a traveller, and heard the "Bismillāh" from my mouth, he called out, "Come forward!" I went and saluted him. He returned my salutation with much kindness. Forthwith he placed on the table a loaf of bread, and butter, and fowl cut in pieces and roasted, and wine, and said, "Eat your fill." I ate and drank a little and fell into a profound sleep. When the night was over, then my eyes opened, and I washed

---

570 All mankind, according to Muḥammadans, are to stand before God at the last day, on a vast plain, to be judged, as in Revelation xx. 13, where, however, there is no mention of the plain.

571 The سُرمه *surmah*, or collyrium, which Orientals apply to their eyes, is, Shakespear tells us, in India, ore of lead, or a galena or sulphuret of lead. For my own part I never saw anything but antimony used. A round bodkin somewhat smaller than a quill is dipped lengthways into the powder, which adheres to it in small quantities. The میل *mīl* or bodkin is then drawn between the eyelids, which are closed upon it, and the powder is thus traced along them just under the root of the eyelashes. This is extremely beneficial to the sight, as I can testify from experience, preventing the lid from inflaming, and it is likewise thought to be ornamental. It is also observed as a custom sanctioned by the Prophet's example. The same practice is thus described by Juvenal:—

> "Ille supercilium madidâ fuligine tinctum
> Obliquâ producit acu, pingitque trementes
> Attollens oculos."

572 بسم اَللّٰه *Bismillāh*, "In the name of God!" should be said at the commencement of every enterprise. Nay, the commonest actions are not done by Muḥammadans without this ejaculation, which, for instance, is uttered when animals are slain for food, before meals, in setting out on a journey, etc.

my hands and face. He again gave me food to eat, and said, "O son! relate thy story." I told him all that had happened to me. He then said, "Why hast thou come hither?" I was amazed and said, "Perhaps thou art mad! I, after toiling for a length of time, have now obtained sight of an inhabited place; God has conducted me thus far, and thou sayest, 'Why hast thou come?'" He said, "Do thou now repose thyself. To-morrow I will tell what I have to say."

"'When the morning came, he said, "In this room are a spade, a sieve, and a bag for feeding horses, bring them out." I said in my heart, "God knows what labour he will exact from me now that he has given me bread to eat." I brought out all those things, and placed them before him. He then said, "Go to that mound, and having dug a hole about a yard deep, sift what comes out in this sieve. Fill the bag with what cannot be sifted, and bring it to me." I took all those things and went there, and having dug just to that depth, I sifted [the earth] and put it in the bag. I saw then that it was all [composed of] gems of various colours. My eyes were dazzled[573] by their brilliance. In the same way I filled the bag to the brim, and brought it to that friendly person. When he saw it he said, "Take thou what is contained therein, and depart hence, for it is not well for thee to stay in this city." I replied, "Your honour has shewn me, on your part, great kindness in giving me such a quantity of pebbles and stones, but of what use will they be to me? When I become hungry, I shall not be able to chew these, nor will they fill my stomach. If then you should give me yet more, still what use would they be to me?" The man laughed, and said, "I feel compassion for thee, for thou, like me, art a native of the country of Persia. On this account I stop thee, otherwise[574] it is thy look out; if, whether or no, thy resolution is no other than this, to enter the city, then take my ring with thee. When thou enterest the

---

573 Forbes has omitted the word چوندھیانا *chaundhiyānā*, "to be blinded," "confused," "dazzled."

574 The sentence should be, نہیں تو تو جان *nahīṅ to tū jān*, "otherwise do thou know." Mīr Amman, doubtless by a *lapsus pennæ*, omitted the تو.

centre of the bāzār, there will be sitting there a person with a white beard, and his appearance and figure bear a strong resemblance to mine.[575] He is my elder brother. Give him this signet, and he will take care of thee; and be pleased to act as he directs, otherwise thou wilt be uselessly put to death; and my control extends just thus far. In the city I cannot interfere." I took the ring from him, and having saluted him, took leave. I entered the city, and beheld that it was a very fine one. The streets and the bāzār were clean, and men and women without concealment were buying and selling amongst one another, and were all well-dressed.[576] I walked on, looking about me. When I arrived in the centre of the bāzār, where the four roads met, there was such a crowd that if you had flung a platter,[577] it would have gone along on the heads of the people. There was such a dense concourse of persons, that it was difficult for one to move. When the crowd dispersed a little, I, too, pushing and jostling, went on. At length I saw my friend, who was sitting upon a chair,[578] and a mace[579] set with jewels was placed before him. I went up and saluted him, and gave him the signet. He looked angrily at me, and said, "Why hast thou come here, and plunged thyself in calamity? I suppose, then, that my foolish brother did not forbid thee?" I said, "He indeed told me, but I did not listen to him." I then related to him all my story from beginning to end. That person rose, and, taking me with him, went towards his house.[580] His dwelling was in appearance like that of kings, and he had

---

575 Before ميرا *merā* there should be a comma or even a full stop.

576 There should be a full stop after لباس *libās*. In Forbes' edition there is none, which makes absolute nonsense.

577 In Forbes' vocabulary the word تهالي *thālī*, "salver," "platter," "flat dish," is omitted.

578 In Bengāl the word چوكي *chaukī* is now used for "a chair," as in Bombay كرسي *kursī* is used. "Chaukī" properly means "bench," and that may be the meaning here.

579 چماق *chumāḳ* is given as a Persian word in the dictionaries, but it is probably originally Turkish. It signifies a club also as well as a baton of office.

580 There should be a full stop at چلا *chalā*.

many servants and attendants. When he had entered a private room and sate down, he said with gentleness, "O my son! what folly is this that thou hast committed, that with thine own feet thou hast entered the tomb? Does any one enter this ill-fated and spell-bound city?" I said, "I have already told you all my story. Now indeed fate has brought me, but have the kindness to acquaint me with the customs of this place, that I may know for what reasons[581] you and your brother opposed my entrance." Then that gentleman said, "The King and all the chiefs of the city are abandoned by God. Their customs[582] and sect are of a strange kind. There is here, in an idol-temple, an idol, from the belly of which the devil announces the name, and caste, and religion of each person, and consequently whatever poor traveller arrives, the King is informed of it. He conducts him to that same temple, and causes him to prostrate himself before the idol. If he bows[583] before it, then it is well; otherwise he causes that helpless one to be drowned in the river. If he tries to escape from the river, and take to flight, then his private parts lengthen to such a degree that they trail on the ground. Such is the spell that fate has fashioned for this city. I pity thy youth; but for thy sake, I will devise a scheme so that forsooth, some days at least, thou wilt survive, and wilt escape this torment." I asked, "What sort of scheme is that? be pleased to direct me." He said, "I will make thee a married man, and for thy sake bring about thy nuptials with the vazīr's daughter." I replied, "When will the vazīr give his daughter to me, destitute as I am! except, indeed, in case I embrace their faith, which is what I never can do." He said, "There is this custom in this city, that whoever prostrates himself before the

---

581 The words کہ اس واسطے *kih is wāsṭe*, "that on this account," should be contracted into کس واسطے *kis wāsṭe*, "on what account?" It is evidently a mere lapsus of Mīr Amman's.

582 The dictionaries omit the word رویّا *rawīyā*, which is the Hindūstānī form of the Persian رویہ *rawīyah*, "custom," for that it is in the singular nominative is proved by the کا *kā* preceding it.

583 The aorist کرے *kare* might be expected here, though the past is more idiomatic.

idol, though he be but a fakīr, and ask for the King's daughter, then, to gratify him, they would give her to him, and forbear to disappoint him. I have, too, credit with the King, therefore all the nobles and great men of this place respect me. And during the week they, for two days, go on pilgrimage to the idol-temple, and perform their devotions. Accordingly to-morrow they will all assemble. I will take thee there." Having said this, he gave me food and drink, and allowed me to go to sleep there. When the morning came, he took me with him, and went towards the idol-temple. On going there, I beheld persons coming and going and worshipping.

"'The King and the nobles were respectfully kneeling before the idol, near the priests, and beautiful unmarried girls and boys, like Hūrīs and Ghilmān,[584] stood ranged in lines on all sides. That kind person then addressed me, saying, "Now do as I tell thee." I assented, saying, "I will perform what you command." He said, "First, kiss the hands and feet of the King. After that, take hold of the skirt of the vazīr."[585] I did exactly so. The King asked, "Who is this, and what does he say?" The man said, "This young man is my relation. He has come from a distance, in the desire of kissing the feet of the King, in the expectation that the vazīr will exalt him in his service, if it be the order of the Great Idol, and the royal pleasure." The King asked, "Will he accept our sect, and faith, and institutions? if so, the request is a fortunate one [and I grant it]." Immediately the music struck up in the orchestra of the temple,[586] and they invested me with a rich robe, and casting a black cord round my neck, dragged me before the throne of the idol, and having caused me to prostrate myself, made me stand there.

"'A voice issued from the idol, which said, "O merchant's son! it is well that thou hast entered my service: now expect my mercy and favour." Having heard this, all bowed down,

---

584 The Hūrīs are too well known to require description. The Ghilmān are beautiful boys who wait on the blest in the blissful abodes of Paradise.

585 There should be a full stop after پکڑ *pakaṛ*.

586 In the original it is, "the music-room sounded."

and began to roll on the ground, and called out, "Praise to thee! why should it not be so? So great a Lord are you!" When it was evening, the King and the vazīr mounted and entered the seraglio of the vazīr, and after the performance of their devotions, delivered over to me the vazīr's daughter, and bestowed on me many gifts as dowry, and said to me, in a tone of great humility, that, in accordance with the command of the Great Idol, they had given her to wait upon me. They settled us both in an abode.[587] When I surveyed that delicate girl, I then found, indeed, that her beauty was like that of a fairy, and perfect from head to foot. Whatever good qualities we hear to be in the Padminī[588] class of women, were all present in her. In perfect freedom from interruption I indulged in amorous delights with her. In the morning I bathed and presented myself at the levée of the King. The King bestowed on me the robe of a son-in-law, and commanded me to remain in constant attendance at his court. At length, after some days, I was admitted into the number of the King's favourites.

"'The King was much pleased with my society, and constantly bestowed on me robes of honour and presents, although I was in affluence as to worldly wealth, because my wife had so much money, and property, and jewels, that there was no limit to them, nor possibility of exceeding them.[589] Two years passed away in much pleasure and comfort. It happened that the vazīr's daughter became pregnant. When the seventh month, and the uncounted[590] (*i.e.* the eighth) month had passed, and her days were fulfilled, her pains began. The nurses and midwives came, when a dead son came forth from her womb, the poison

537 There should be a full stop after رکھا, *rakhā*.

588 The Hindūs divide women into four classes,—first, the पद्मिनी *Padminī*, which is the most beautiful and excellent; second, the चित्रिणी *Chitrinī*; third, the शङ्खिनी *Shaṇkhinī*, described as tall with long hair, neither stout nor thin, of irascible disposition and strong passions; fourth, the हस्तिनी *Hastinī*, which is the worst of the four classes.

589 This appears to me the only way of rendering the word نہایت *nihāyat*.

590 As the child is seldom born in the eighth month, it is called "the uncounted," in opposition to the seventh and ninth.

of which infected the mother, and she too died. I became distracted with grief, saying to myself, "What calamity is this which has come upon me?" Seated at her head I was weeping. All at once the sound of lamentation rose on high from the females' apartments, and from all sides women began to come in. Each that entered smote both her hands on my head,[591] and stood opposite my face, and began to weep. So many women came that I was hidden by their hips. I was almost expiring.

"'Meanwhile some one pulled my collar from behind, and dragged me along. When I looked, it was the same Persian who had effected my marriage. He began to say, "Idiot! wherefore weepest thou?" I said, "O cruel one! what word is this thou hast spoken? my kingdom has been spoiled. The comfort of my housekeeping has gone—is passed, and thou sayest, 'Why dost thou grieve?'" That friendly person smiled, and said, "Now weep for thine own death! I told thee from the first that thy destiny had probably conducted thee into this city, which truly was the case. Now, except death, there is no escape for thee." At length people seized me and led me to the idol-temple. I saw there the King, and the nobles, and the thirty-six orders of the subjects assembled, and the wealth and effects of the vazīr's daughter were all placed there. Whoever fancied anything, took it, and deposited the money it was valued at.

"'In short, all the effects were turned into ready money, and with the money jewels were purchased, and these were fastened up in a casket, and they brought bread and sweetmeats, and roast meat, and fruit dried and fresh, and articles of food, and filled a box with them, and having placed the corpse of that lady in another box, they loaded a camel with the box of food, and made me mount on it, and put the casket of jewels under my arm, and all the Brāhmans proceeded on and on, performing their religious rites and blowing horns, and in the rear a crowd

---

591 I cannot see why the indecencies in this passage and in other parts of the book, which I forbear to translate, should not be omitted. They add nothing to the sense, though much to the sensuality of the story.

of people, uttering congratulations, accompanied us. In this manner I issued forth from the city by the same door in which I had entered on the first day. As soon as the eyes of the superintendent of that quarter fell upon me, he began to weep, and said, "O ill-fated one! overtaken by fate! thou didst not listen to my words, and having entered that city, hast uselessly given up thy life. It is not my fault. I forbade thee." He spoke thus, but I remained struck with confusion. Neither did my tongue aid me to give an answer, nor had I presence of mind left to say, "Let us see what is to be the end of me?"

"'At length they conducted me to that same castle the door of which I had seen closed on the first day, and a number of men, by their united efforts, opened the door, and carried in the bier and the box. A priest came up to me and began to admonish me, saying, "Man receives his nativity one day and one day expires. Such is the transitory condition of the world. Now this thy wife, and thy son, and thy wealth, and food for forty days, are before thee. Take this and remain here until the Great Idol has compassion on thee." I in my fury was about to heap curses on that idol, and on the inhabitants of that place, and on that custom, and to inflict blows and buffets on the Brāhman. The same Persian forbade me in his own language, saying, "Take care! never utter a word; if thou sayest anything, then that very moment they will burn thee alive. Well! what was in thy destiny, that has happened. Now place thy hope on the mercy of God. Perhaps God my bring thee forth hence alive."

"'At length all left me alone and went forth from that fortress and again locked the door upon me. At that time I involuntarily wept at my lonely and helpless state, and began to kick the corpse of that woman, saying, "O carrion! if thou wast to die in parturition, why didst thou marry? and why didst thou become pregnant?" After beating and thumping her, I again sate down silent. Meanwhile the day advanced and the sun waxed hot, and the brain of my head began to boil, and, through the stench, I began to give up the ghost. Wherever I looked, the bones of dead men and boxes of jewels were heaped up. Then I took some old chests and placed them below and above, in order that there might be a refuge from the heat by day, and from the dew at night. I myself began to search for water. On one side I saw a sort of spout, which was cut out of stone in the wall of the fort, and resembled the mouth of an earthen jar. In fact, I subsisted some time on that water and the food.

"'At length my food was finished. I was dismayed, and uttered my complaints to God. He is so merciful that the door of the castle opened, and they brought in a corpse. With it came in an old man. When they had departed, leaving him too alone, it occurred to me that I would kill that old man, and take away every bit of his box of food. I took the foot of a box in my hand, and went up to him. That helpless one was seated, resting his head on his knees, in a state of stupor. I came behind him and gave him such a blow on his head that his skull was smashed, and his brains fell out, and he immediately resigned his spirit to God. I took his food and began to eat. For a long time this was my employment, that whatever living person accompanied a corpse, I slew him, and taking his provisions, lived in plenty.

"'After some time, on one occasion, there came in along with a bier, a girl of very beautiful form. My heart did not wish to kill her also. She saw me, and, through fear, became insensible. I took up her food also, and carried it to my own place. But I did not eat alone. When I felt hungry, I took some food to her, and ate with her. When that woman saw that I did not hurt her, her fear became less day by day, and she grew more and more sociable, and began to frequent my abode. One day I inquired her story, saying, "Who art thou?" She replied, "I am the daughter of the King's principal minister.[592] I was betrothed to the son of my father's brother. On the day of the bridal-night he was seized with colic. Such was the pain with which he was convulsed, that in the space of an hour[593] he died. They brought me along with his bier,

[592] The وکیل مطلق *vakīl-i muṭlak* is an office under the Mughal Emperors equivalent to viceroy, and consequently belongs to some great noble in the provinces at a distance from Delhi, as to Sindhya. In Forbes' vocabulary the word is omitted.

[593] The double meaning of آن *ān* here would be considered a beauty in style. Forbes has omitted the second meaning.

and left me here." She then inquired my story.[594] I too gave a full and complete account of myself, and said, "God has sent thee here for my sake." She smiled and remained silent.

"'In this same manner, after some days, our mutual attachment increased. I taught her the fundamental[595] doctrines of the Musalmān religion, and made her recite the Creed, and going through the form of a temporary[596] marriage, I cohabited with her. She, too, became pregnant.[597] A son was born. Our life[598] passed for nearly three years in this same manner. When the child was weaned,[599] I one day said to the lady, "How long shall we remain here? and in which way shall we get forth hence?" She said, "If God brings us forth, we shall get out, else we shall one day die here." At what she said, and at my detention, I wept bitterly; and as I wept, I fell asleep. I beheld in a dream a person, who said to me, "It is possible to make thy egress by the drain; do thou do so." I started up through joy, and said to my wife, "Collect and bring to me the iron nails and bolts which were in the old chests, then I will widen it." In short, I placed a nail in the mouth of that sewer, and hammered it with stones, so that I wearied myself.

---

594 There should be a full stop after پوچھا *pūchhā*.

595 Forbes has given this meaning of ارکان *ārkān* in his vocabulary, but omitted it in his dictionary, as Shakespear has in his. It is a rare sense of the word, which occurs very frequently in the expression ارکان دولت *ārkān-i daulat*, "Pillars of the state."

596 Forbes writes the word متعہ *mutā*. Johnson, in his Persian Dictionary, makes it متعۃ *mitāṭ*. Shakespear restricts it to the Shiāhs, while Forbes more indulgently extends the privilege to all good Musalmān. It corresponds to the गान्धर्व्व विवाह *gandharvva vivāha*, that is, intercourse by mutual consent without ceremonies, or ceremony.

597 This is the refined expression. The vulgar term is پیٹ رهنا or هونا *peṭ rahnā* or *honā*, which occurs two pages back.

598 زندگی *zindagī*, "life," or مدّت *muddat*, "interval," must here be understood as the nominative to گذری *guzrī*.

599 Forbes has omitted this sense of بڑهانا *baṛhānā*. Both here and in the meaning given to the word at p. 130, l. 8, viz. that of "closing a shop," we trace the superstitious feeling referred to in note 255, *q.v.*

By the labour of a year, that aperture became large enough for a man to issue from it.

"'After that I selected the best jewels, and filled the sleeves of the dead with them, and taking them with us, we three sallied forth by that same passage. I returned thanks to God, and seated my son on my shoulder. A month has elapsed since, avoiding the high road through fear, I have come along by way of the forests and mountains. When hunger arises, I eat grass or leaves. I have no strength to talk. This is my story, which you have heard.'

"Health to the King! I felt compassion for his state, and having caused him to take a warm bath, and to put on good apparel, I appointed him my deputy: and in my house several boys were born to me from that Princess, but they died in their infancy. One son died after reaching his fifth year, and in grief for him the Princess also died. I suffered excessive sorrow, and without her that country began to be wearisome[600] to me. My heart became dejected. I determined to set out for Persia. By a representation to the King, I caused the office of superintendent of that port to be given to that young man [my deputy]. In the meanwhile, the King too died. I, bringing with me that faithful dog, and all my property, treasure, and jewels, came and stopped[601] in Naishāpūr. In order that no one might become acquainted with the story of my brothers, I have suffered myself to become known as the dog-worshipping merchant, and, under this infamous character, I to this day have to pay double taxes to the government of the King of Persia.

"It happened that this merchant's son came there; by this means I have kissed the feet of the Asylum of the world."

I[602] inquired, "What! is not this thy son?" The merchant

---

600 A very rare sense of کاٹنا *kāṭnā*, which has passed unnoticed by both Forbes and Shakespear.

601 Instead of the comma in Forbes' edition, a full stop is imperatively required after رہا *rahā*; and the full stop after ہووے *howe* must be expunged. As the text now stands, it is little better than nonsense.

602 Āzād-Bakht again speaks in his own person.

replied, "Point to which the world turns in prayer! this is not my son, he is a subject of your own royal self, but now the master of my property, and my heir; in short, he and he alone is everything to me you can mention." When I heard this, I inquired of the merchant's son, "Of what merchant art thou the son? and where do thy parents dwell?" The boy kissed the ground and begged that his life might be spared, and said, "This handmaid is the daughter of the vazīr of Your Majesty. My father fell under the royal displeasure by reason of the rubies of this very merchant, and the command was thus given —that if in a year his word was not proved true, he should be put to death. I, having heard it, assumed this disguise, and conveyed myself to Naishāpūr. God has brought the merchant with his dog and the rubies into the royal presence. Your Majesty has heard the whole history. I hope that my aged sire may be released."

When the merchant heard this explanation of the vazīr's daughter, he heaved a sigh, and fell powerless. When rose-water had been sprinkled over him, he recovered his senses, and said, "Alas! ill-fortune! I had come such a distance, enduring all the toil and trouble, in the hope of adopting this merchant's child, and of writing and bestowing on him a deed of gift of all my property, that then my name might continue, and all the world would call him my child, and now my thought has turned out vain, and the thing has proved the opposite [to my wishes]. By proving to be a woman, she has ruined me, the old man. I have been caught by female arts,[603] and now the proverb[604] applies to me—

He stopped at home, and with the pilgrims went not he,
With shaven head, a mark for scorn and obloquy."

In short,[605] I compassionated his distracted state, and was moved to pity by his weeping and lamentations. I called him

---

[603] This sense of چرتر *charitr* has been omitted in the dictionaries.

[604] Those who go as pilgrims to Makkah shave their heads on arriving there. The merchant compares himself to one who makes himself ridiculous by undergoing the shaving without any of the merit or advantages of a pilgrim.

[605] Āzād-Ba<u>kh</u>t speaks again.

to me and whispered to him the joyful tidings of his union, saying, "Be not sorrowful; I will cause your nuptials to take place with this very girl. God willing, thou wilt have children, and this very girl shall be thy mistress." At hearing this good news, he was upon the whole[606] consoled. I then directed the vazīr's daughter to be taken to the women's apartments, and the vazīr to be brought from the prison and bathed in the warm bath, and dressed in a robe of honour, which marked his restoration to favour, and brought to me with speed. When the vazīr came, I condescended to go to meet him as far as the edge of the carpet,[607] and regarding him as my senior, I embraced him, and bestowed on him afresh the writing-case which was the insignia of his office as vazīr, and I gave to the merchant also a grant of land and a title, and having observed an auspicious moment, I caused the nuptial ceremony to be performed, and wedded him to the vazīr's daughter.

In the space of some years two boys and a girl were born in his house, and in fact his eldest son is now the chief merchant, and the younger the comptroller of my household. O darweshes! I have on this account related this story in your presence, because I last night heard the adventures of two faḳīrs, and now you two who remain, consider that we are seated in the same place and look on me as your servant, and this place as your faḳīr's hut. Without scruple or hesitation relate each his own adventures, and stay a little while with me.

When the faḳīrs found such strong encouragement on the part of the King, they began to say, "Well! since you have evinced a kindness for us mendicants, we two also will relate our story. Be pleased to listen."

---

606 Forbes in his vocabulary has translated في الجملة *fī 'l-jumlah*, "in short," a meaning which I believe it can never bear. The sense is that the merchant recovered a little from his excessive disappointment, though he would rather have had an adopted son in the vazīr's daughter, than the chance of begetting one.

607 A most unusual condescension on the part of Eastern princes, which, in the opinion of their grovelling slaves, would quite atone for years of imprisonment. The carpet generally extends over but a small part of the audience-chamber.

TRAVELS OF THE THIRD DARWESH.

THE third Darwesh sate down with his hands clasped round his knees,[608] and began to relate his travels in the following manner:—

Hear then, O friends! the tale of this faḳīr;
To all that has befallen me, give ear!
All that the God of Love has done to me,
I'll fully tell—do ye attentive be!

This humblest of individuals is the son of the King of Ăjam.[609] My father was the King of that country, and had no son but me. I, during the season of my youth, amused myself in playing with my companions at oblong dice, cards, chess, and backgammon; or, mounting my horse, employed myself in riding and the chase. This is what befell me one day. I had caused my steed to be got ready, and taking with me all my friends and acquaintances, went out towards the plain. I proceeded to a distance, letting fly hawks, falcons, and kestrels at the Brāhmanī ducks and partridges. [Then] a spot of wonderful beauty met my gaze, for wherever the eye was

---

[608] The first darwesh is said دو زانو هو بیٹھنا *do zānū ho baiṭhnā*, which is a position used in prayer, and is simply sitting on your heels. The second darwesh sits down چار زانو هو *chār zānū ho*, which I believe to be equivalent to what we call sitting cross-legged. The expression here used of the third darwesh, گوٹ باندھ بیٹھنا *goṭ bāndh baiṭhnā*, means to sit with the arms clasped, or the girdle bound round the knees. In Forbes' text, کوٹ باندھ *koṭ bāndh*, I believe to be an error for گوٹ باندھ *goṭ bāndh*; گوٹ *goṭ* being the hem of a garment.

[609] The second darwesh was the son of the King of Fārs, which is that part of Persia of which Shīrāz was the capital. Here we find the third darwesh the son of the King of Ăjam, *i.e.* of Persia generally. Mr. Smith, impaled on the horns of this cruel dilemma, has made both darweshes "Princes of Persia." I prefer being more literal and leaving the author and reader to unravel the node together.

directed, the ground appeared for miles green [with verdure], and blushing with flowers. Surveying this scene, we dropped the reins of our steeds and proceeded on slowly, step by step, looking about us. All of a sudden I saw in that wilderness a black stag, on which was a cloth of brocade and a head-stall set with jewels, and from whose neck were hung bells of gold stitched to a gold-embroidered collar, which was moving about grazing at its ease in that place (where man had never entered nor bird had flapped its wing). Hearing the sound of the hoofs of our steeds, it was on the alert, and raising its head, looked, and then slowly made off.

At sight of it, such a desire [of getting possession of it] arose, that I said to my companions, "Do you stand here; I will take it alive. Take care not to advance a step nor to follow me;" and the steed I bestrode [*lit.* "under my thighs"] was so swift that I had frequently galloped it past deer, and causing them to forget their bounds,[610] had seized them, from time to time, and taken them. I galloped after it. It, when it saw me following, bounded off [*lit.* "began to fill its springs"] at speed, and fled like the wind.[611] My steed too matched [*lit.* "was conversing with"] the wind, but did not come up even with its dust. That fleet courser too became covered with sweat, and my tongue also began to crack with thirst, but no efforts of mine were of any avail. Evening drew on, and I knew not whence or whither I had come. Having no alternative, I employed a stratagem against it, and having taken out an arrow from my quiver, and resting my bow on the bow-case,[612] I fitted it to the string, which I drew to my ear, and taking aim at its

---

[610] The deer, when pursued by a well-mounted horseman, cross backwards and forwards in front of him, by which they allow him to come up, so that such a feat as is here described is by no means impossible.

[611] Literally, "became wind." I prefer the translation given above to that in Forbes and Shakespear, viz. "disappeared," as the sequel shews that the Prince kept the stag in sight, and, in fact, wounded it.

[612] The تکش *tukkash* is evidently a mere corruption of تیر کش *tīr kash*, "arrow-holder," or "quiver," which occurs at p. 209, l. 18, of the text, but the قربان *kurbān* is perhaps what I have rendered it, "a bow-case."

thigh, said, "God is most great," and discharged the shaft. In fine the very first arrow lodged in its leg.[613] It then moved limpingly towards the foot of a mountain. I too dismounted from my horse, and followed it on foot. It made for the mountain, and I too pursued it. After some ascents and descents, a cupola appeared. When I came near it, I saw a little garden and a spring[614] of water. The stag indeed had vanished from my sight.[615] I was much exhausted, and began to wash my hands and feet.

All at once the sound of weeping came to my ears from the interior of that tower, as if some one was saying, "O my child! may the arrow of my sighs transfix the heart of him who wounded thee with his shaft; may he derive no fruition from his youth! and may God make him as afflicted as I am!" Having heard this, I went there. I saw then that a venerable old man with a white beard, and dressed in good apparel, sate there on a cushion, and before him lay the stag, from the thigh of which he was drawing out the arrow, and uttering imprecations. I saluted him and respectfully joining my hands, said, "Health, venerable sir! this fault has been unwittingly committed by this slave. I knew not of this; for God's sake excuse me." He replied, "Thou hast tortured a dumb animal; if this bad deed was unknowingly done by thee, God will forgive thee." I went up and sate beside him and took part in extracting the arrow, which we got out with great difficulty, and after covering the wound with plaster we let [the stag] go. After that the old man, having washed his hands, gave me some breakfast to eat, of what was then ready.

---

613 I always suspected a mistake here in the text of Forbes' edition, which gives پانوں میں *pānoṅ meṅ*, "in the legs," as the stag could hardly have escaped at all had both legs been transfixed. On looking at Mr. Romer's MS., I find my suspicions were just, as the word there is in the singular, پانو میں *pānw meṅ*.

614 چشمہ *chashmah* corresponds to "*fons*," and not to our word "fountain," which is فوارہ *fauwārah*.

615 Forbes, in his vocabulary, has (probably by a typographical error) given this word wrongly,—چھلوا *chhalwā* instead of چھلاوا *chhalāwā*. It comes from چھلنا *chhalnā*, "to deceive."

When I had eaten and drunk, I stretched myself out at length on a bedstead.

By reason of my fatigue, and from having well filled my stomach, I slept. In that slumber the sound of lamentation and wailing reached my ears. On rubbing my eyes and looking about me [I found] that neither that old man nor any one else was in the apartment. I was lying alone on a bed, and that vestibule was vacant. Feeling alarmed I began to look on all sides. In one corner a curtain was let down. I went there and lifted it up. I saw then a throne spread with cushions, and on it a fairy-born female of about fourteen years old, with a face like the moonbeams, and ringlets loosely flowing on each side, who, with smiling countenance, and dressed in European garments, was looking [towards me] with wondrous blandishments, and sitting there. And the old man, resting his head on her feet, continued helplessly weeping and bereft of sense. Beholding this condition of the old man, and the beauty and loveliness of that delicate girl, I swooned and fell without life like one dead. The venerable senior, seeing this my state, came to me with a bottle of rose-water, and began to sprinkle it on me. When I rose up with renewed life, I went before that lovely girl and saluted her. She[616] never moved hand nor lip. I said, "O roseate form! what sect sanctions such pride, and the non-return of a salutation?

> Graceful is silence,—aye! but not to this degree.
> What though the lover's eye should close despairingly?
> E'en then she speaks not, [but looks on unpityingly].

For the sake of that God who created thee, say somewhat. I have found my way here fortuitously, [and] to oblige a guest is an imperative duty." I pleaded long, but in vain; she sate and listened in silence like an image. I then advanced and touched her feet with my hand. When I touched them, I

---

616 Forbes has a misprint here, اُس بي *us be*, for اُس نے *us ne*. Even these trifling blunders become of importance in a stereotyped edition. In the next line is کرتا *kartā* for کرنا *karnā*.

felt that they were hard. At length I discovered that some skilful statuary[617] had carved this gem[618] out of stone, and had fashioned it into an image. I then interrogated that idol-worshipping old man, saying, "I fixed a shaft[619] in the leg of thy stag; thou hast with this dart of love wounded my heart and pierced it through and through. Thy prayer has been accepted. Now give me a circumstantial explanation of these circumstances, as to why this talisman has been made? and why thou, abandoning the habitations of men, inhabitest the forest and the mountain? Tell me what has happened to thee."

After I had importuned him much he made answer, "This thing has ruined me, indeed. What! dost thou also wish to be destroyed by hearing it?" I said, "There! thou hast made excuses and evasions more than enough! say what I want to hear, otherwise I will slay thee." Seeing me persist resolutely, he said, "O youth! may God Most High keep every mortal from the flame of love! Lo, now! what calamities this love has occasioned! It is through love that the wife endures cremation with the husband, and perishes by her own consent; and the story of Farhād and Majnūn is known to all. What fruit wilt thou obtain by hearing that story? Thou wilt uselessly abandon thy family, thy fortune, and the world, and go forth [as a faḳīr]." I replied, "Enough! now fold up and put away your friendship; at this time look on me as your foe. If life is dear to you, then tell me distinctly." Having no resource, he wept, and began to say, "This is the story of me ruined. The name of your slave is Nīmān Saiyāḥ.[620] I was a great merchant. During this my life I have traversed the seven

---

[617] In the text it is, "they had carved and Āẕur had fashioned." Āẕur signifies "fire," and is said by Muḥammadans to have been the name of Terah, Abraham's father, who was, according to them, a statuary and maker of idols.

[618] The word لعل *lāl* means "ruby," "precious stone," but it is here used to signify "any precious work of art," exactly as we use the word "gem" when we say—such a thing is "quite a gem."

[619] The word کهپرا *khaprā* signifies "an arrow with a broad point."

[620] نعمان *Nīmān* is the name of the Arabian kings of حيرة *Ḥiraṭ*. *Vide* note 303. سياح *Saiyāḥ* signifies "traveller" or "pilgrim."

regions of the earth for the sake of traffic, and have obtained access to the presence of all kings. On one occasion this thought occurred to my mind, that I had indeed wandered over countries in the four quarters of the horizon, but had not gone towards the island[621] of Europe, nor had seen the King of that place and his subjects and soldiery, nor gained any information as to the customs and institutions there; that I ought, therefore, for once to go thither also. I took counsel with my companions and friends, and made a firm resolve [to set out thither], and took curiosities and presents from various places, such as were fit for that country, and having assembled a caravan of merchants, I embarked on board a ship and departed. Meeting with a favourable wind, we arrived at that country in a few months, and alighted in the city. It was a wondrous city we beheld, for no city equals that in beauty. In every bāzār and street there were paved roads, and water was sprinkled there. The cleanliness was such that not even a straw was anywhere to be seen, why speak of dirt then?—and the buildings were of various colours,[622] and in the roads at night there were on each side the way lights at the interval of a pace, and without the city were gardens in which were seen wondrous flowering shrubs and fruits, which, except in paradise, are perhaps nowhere else to be found. Whatever praise I should bestow on that place would be deserved.

"In short, the report spread of the arrival of merchants. A confidential eunuch, attended by several body-servants, came to the caravan and inquired of the merchants who was their chief. All pointed to me. The eunuch came to my room, and I received him with respect. Salutations were interchanged. I seated him on the cushion and offered him the pillow.[623] After

---

621 The Persians, according to this, believe Europe to be an island. This does not agree with what Morier tells us of the determination of the Persian princes not to visit England by water.

622 رنگ به رنگ کی *rang bah rang kī* may also mean "of various kinds," and I should feel inclined to adopt this latter interpretation.

623 To an inferior a part of the cushion is given as a seat; to an equal a part of the large pillow for the back is offered; while to a superior the whole pillow is surrendered, and the host retreats to the cushion.

that I inquired, 'What is the cause of your honour's coming? Be pleased to tell me.' He replied, 'The Princess has heard that merchants have arrived, and have brought much merchandize; wherefore she has ordered me to bring them to her presence. Do you then take with you such articles as you think fit for the use of kings, and obtain for yourself the happiness of kissing the imperial threshold.'

"I replied, 'To-day, indeed, I am unable,[624] from fatigue. To-morrow I shall be ready with my life and effects. Whatever this weak person possesses I will present as an offering; whatever is approved of shall be the property of the Government.' Having made this promise, and having given him ãṭr-of-rose and betel, I dismissed the eunuch, and, having called all the merchants to me, I collected from them all the rarities which each possessed; and I brought also whatever was in my house; and in the morning I presented myself at the door of the royal palace. In fine, the doorkeepers announced my coming, and an order was given to bring me into the presence. The same eunuch came forth, and, taking my hand in his, and conversing in a friendly manner, led me in. We first passed through the chambers occupied by the retinue,[625] whence he took me into a magnificent apartment. O my friend! thou wilt not believe the splendour that met my sight; it was as if you had clipped the wings of fairies and let them loose. To whichever side I looked my gaze was riveted, and my feet gave way under me.[626] I supported myself by an effort and advanced in front of the Princess. As soon as my sight fell on her, I experienced a swooning sensation, and a tremor pervaded my hands and feet.

"Somehow or other I managed to offer my respects. On both sides, on the right hand and on the left, rank upon rank,

---

[624] Forbes has omitted this sense of قاصِر *ḳāṣir*, in his vocabulary.

[625] Forbes, in his vocabulary, has omitted the word خواصّ پُرا *khawāṣṣ purā*, and Shakespear marks it with a note of interrogation. The sense, however, here, is evidently "the ante-chambers occupied by servants, etc."

[626] There is a very insipid play on words here, گڑنا *gaṛnā*, signifying "to be buried," and اکھڑنا *ukhaṛnā*, "to be torn up by the roots," as though he planted his eyes instead of his feet.

fairy-faced delicate ladies were standing with arms respectfully crossed. When of the different kinds of jewels and pieces of wearing apparel and rarities which I had taken along with me, several trays had been arranged in the royal presence (inasmuch as every article was worthy of being approved), the Princess was pleased, gave them in charge[627] to the steward of her household, and said, 'The price of this shall be paid to-morrow, according to the invoice.' I made my obeisance, and was pleased at heart, saying to myself, 'Well! there will be this excuse for coming to-morrow also.' When, after taking leave, I had come out, I was talking like a deranged person; what issued from my mouth was altogether irrelevant[628] to the subject. In this same way I entered the caravanserai, but my senses were unsettled. All my acquaintances[629] and friends began to ask, 'What is this your state?' I said, 'My brain is heated with so much business.'[630]

"In short, I passed that night in a state of excitement; in the morning I went again and presented myself, and with the same eunuch re-entered the palace. I saw the same splendour that I had seen the day before. The Princess, when she saw me, dismissed every one to his respective employment. When

---

[627] It is impossible to conceive a more confused and ungrammatical sentence than this. We begin with understanding اُن كي *un kī*, to make the first member of it intelligible; then the nominative to فرمايا *farmāyā*, viz.: بادشاهزادي نے *pādshāhzādī ne*, is omitted, and حوالے هوئي *ḥawāle hūe*, is a sad blunder for حوالي كئي *ḥawāle kiye*, which again ought to be in the feminine to agree with كشتيان *kishtiyān*. Forbes, too, by putting only a comma at دي جائيگي *dī jāegī*, has increased the confusion. Altogether it is one of the clumsiest sentences ever perpetrated.

[628] Literally, "It was something, and from my mouth another thing was issuing." There should be a comma after كہتا *kahtā*, as one unacquainted with the idiom of the language might otherwise be inclined to take the كہتا *kahtā* and the تها *thā* together.

[629] The young student will do well to remember this distinction between آشنا *āshnā* and دوست *dost*, words which the dictionaries confound with one another.

[630] Literally, "From so much coming and going heat has ascended into my brain."

the crowd had dispersed,[631] she rose and went into a private apartment, and sent for me. When I went there, she gave me an order to sit down; I bowed and took my seat. She said, 'Since thou hast come hither, and brought these articles, what profit dost thou wish thereupon?' I stated that I had had a strong desire to behold her royal feet, which God had granted; and, with regard to the prices which were written in the invoice, half was the cost price and half profit. She said, 'Nay! the price which thou hast written shall be given to thee, and more besides shall be given as a present, on condition that one thing can be done by thee that I will command thee.'

"I said, 'I shall consider it my good fortune if your slave's life and property can be of any service to Your Majesty, and I will gladly [*lit.* 'with my eyes'] do it.' When she heard this, she sent for a writing-case, wrote a note,[632] and having placed it in a bag[633] ornamented with pearls, and having wrapped over it a handkerchief of the finest muslin,[634] gave it into my charge, and, having taken off from her finger a signet, gave it me, for a token, and said, 'In that direction is a large garden. The name of it is Dil-kushā [*i.e.* 'heart-expanding'], do thou go there, and be pleased to put into the hand of a person named Kaikhusrau,[635] who is the superintendent, this signet, and give him my blessing, and ask for an answer to this letter, but come back quickly; if you eat your dinner there, drink water here.[636]

---

631 The meaning given by Forbes for پرچھا *parchhā* will not apply here.

632 شقه *shuḳḳah* is a letter from a superior, خط *khaṭṭ* one from an equal, عرضي *ărẓī* one from an inferior.

633 The word دلمیان *dulmiyān* occurs in Forbes' vocabulary out of its alphabetical order. The sense of "bag for a "letter" or letter-cover" has been omitted in the dictionaries.

634 Literally, "night-dew," a very poetical expression.

635 This is also the name of the third king of the Kaianian, or second dynasty of Persia. Rustam was one of his generals, and his war with Afrāsyāb, King of Turkestān, is celebrated in the "Shāh-Nāmah."

636 A proverbial expression, the sense of which is, that he was to consider haste so necessary that every delay was to be avoided, and even the most urgent affair, such as drinking water after his food, was to be postponed till he came back; or, his stay was to be so short that he might seem to eat there and drink here.

I will give thee such a reward for this service that thou shalt see!' I took leave, and went on inquiring my way. After going nearly two *kos*, that garden appeared in sight. When I had reached it, a person fully armed took me and conducted me in by the garden gate. I beheld there a young man of lion-like form, seated with much dignity on a chair of gold, wearing a coat of mail such as those made by Dāūd,[637] and a cuirass, and back and side-pieces,[638] and a helmet of steel on his head, and five hundred eager[639] young warriors, holding shields and swords in their hands, and girt with quiver and bow, stood ready, formed in line.[640]

"I saluted him; he called me to him. I gave him that signet, and, with flattering words, showed him that handkerchief, and told him the circumstances of my bringing the note. He, immediately on hearing it, bit[641] his finger with his teeth, and, smiting his head, said, 'Perhaps thy appointed doom has brought thee here. Well! enter the garden; in a cypress-tree an iron cage is suspended, in which a young man is confined. Give him this letter, and come back quickly with his answer.' I pushed on hastily into the garden; a garden of what beauty! it was, as you might say, entering in this life into Paradise. Each parterre blushed with a different colour, and fountains continued springing up, while the birds kept up a constant warbling.[642] I went straight on, and saw that cage in the tree, in which a handsome young man was visible. I approached, bowing my

---

637 I am not aware that the Muḥammadans have any tradition as to the sort of armour that David wore. I therefore suppose that Dāūd, or, *Anglicè*, David, was some famous smith, who manufactured superior armour.

638 This expression has occurred before, *vide* note 466. The چار آئینه *chār āīnah*, or "four mirrors," are (1) the cuirass in front; (2) (3) the side-pieces under the arms; (4) the back-piece; all of burnished steel.

639 An idiomatic sense of تیار *taiyār*, which has been lost on the lexicographers.

640 This obvious sense of پرا *parā*, is not to be found in the dictionaries.

641 *Vide* note 140.

642 I have taken a liberty in translating چہچہا *chahchahā* "warbling," as the birds in India can hardly be said to warble; and the word is, no doubt, one formed by imitation, and approaches more closely to our "chirp."

head respectfully, and saluted him, and gave him, through the bars of the cage, that letter, sealed up. That dear person opened the letter, and began to read, and to inquire of me with eagerness after the welfare of the Princess.

"The conversation was yet unfinished when a host of negroes appeared, and came and fell upon me on all sides, and smote me unsparingly with their spears and swords. What strength has a single unarmed man [to resist]? In a moment they mangled me with wounds, and I had no consciousness left. When I recovered my senses, I found myself on a bedstead which two men on foot were taking along, and talking to one another [as they went]. One said, 'Fling down the carcase of this dead fellow in the plain; the dogs and the crows will eat him.' The other said, 'If the King causes inquiry to be made, and this information reaches him, then he will have us buried alive, and our families crushed to death in an oil-press. What! are we sick of our lives, that we should act so unreasonably?'

"I, hearing this dialogue, said to the two Gog and Magog,[643] 'For God's sake have pity on me; I have still a little life left in me; when I am dead do with me what you will. The dead is in the hands of the living;[644] but at least tell me this, what has befallen me? why did they smite me? and who are you? Come now, tell me thus much at least?' They then took pity on me, and said, 'That young man who is confined in the cage is the nephew of the King, and his father formerly sate on the throne. When his father died, he left this bequest to his brother, that as his son, who was the heir of the empire, was still a lad, and his mind was not yet matured, he [the brother] was to carry on the government with loyalty and vigilance, and when the Prince came of age, he was to marry him to his daughter, and make him master of all the realm and treasure. With these words he expired, and the succession to the empire devolved on his younger brother. He did not act in accordance

---

643 ياجوج *Yājūj* and ماجوج *Mājūj* are the eastern Tartars, who, according to Muḥammadans, are to do great things in the history of the world hereafter. Here the expression means any savage truculent fellow.

644 A proverb in pure Persian. The sense is obvious.

with the will, but on the contrary, giving out that the Prince was deranged and insane, thrust him into a cage, and placed a strong guard on all sides of the garden, so that a bird could not fly there, and has several times given him deadly poison, but life is too strong in him, and the poison has no effect. Now these two, the Princess and this Prince, have become lover and mistress. She suffers the disquietude of love in her palace, and he in his cage. She sent by thy hand a love-letter, full intelligence of which the spies carried to the King. He despatched a body of negroes, who brought you to the state you are in, and he asked counsel of his vazīr as to the means of slaying the imprisoned youth. That traitor has persuaded the Princess[645] to slay with her own hand that innocent person in presence of the King.'

"I said, 'Come on! before expiring, let me see this sight at least.' At length, being persuaded, those two and I, wounded as I was, went silently and stood in a corner. I saw then that the King was seated on his throne, and a naked sword was in the hand of the Princess, and that they had taken the Prince out of the cage, and had placed him before [the King]. The Princess, assuming the character of executioner, and holding a naked sword, advanced to slay her lover. When she came near him, she threw away the sword, and clung to his neck. Then her lover said, 'I am content to die thus. I both wish for thee here, and shall continue to long for thee there.' The Princess said, 'It was by this pretext that I came to see thee.' The King, beholding this action, was much incensed, and threatened the vazīr, saying, 'Hast thou brought me to shew me this spectacle?' The eunuchs separated the Princess, and took her into the palace, and the vazīr, being enraged, raised his sword and ran upon the Prince, in order that by one stroke he might

[645] This part of the plot is most ridiculous and unnatural, and Mīr Amman seems to have done his best to make it more confused by interchanging the words ملکه *malikah* and شہزادي *shahzādī*, the former of which properly means "queen-consort," or "queen," and the latter "princess." In this sentence, if we translated literally, we should have, "The traitor persuaded the queen that the princess should slay the innocent prince." The شہزادي *shahzādī* ought to be omitted.

finish that helpless one. When he was about to smite with his sabre, an arrow from an unseen hand entered his forehead, so that his head[646] was split in two, and he fell down.

"The King, beholding this circumstance, hastily entered his palace. The young Prince was quickly confined in his cage, and taken back to the garden; and I too departed thence. On my way, a person called me and took me into the presence of the Princess, who, seeing that I was wounded, summoned a surgeon, and, with the strictest injunctions, said, 'Restore this young man to health quickly, and cause him to take the bath of convalescence;[647] this is thy task;[648] in proportion to the pains thou takest with this person shall be the reward and promotion thou shalt receive.' In short, the surgeon, in accordance with the command of the Princess, by excessive [*lit.* "making running and running"] attention, in the space of forty days, caused me to bathe and wash, and led me into the presence. The Princess asked, 'Pray, have you now no suffering?' I said, 'By the kindness of your royal self I am now strong and vigorous.' Then the Princess bestowed on me a robe of honour and a large sum of money, which she had promised, nay, twice as much as that, and gave me leave to depart.

"I collected all my companions and servants, and set out from thence. When I arrived at this place, I said to them all, 'Do you go to your own country,' and I having made, on this mountain, this place, and this image of her, have fixed my abode here, and, after giving money to my servants and slaves, according to their respective merits, have set them at liberty, and told them that as long as I survive it is incumbent on them to provide for my subsistence; after that, they are free to do as they like. Now, these same persons faithfully provide me with

---

[646] One would have expected هو گيئي *ho gaiī*, to agree with پيشاني *peshānī*. As it is, we must understand سر *sir*, "head."

[647] The same expression has occurred before, *vide* p. 31, l. 6. While on a sick bed the customary ablutions must, of course, be suspended. The first bath, therefore, marks the perfect recovery of the Muḥammadan.

[648] مجرا *mujrā* is the Latin *officium* here.

food, and I, at my ease, worship this image, and, as long as I live, this will be my employment. This is my history, which thou hast heard." O faḳīrs! after hearing this story, I forthwith put on my neck the faḳīr's [649] garb, and assumed the wandering ascetic's dress, and set off in the desire of seeing the country of Europe. In the space of some time, wandering on through forests and mountains, my appearance became like that of Majnūn [650] and Farhād.[651]

At length my longing carried me to that city, in the streets and alleys of which I began to wander about like one demented. For the most part I stopped in the vicinity of the palace of the Princess, but I found no means of access there. Marvellous was my dismay, that the object for which I had endured such labour was not attained. One day I was standing in the bāzār, when all at once the people began to fly, and the shopkeepers, closing their shops, went away. Just before [652] there had been this display, and now all was deserted. In one direction appeared a youth resembling Rustam [653] in his head and the lower part of his face, roaring like a lion, and flourishing a two-handed sword, wearing ring and plate armour on his body [*lit.* "on his neck"], and a helmet, with a fringe of mail to guard the neck,[654] on his head, and a pair of pistols in his girdle, and muttering to himself like one inebriate; and behind him came two slaves dressed in garments of cloth, and carrying on their heads a bier covered with velvet of Kāshān.[655]

---

[649] The same expression has occurred at p. 21, l. 18. كفن *kafan* signifies "a shroud," whence كفني *kafnī*, a white garment like a shroud worn by faḳīrs, emblematic of their being dead to the world, and also their actual shroud when they perish alone in their wanderings.

[650] *Vide* note 141.

[651] *Vide* note 263.

[652] A very idiomatic use of يا *yā*, not explained in the dictionaries. The word thus repeated signifies "at one time," "at another time."

[653] *Vide* note 323.

[654] I have been obliged to translate جهلم *jhilam*, by a periphrasis of nine words. Those who have seen a Sikh or Afghān helmet, will readily comprehend what the *jhilam* is.

[655] Kāshān is a city of Persia in N. lat. 34° 10′; E. long. 51° 15′, famous for its velvets, and also for its scorpions.

When I saw this sight, I determined to go with him. Every person I saw tried to keep me back, but I would not listen to them.[656] Proceeding on, that young warrior arrived at a magnificent edifice. I, too, went with him. He, on turning about, was on the point of giving me a blow and cutting me in two pieces. I adjured him, saying, "I too desire this. I pardon you my blood; by any means release me from the torment of this life, for I am utterly weary of it. I have intentionally cast myself in thy way; do not hesitate." Seeing that I was firmly intent on dying, he felt pity for me, with which feeling God inspired him,[657] and his wrath was cooled. With much courtesy and kindness he asked, "Who art thou? and why art thou become weary of thy life?"

I said, "Be pleased to sit a little that I may tell you. My story is a very long one; and I am a captive in the grasp of love, for which cause I am desperate." When he heard this, he unbelted himself, and having washed his hands and face, ate some breakfast, and prevailed on me to eat. When, after finishing his repast, he had taken his seat, he said, "Speak! what has befallen thee?" I recounted to him all the story of that old man, and of the Princess, and of my going thither. At first, when he heard it, he wept, and said, "How many families has not that ill-fated one rendered desolate! but marry! thy cure is in my hands. It is probable that by means of this sinful person [*i.e.* myself] thou wilt arrive at thy desire; and be not thou anxious, but compose thyself." He commanded the barber to shave me, and cause me to take the warm bath. His slave brought me a suit of clothes, in which he dressed me. Then he began to say to me, "This bier which thou hast seen is the coffin of that very Prince, now deceased,[658] who was confined in the cage. Another vazīr slew him by a stratagem.

---

656 Literally, "When was I listening?"

657 An ungrammatical sentence. Here دیکھکر *dekhkar* ought to agree with خدا *khudā*, which is the nominative to the verb, for we cannot say in Urdū, any more than in our own language, "He having seen, God inspired him."

658 The Muḥammadans, by a charming euphonism, call a defunct person مرحوم *marḥūm* or مغفور *maghfūr*, "one on whom God has had pity—whom God has pardoned."

He indeed has obtained deliverance, since, after suffering cruel oppression, he has been put to death. I am his foster-brother, and I slew the vazīr with a blow of my sword, and resolved to slay the King, but he supplicated for his life, and began to protest with oaths that he was innocent. I, looking on him as a coward, released him, and since then this is my practice, that at the new moon of each month on Thursday, I go through the city carrying the bier in this same manner, and mourn for him."

On hearing from his tongue this account, I felt comforted, and said to myself, "If he is willing, my wish will come to pass. God has done me a great kindness in making such a furious person kind to me. It is true if God is kind, then every one is kind." When the evening came and the sun had set, that young man brought forth the bier, and set it on my head instead of that of one of the slaves, and taking me with him, went on. He then began to say to me, "I am going to the Princess; I will speak in recommendation of thee to the utmost of my power; do not thou utter a word; sit silent and listen." I said, "I will do exactly as Your Highness says; God keep you well, for that you take pity on my condition." The young man then set out for the royal garden. When he got inside, there was an octagonal platform of marble in the grass-plot[659] of the garden, and on it was a canopy of white tissue with a fringe of pearls supported on pillars of diamond, and there a cushion of rich brocade was placed, beside which were large pillows and pillows for the arm. He caused the bier to be placed there, and told us two[660] to go and sit under a tree.

After a short time, the gleam of torches appeared, and the Princess herself, with several female attendants guarding her in front and in rear, came forward, but dejection and displeasure were visible in her countenance; she approached and took her seat on the cushion. This foster-brother of the Prince stood before her, with his hands respectfully folded, and he then seated himself humbly at a distance on the edge of the carpet.

---

659 صحن *ṣaḥn*, I think, may be translated thus here. It also means "open space," "area," which also makes good sense in this passage.

660 The faḳīr and the other slave.

They read the prayer for the dead, and then began to converse. I continued listening with attentive ears. At length the youth said, "Queen of the world, health! the Prince of the realm of Persia, having heard, without seeing you, the good and amiable qualities you possess, has given his sovereignty to the winds, and becoming a faḳīr, and reducing himself to wretchedness like Ibrāhīm Adham,[661] and enduring much hardship, has come hither;

Lord! for thy sake I left the town of Balkh;[662]

and for many days has wandered about this city, distressed and afflicted. At length, having determined to die, he followed me close. I menaced him with my sword, but he stretched forth his neck, and adjured me with an oath not to delay, as he himself desired nothing else. In short, he is firmly attached to you. I have tried him well, and found him in all respects perfect. I have, therefore, introduced the mention of him. If Your Highness, regarding him as a traveller, will condescend [to inquire into] his circumstances, it will not be inconsistent with the fear of God and the recognition of what is right."

When the Princess heard this discourse, she said, "Where is he? If he is a prince, then, of course, let him come into my presence." The foster-brother arose up thence, and came and took me with him. I was excessively delighted at seeing the Princess, but my reason and senses were given to the winds; I was reduced to silence and had no courage to say anything. In a moment the Princess departed, and the foster-brother returned to his own abode. When he reached home he said, "I have related to the Princess all the facts concerning thee, from beginning to end; and I have also spoken in thy favour; now,

---

[661] A King of Khurāsān, who abandoned his capital Balkh, and became a faḳīr.

[662] سائں Sāīn is the Sindhī form of صاحب Ṣāḥib, "Sir!" "Lord!" This is what Ibrāhīm Adham is supposed to have said, addressing himself to God. Forbes has omitted the word کارن kāran, "a cause," which, with ي ī, "emphatic," signifies "for the very cause." Balkh is the capital of Bukharia, and lies in E. long. 65° 20′; and N. lat. 37°. It is the ancient Bactra, and was founded by Kaiumarz, the first King of Persia. It is inhabited by the Uzbak Tartars.

do thou go every night, without fail, and enjoy delights and pleasure." I fell at his feet, and he embraced me. I remained all day counting the hours, saying, "When will it be evening, that I may go?" When it was night, I took leave of that young man, and went my way, and, having gone into the garden close to the palace of the Princess, I seated myself there, leaning on a pillow on the terrace.

After a short interval the Princess, alone, with but one attendant, came forward slowly, and sate down on a cushion. My good fortune obtained for me this day. I kissed her feet. She raised my head, embraced me, and said, "Look on this opportunity as precious, and observe what I say. Conduct me hence, and go to some other country." I said, "Let us go." With these words we both of us issued from the garden; but from confusion and joy, our hands and feet swelled,[663] and we missed our way, and were going on in one direction, but did not find any place to rest in. The Princess was chagrined, and said, "Where is thy abode? Go on quickly and reach it, else what wouldest thou do? my feet are blistered; I will sit down in the road somewhere."

I said, "The house of my slave is near, we shall be there directly; be of good cheer and step out." I spoke, indeed, an untruth; but I was perplexed at heart where to conduct her. In the midst of the road appeared a door fastened with a padlock. We quickly broke the padlock and entered the house. It was a good house, with carpets spread, and bottles filled with wine, ranged in order in the recesses, and, in the kitchen, bread and roast meat were ready. We were completely exhausted, and took, each of us, a bottle of Portuguese wine along with that relish,[664] and we passed the whole night together in pleasure. When, after that repose, the morning dawned, a com-

---

[663] A proverbial expression to denote rapture is to say, "that one swells so as not to be contained in one's clothes," as we say of a person that "he could not contain himself." All that is meant here is, that they were too overcome with joy to be capable of exertion.

[664] گزک *gazak* is here our "snack," a slight repast, or as we say "a relish." It generally means something highly peppered, a "devil."

motion arose in the city that "the Princess was lost." From quarter to quarter and street to street a proclamation went round, and procuresses[665] and spies were let loose to recover her, wherever they could lay hands on her, and to all the gates of the city patrols of the royal guards[666] came and took post there. Those in charge of the gates received command that not even an ant should find egress from the city without a pass; and that whoever brought information of the Princess should receive a thousand pieces of gold and a dress of honour, as a present. Through the whole city procuresses began to be on the alert, and to enter every house.

As my ill-fortune would have it, I had not shut the door. An old woman, the maternal aunt of Satan (may God blacken her countenance!),[667] with a rosary dangling from her hand, and wrapped in a mantle, finding the door open, entered boldly, and standing in front of the Princess, lifted up her hands, and began to utter a benediction, saying, "May God keep safely the nose-ring and bracelets of thy good fortune![668] and may the turban of him who supports thee continue unremoved [by death]! I am a poor widow beggar-woman, and have one daughter, who, her days being fulfilled, is dying, in parturition, of the pangs of childbirth; and I have not sufficient means to get half a damrī's worth of oil to burn in a lamp; food and drink are out of the question. If she dies, whence shall I procure burial or a shroud for her? and if she brings forth, what shall I give to the nurse and the midwife? and whence shall I

---

[665] The كتني *kuṭnī*, or "procuress," is not quite so infamous as with us, seeing that her services are commanded even by the votaries of Hymen, who invariably employ an old woman, first as an avant-courier, and then as a go-between.

[666] The noble name of "the Guards" must, alas! be rendered into Persian by the word "slaves." Thus غلام نادر *ghulām-i Nādir* (literally, "slave of Nādir") signifies one of the body-guard of Nādir the Great.

[667] Here is an insipid attempt at punning on the words خالا *khālā*, "a maternal aunt," and كالا *kālā*, "black."

[668] The nose-ring and bracelets are the mark of a married woman, and are laid aside on the death of a husband. This benediction therefore implies, "May God preserve thee from widowhood!"

give the lying-in woman sathwārā[669] or caudle[670] to drink? Two days have passed, to-day, since she has been lying hungry and thirsty. O lady! give me of your bounty[671] a morsel that I may have the means of giving her water to drink."

The Princess, taking pity on her, called her near, and gave her four loaves and some meat, and a ring, which she took off from her little finger, and said, "Sell this, and make and give to her ornaments, and pass thy life in peace, and sometimes visit us; the house is thine." She had exactly obtained the wish of her heart, in search of which she had come. Uttering benedictions and expressing her devotion, she joyfully made off. The bread and meat she threw away on the threshold, but the ring she took in her clenched hand, saying, "A token from the hand of the Princess has fallen into my possession." Since, however, it was God's pleasure to save us from that calamity, the owner of that mansion, a young warrior, mounted on an Arabian steed, arrived, holding a spear in his hand, and carrying suspended from the cord for tying game, a stag. He found the lock of his house broken, and the door open, and saw the procuress as she issued forth. In anger he seized her back hair with one hand, and took her off her legs, and entered the house. He then tied a cord to her two legs, and suspended her from the branch of a tree, putting her head downwards and her feet up, in which position, after a short convulsion, she expired. On beholding the form of that man, such a terror overpowered me that my colour changed and my heart began to quake with

---

669 ستهوارا *sathwārā*, or, as it is written in the Ḳānūn-i Islām, ستواڑا *satwāṛā*, or ستهوڑا *sathwaṛā*, is made of wheat flour, dried ginger, soft sugar, and clarified butter, mixed together over a fire. It is given especially to puerperal women. *Vide* Ḳānūn-i Islām, Glossary, p. xcviii.

670 اچهوانی *achhwānī*, or اجواینی *ajwāenī*, is made of the following ingredients:—black pepper, long pepper and the root of pepper, turmeric, dry ginger, garlic, greater galangal, bāī-barrang (a kind of medicinal seed), cloves, attivassa (a kind of medicinal root), black henbane, viscid cleome, of each of these an equal weight, and a weight of bishop's-weed seed equal to the weight of all the above put together. These, reduced to a fine powder and mixed with warm water, are given to puerperal women. *Vide* Ḳānūn-i Islām, Glossary, p. lx.

671 This obvious sense of خیر *khair* is not given in Forbes' vocabulary.

dread. That dear person, seeing us both alarmed, encouraged us, saying, "You have acted very imprudently to do what you have done, and leave the door open!"

The Princess smiled, and said, "The Prince told me it was the house of his slave, and brought me and persuaded me." He answered respectfully, "The Prince has spoken truly; all mankind are the slaves and handmaids of kings. It is by their blessing and generosity that all are provided for and supported. I am your purchased slave, though no money has been given[672] for me. But reason requires that a secret should be concealed. O Prince! the coming of yourself and of the Princess to this poor house is to me happiness in this world and the next, and you have bestowed honour on your devoted servant. I am ready to sacrifice myself for you. I will not in any way withhold my life or property; do you repose yourself at your ease; there is now not the slightest particle of danger; if this carrion procuress had escaped alive, she would have brought calamity upon us. Now be pleased to rest as long as your illustrious mind wills, and inform this your servant of whatever you may require; he will bring everything,—and what is a king! not even an angel shall get intelligence of you." That brave man uttered such encouraging words that we, to a slight extent, recovered our tranquillity. I then said, "Bravo! you are a noble fellow. We too, when we have it in our power, will requite you for this courtesy; what is your name?" He replied, "The name of your slave is Bihzād Khān." In short, for six months he performed with heart and soul all the service we required, and our life passed in complete repose.

One day I called to mind my own country and my parents, wherefore I sate very pensive. Seeing my countenance sad, Bihzād Khān joined his hands and stood before me, and began to say, "If any fault has been committed by this devoted servant

[672] Literally, "neither دام *dām* nor درهم *dirham* have been given." The former is the twenty-fifth part of a small copper coin called a pice. The latter is about the one-fifth of a penny. It is this expression which figures in the Sindh papers, printed by order of Parliament, as "a dam and a drain"!! So much for authorized translations! *Vide* "Dry Leaves from Young Egypt," p. 254, note ‡.

in the discharge of his duties, be pleased to signify it." I said, "For God's sake, what discourse is this? You have so behaved to us that we have remained in this city as one remains in his mother's womb; otherwise we had done such a deed that every straw was our foe. Who was such a friend to us that we could obtain [through his means] a little rest? May God keep you happy! you are a noble man." He then said, "If your heart is estranged from this place, then I will convey you in safety whithersoever you command." I said, "If I could arrive at my own country, I should see my parents; my position indeed has become such as it is, but God knows what theirs may have become. The desired object for which I expatriated myself has indeed been accomplished. Now it is incumbent on me to kiss their feet also. They have no intelligence of me whether I be dead or alive; what anxiety they will be suffering in their hearts!" That gallant man said, "Excellently well! let us go." With these words he brought a Turkish horse which could travel two hundred miles [without a halt], and a swift but gentle mare, whose wings had not been clipped [*i.e.* very speedy], for the Princess, and caused us both to mount. Then, putting on his ring and plate armour, and girding himself with his weapons, being fully accoutred, he mounted his own steed, and said, "Your slave will precede you; do Your Highnesses follow at your ease, keeping in your horses."

When he reached the gate of the city, he uttered a yell, and broke the lock with his axe, and shouted menacingly to the warders, "Villains! go and tell your lord that Bihzād Khān with open defiance [*lit.* "shouting and brawling"] is carrying off the Princess Mihrnigār[673] and the Prince Kāmgār,[673] who is his son-in-law; if he has the least feeling of courage,[674] then let him come out and take away the Princess. Let him not say that I carried her off by stealth; but if he will not do this, let

[673] مہرنگار *Mihrnigār* may be translated "idol of love;" and کامگار *Kāmgār*, "fortunate."

[674] The meaning given to نشه *nashah*, in Forbes' vocabulary, "intoxication," is altogether inapplicable here. It means "perception in a very slight degree," "*soupçon*."

him repose himself seated in his castle." This intelligence quickly reached the King. The vazīr and the commander of the forces received command to bind the three wicked rebels and bring them, or to cut off their heads and send them to the royal presence. In a short time a dense[675] host made its appearance, and the whole earth and sky was enveloped in dust. Bihzād Khān caused the Princess and me the faḳīr to stand in the arch of a bridge which had twelve arches, and was like the bridge of Jaunpūr;[676] and he himself, encouraging his horse, turned towards that army, and, roaring like a lion, urged his steed at the gallop among the ranks. The whole army was dissipated like the green scum that floats on water,[677] and he, reaching the two commanders, cut off their heads. When the generals were slain, their troops dispersed, according to the proverb, "The guidance of a thing depends on the head; when the pod is burst, the seeds are scattered." Thereupon the King himself, attended by some cuirassiers, came to the rescue, and that incomparable youth, having broken their array, also gave them a complete defeat. The King retreated. It is true that victory is the gift of God, but Bihzād Khān displayed such prowess as would perhaps have exceeded even Rustam's power. When Bihzād Khān saw that the field was clear, and that none remained to pursue us, he came, free from doubt, and with mind at ease, where we stood, and went on, taking the Princess and me with him. The interval of a journey soon passes; in a short space of time we arrived in the confines of my own country. I wrote and despatched a letter announcing my return in perfect health and safety to the presence of the King who was my

---

675 I believe the word غٹ *ghaṭ* to be a corruption of the Sanskrit word घट *ghaṭ*, "a crowd."

676 Jaunpūr is a town in the province of Allahābād, on the banks of the Gumtī river. It lies in N. lat. 25° 45′, and E. long. 82° 39′. It is said to have been built by Sulṭān Fīrūz of Dihlī, who named it after his cousin Faḳīru'd-dīn Jawna. It has a bridge of considerable extent divided into two parts, one of which consists of ten arches and spans the channel of the river during the dry season, but is so much submerged during the rains that the troops under Sir R. Barker in 1773 sailed over it. It was built during the reign of Akbar by the governor of the province, Munawwar Khān.

677 These six words express the meaning of کاي *kāī*.

father. The Asylum of the world, when he read it, rejoiced. He performed a double thanksgiving, and, as when water has fallen in the dried rice-crop,[678] he revived, and taking all his nobles in his train, he came to meet this weak person, and halted on the margin of the river, and gave an order to the admiral to provide vessels. I, from the other side, saw the cavalcade of the King standing there, and in the desire of kissing his feet I made my horse plunge into the stream, and arrived, by swimming, in the royal presence. My father affectionately embraced me.

Now another sudden calamity occurred, for perhaps the horse on which I rode was the colt of that very mare which carried the Princess, or, by reason of its homogeneousness, the mare, too, when it saw my horse, with a rapid movement, threw itself, along with the Princess, into the river after me, and began to swim. The Princess, losing her presence of mind, pulled the reins, and, as the mare had a tender mouth, she turned over. The Princess, after several submersions, sank, together with the mare, in the stream; nor did we see any further trace of them. Bihzād Khān, seeing this state of things, threw himself, with his horse, into the stream, to assist the Princess; and he too was caught in the same eddy, and was unable to extricate himself; he struggled much with hand and foot, but could do nothing, and he too sank. The Asylum of the world, beholding these occurrences, sent for a great net, and caused it to be cast in, and commanded the mariners[679] and divers [to search for the bodies]. They dragged the whole river, and brought up, from time to time, the dirt from the bottom; but those two [Bihzād Khān and the Princess] were not recovered. O faḳīrs! such was the effect of this occurrence

---

678 The word دهان *dhān* or دهان *dahān* is capable of two renderings. The one given above is doubtless correct, but it might also, if a dissyllable, signify "mouth," which would also make good sense, and this ambiguity is a beauty with Oriental writers.

679 The word ملاح *mallāḥ*, "a waterman," "a sailor," has been omitted in Forbes' vocabulary.

upon me that I became melancholy and insane, and assuming the habit of a faḳīr, went about saying,—

"One fate has waited on all three:
That you have seen, now this too, see!"

Had the Princess been lost anywhere, or had she died, then my heart could have found some comfort. I should then have issued forth in search of her, or had recourse to patience; but, when she sank before our eyes, I lost all power.[680] At length the idea entered my mind that I would drown myself in the river; perhaps in death (thought I) I shall find my beloved one.

One day, at night, I entered that same stream, and, having resolved to drown myself, I advanced into the water up to my neck. I was about to step on and submerge myself, when that same veiled horseman, who gave you good tidings, arrived. He seized my hand and encouraged me, saying, "Be of good cheer! the Princess and Bihzād Khān are alive. Why dost thou uselessly throw away thy life? Such is the course of this world; despair not in the court of God. If thou survivest, thou wilt, some day or other, meet with those two. Go now towards Rūm. Two other heart-sore darweshes have already gone there; when thou meetest them, thou too wilt attain thy desire." O faḳīrs! in accordance with the command of my spiritual guide, I, too, have come and am present in your illustrious service. I have a strong hope that each will gain his wish. These are the adventures of this mendicant, which he has entirely and fully related.

---

680 A very foolish sentence, which it would be waste of time to endeavour to render lucid.

TRAVELS OF THE FOURTH DARWESH.

THE fourth faḳīr began, with tears, to relate the story of his wanderings in the following manner :—

> To the sad tale of wretched me, give ear!
> Attend a little and my story hear!
> Wherefore I came thus far in pain and woe
> I'll fully tell—hear, and the reason know!

O divine preceptors! be attentive a little. This faḳīr who is overtaken in this [calamitous] state, is the son of the King of China. I was reared in luxury and indulgence, and was well instructed. I was wholly unacquainted with the good and evil of the world, and thought it would always continue thus. In the midst of my tranquillity this event occurred—the King, who was the father of this orphan, died. In the agonies of death he called his younger brother (who was my uncle), and said, "I truly leave all my wealth and dominion and depart, but do you perform this my will, and act with magnanimity. As long as the Prince, who is the rightful occupant of this throne and canopy, is young, and has yet to acquire discernment and the ability to manage his own house, do you discharge the duties of viceroy, and suffer not the soldiers or the people to be oppressed. When he has come to years of discretion, make over the throne to him with full explanation of everything, and Roshan Akhtar,[681] who is your daughter, to her espouse the Prince, and withdraw yourself from the government. By this procedure the imperial sway will continue firm in my family, and no interruption will occur." With these words he indeed rendered up his spirit to God; his younger brother became

[681] روشن اختر *Roshan akhtar*, that is, "Bright star."

king, and began to administer the empire. He ordered me to continue in the female apartments, and not to come forth thence till I grew up to be a young man. Till the age of fourteen I was reared among the ladies of the royal family and their attendants, and continued to play and divert myself. Hearing the news of my intended marriage with the daughter of my father's younger brother, I was glad, and in this hope remained free from care, and said in my heart, "Now, after a short time, the kingdom too will pass into my hands, and my marriage also will take place." The world is supported by hope. There was an Abyssinian named Mubārak, who had been brought up in the service of my deceased father, and in whom much confidence was placed, and who was a man of quick parts, and faithful: to him I often went, and seated myself by him. He too was shewing much kindness to me, and, when he surveyed my youth, rejoiced, and said, "Praise be to God! O Prince! you have now become a young man; if it please God Most High, your paternal uncle will shortly carry into effect the injunctions of the shadow of the Most High [that is, "the late king"]. He will give you his daughter and the throne of your father."

One day it happened that one of the inferior female attendants had given me such a slap, though I had committed no offence, that the mark of her five fingers rose up on my face. I went sobbing to Mubārak. He embraced me, and wiped away my tears with his sleeve, and said, "Come! I will to-day take you to the King. Perhaps when he sees you he will be kind, and regarding you as capable of receiving your rights, will hand them over to you." He immediately took me into the presence of my uncle, who shewed me much kindness in the open court, and asked, "Why are you sad? and why have you come hither?" Mubārak said, "He has come to make a petition." When he heard that, he said of his own accord, "I will now celebrate the marriage of the young prince." Mubārak said, "It is very auspicious." [The King] immediately summoned before him the astrologers and soothsayers, and asked them, with feigned sincerity, "In this year, which month and which day and hour and part of an hour is auspicious in order for me to make preparations for the marriage?" They, perceiving what his real wishes were, after calculations, said, "Point to which the world turns in prayer! this entire year is unlucky: no day in any month can be fixed on as fortunate. If this whole year passes away prosperously, the next year will be better for the happy ceremony." The King looked towards Mubārak, and said, "Conduct the Prince into the seraglio. If God wills, after this year has passed, I will deliver over that which I hold in charge for him, let him keep up his spirits and employ himself in reading and writing." Mubārak made obeisance, and took me with him and conveyed me to the seraglio. After two or three days I went to Mubārak, who, as soon as he saw me, began to weep. I was amazed, and asked him, saying, "Papa! art thou well? what is the cause of thy weeping?" Then that faithful friend (who loved me with heart and soul) said, "Would that I had known this on the day when I took you to that tyrant, then I would not have taken you." I said, in consternation, "What such great impropriety was there in my going? do just[682] tell me." He then said, "All the nobles and vazīrs and pillars of the state, both small and great, of your father's time, were pleased when they saw you, and began to return thanks to God, saying, 'Our young master has now become a man and fit to reign. Now, after some days, the rightful heir will have his rights, and he will then appreciate our merits, and understand the worth of his hereditary servants.' This intelligence reached that faithless one; the serpent began to move in his bosom. He called me apart, and said, 'O Mubārak! now act so as to slay the Prince by some stratagem or other, and relieve my mind of danger from him, in order that I may be at peace.' From that time I have been distracted with the knowledge that thy uncle is thy deadly foe." As soon as I heard this inauspicious[683] news from Mubārak, I died without a blow, and in deadly terror fell down at his feet, saying, "For God's sake! I relinquish the throne; let my life in any way be saved." That faithful servant

---

682 صحیح *ṣaḥīḥ* signifies "exact," "perfect," but it is here used in a very idiomatic way, which may perhaps be rendered by our "just," as above.

683 There is here an insipid pun on the name Mubārak, which cannot be preserved in the English.

raised my head and clasped me to his breast, and replied, "There is no danger; I have thought of a plan; if it succeed, then never mind; when life remains, all is safe. It[684] is probable that by this contrivance both thy life will be preserved and thy wishes attained."

After giving me this encouragement, he took me with him, and went to the place where the deceased king, that is to say, my father, used to sleep and sit, and said much to console me. A seat was placed there. He directed me to take hold of the chair on one side, and laying hold of it himself on the other, he moved it away, and lifted up the carpet which was under the seat,[685] and began to excavate the ground. All at once a window appeared, which was fastened with a padlock and a chain. He called me. I felt sure in my heart that he had dug this hole in order to slay me and bury me in it. Death hovered before my eyes, but, having no alternative, I approached him, repeating inaudibly the creed.[686] I beheld then that within that casement was a building and four rooms. In each apartment were ten golden jars[687] suspended by chains to which they were fastened. And on the mouth of each jar was a brick of gold, and a monkey made of jewels sitting on it. I counted thirty-nine jars in the four rooms, and I observed one jar which was filled to the brim with gold coins, but on which was neither monkey nor brick, and I saw a reservoir filled brimful with jewels. I asked Mubārak, saying, "O papa! what talisman is this? and whose place is it? and of what use are these?" He said, "These monkeys which you behold, their story is this, that your father from his

---

684 There ought not to be the new paragraph here which appears in Forbes' edition, as to begin one in the middle of a short speech is obviously absurd. The paragraph should begin at یہہ بهروسا دیکر *yih bharosā dekar*.

685 Either كرسي *kursī* and صندلي *ṣandalī* are different things,—differing not simply as genus and species, which difference is acknowledged on all hands,—or Mīr Amman has very foolishly created an ambiguity by introducing both into one sentence.

686 *Vide* note 453.

687 Or it may be, "ten jars suspended by chains of gold." The collocation renders the sense doubtful.

youth had formed a friendship and intimacy with Malik Ṣādiḳ, who is the king of the genii.

"Accordingly once in every year he used to take several kinds of curiosities, perfumes, and rarities such as this country produces, and used to stay with him for nearly a month. When he took leave, Malik Ṣādiḳ used to give him a monkey of emerald, which our king brought and deposited in this subterraneous chamber. No one but myself was acquainted with this matter. One day this slave made representation as follows, 'Asylum of the world! you are taking these costly things worth hundreds of thousands of rupees, and bring back thence for yourself a lifeless monkey of stone; pray what profit will result from this?' He smiled, and replied to these words of mine as follows: 'Take care! do not reveal this anywhere; caution is absolutely necessary. Each[688] of these lifeless monkeys that thou seest has a thousand powerful Devs subject and obedient to it, but until I have collected forty monkeys complete, all these are useless and of no service.' Well! there was one monkey deficient, and in that same year the King died. All[689] this labour was of no good, the advantage of it was not rendered evident. O Prince! seeing this thy friendless condition, I remembered the circumstance, and determined in my mind to take thee to Malik Ṣādiḳ, and state the tyranny of thy father's brother. It is probable that, calling to mind his friendship for thy father, he will give thee the monkey that is wanting; then by their aid thy realm will come into thy possession, and thou wilt reign at thy ease over China and Māchīn,[690] and at the present moment

---

688 The student will do well to notice, in order to avoid, the style of expression used here. یہہ ایک ایک میمون *yih ek ek maimūn* is a nominative without a verb, and were it a genitive, as it ought to be, هر ایک *har ek*, which follows, would not be required.

689 The paragraph is very absurdly closed at وفات پائي *wafāt pāī*. It ought to end eight lines further on, at نظر نہیں آتي *naẓar nahīn ātī*, and the next should commence with میں نے اُس کي زباني *main ne us kī zabānī*, or else where it is here made to commence.

690 The common Persian term for China is "Chīn and Māchīn." Which part is called ماچین *māchīn*, महाचीन *mahāchīna*, "Great China," does not appear. In Richardson's Persian Dictionary we have ماچین *māchīn* rendered by "The Emperor of China," on what authority I know not.

thy life will be saved by this procedure; and should nought else result, this is the only means of escape from the hands of the tyrant that seems possible." When I had heard all this statement from his lips, I said, "Dear papa! now thou art the disposer of my life; whatever is for my welfare, that do." He then encouraged me, and went himself to the bāzār to purchase extract of rose and frankincense, and whatever he thought proper to take thither.

The next day he went to that miscreant uncle of mine, who was to me in the place of Abū Jahl,[691] and said, "Asylum of the world! I have fixed in my mind a plan for slaying the Prince; if you command, I will state it." The wretch being pleased said, "What plan is that?" Then Mubārak said, "In putting him to death Your Highness would in every way incur dishonour; but I will take him into the jungle, kill him, and after burying him, come away; no one will get the slightest inkling of what has taken place." When he heard this plot from Mubārak, he said, "Most admirable! what I wish is that he should not continue safe, for distrust on his account rankles in my heart; if thou wilt free me from this anxiety, then thou shalt receive, in requital of this service, an ample return. Wherever thy mind wishes, take him, and make away with him, and bring me the glad intelligence of the event."

After Mubārak had taken these steps for his security as regarded the King, he took me with him, and with those presents departed from the city by night, and proceeded in a northerly direction. He journeyed incessantly for a month. One night, as we were travelling on, Mubārak said, "Thanks to God! we have now reached the place we had in view." When I heard this, I said, "Papa! what is this thou hast said?" He said, "What, O Prince! dost thou not see the host of the genii?" I said, "I see no one except thyself." Mubārak took out a box for holding collyrium, and drew through my eyes needles smeared with the collyrium of Sulaimān. Instantly the people of the genii and the tents and canvas inclosures of their host began to ap-

---

691 ابو جہل *Abū Jahl*, that is, "the father of ignorance," was the uncle of Muḥammad, who opposed his mission, and thus procured for himself this soubriquet.

pear; all, however, were pleasant-looking and well-apparelled. Recognizing Mubārak, each in a friendly way embraced him and cracked jokes with him.

At length, proceeding on, we approached the royal pavilions, and entered his court. I saw then that lights were ranged in order, and seats of various kinds were spread in double rows, and on them were seated the wise and the excellent, darweshes and nobles, vazīrs and generals; and the state-messengers and ushers, soldiers and attendants, stood with arms respectfully crossed, and in the midst was spread a throne set with jewels, on which sate, with an air of great dignity, Malik Ṣādiḳ on a cushion propped with pillows, and wearing a crown and a tunic. I went near and saluted him; he kindly ordered me to be seated, after which we occupied ourselves with a repast. After we had finished, the table-cloth was removed, whereupon he turned to Mubārak, and inquired my story. Mubārak said, "In the place of his father his father's younger brother now rules over his empire, and has become his deadly foe; wherefore I have carried him off thence, and having had recourse to flight, have brought him to Your Highness's service, for he is an orphan and the kingdom is his by right. No one, however, can do anything without a protector. With Your Majesty's aid he will be supported. Remember the claims of his father's services, and give him assistance, and bestow on him that fortieth monkey, that the entire forty may be completed, and this prince, having obtained his rights, may offer up prayers for your life and prosperity. Except Your Highness's protection, there appears to be no asylum for him."

When Ṣādiḳ had heard all this narrative, he said, after some reflection, "In truth, I am much indebted for the services and friendship of the late king, and this helpless person, reduced to misery, has left his hereditary kingdom, and has come hither to save his life, and has taken refuge under the skirt of my fortune. As far as I am able I will in no respect fail him, and will not omit to serve him; but I have one thing for him to do, which if he can do and does not act perfidiously, and brings it to a happy termination, and comes out perfect from the trial, I give him my positive promise that I will act with more kindness to him than I shewed to his father, and will give him whatever he wants." I joined my hands, and respectfully stated, "Whatever service can be rendered to Your Majesty by this devoted servant, as far as my ability goes, shall be performed most zealously, and well and faithfully and carefully accomplished, and I shall regard it as my happiness in this life and in that which is to come." He said, "Thou art yet but a boy, wherefore I enjoin thee again and again, take care that thou dost not act perfidiously and fall into calamity." I said, "God will make it easy through the auspicious fortune of the King, and I will exert myself to the utmost of my power, and bring my charge safely and untouched to the royal presence."

When he heard this, Malik Ṣādiḳ called me to him, and took a paper out of his pocket-book, and shewed it to me, and said, "Search out wheresoever you can, and find and bring to me the person of whom this is the portrait, and when thou findest her direction and encounterest her, make known to her on my part the warmest attachment. If this service is accomplished by thee, then thou shalt receive greater attention than thou couldst entertain a hope of; otherwise thou shalt receive according to thy deserts. When I looked on that paper, I saw a picture of such a kind that I began to faint. By a violent effort, owing to the terror I felt, I supported myself, and said, "Very good! I will take my leave. If God wills me success, I shall then act in accordance with the royal orders." With these words I took the way to the jungle, accompanied by Mubārak. I wandered on from village to village, from town to town, from city to city, from country to country, and inquired of every one her name and abode. No one said, "Yes, I know her, or have heard of her from any one." After enduring for seven years distress and perplexity, I arrived in a city of which the buildings were lofty, and which was well populated, but every living person there was repeating the Great Name of God, and performing worship and service to him.

Then I saw a blind Hindūstānī faḳīr begging alms, but no one gave him a kauṛī[692] or a morsel. I was surprised, and felt pity for him, and taking out a gold coin from my pocket, put it

---

[692] The kauṛī is a small shell (*cyprea moneta*) used as money.

into his hand. He took it, and said, "O benefactor! God requite thee well! perhaps thou art a traveller, and not an inhabitant of this city?"[693] I said, "In truth, I have been suffering misery for seven years. I find no trace of that for which I issued forth. To-day I have arrived in this city." The old man, after uttering benedictions, went away. I followed him. Outside the city a stately mansion appeared. He entered it, and I too went in. I saw then that the building had fallen down in various places and had continued unrepaired.

I said in my heart, "This palace is fit for kings. When it was in repair, what a heart-delighting abode it must have been! and now truly, from being deserted, what a state it has fallen into! But I know not why it has been deserted, and why this blind man dwells in this palace." The blind man was going on, feeling his way with his stick, when a voice reached me as if some one was saying, "O father! is all well? why have you returned so early to-day?" When the blind man heard [these words], he replied, "Daughter! God made a young traveller compassionate my state. He[694] gave me a gold coin. For many days I have not eaten a good dinner and filled my stomach well; wherefore I have bought flesh, spices, butter, oil, flour, and salt, and I have also purchased the clothes you required. Now cut them out, sew them, and put them on, and cook the dinner, that, after having eaten and drunk, we may offer up benedictions for that liberal man. Though I know not the desire of his heart, yet God is wise and all-seeing; he will accept the prayer of us destitute." When I heard this account of the privations he had undergone, it involuntarily occurred to me that I would give him twenty more gold pieces; but when I turned my attention in the direction of the voice, I saw a woman who was evidently the lady of whom I had received a portrait.[695] I took out the picture and compared it, and saw that there was

---

[693] This sentence ought to have the mark of interrogation.

[694] A new paragraph ought not to begin here, but after قبول کرے *ḳabūl kare*, five lines further on.

[695] I have here translated this passage freely. The literal translation is this, "I saw a woman that that portrait was exactly the one of that very lady."

not the difference of a hair's point.[696] A cry escaped from my heart, and I became insensible. Mubārak took me in his arms. sate down, and began to fan me. I recovered my senses a little, and continued gazing in that same direction, until Mubārak asked, "What has happened to you?" My answer had as yet not issued from my lips, when that lady said, "O youth! fear God, and look not on a strange female; modesty and a proper sense of shame are incumbent on all."

She discoursed with such propriety, that I became infatuated with her beauty and her disposition. Mubārak did all he could to cheer me, but what perception had he of the state of my heart? Having no resource, I called out, "O servants of God! and dwellers in this abode! I am a poor traveller; if you will invite me to be with you, and give me a place to stop in, it will be a great thing for me." The blind man called me to him, and, recognizing my voice, embraced me, and took me into that apartment where that delicate girl sate. She went and hid herself in a corner. The old man asked me, saying, "Relate thy adventures, and why thou hast left thy family, and wandered about thus alone? and of whom thou art in search?" I did not mention the name of Malik Ṣādiḳ, nor did I refer to anything that had transpired there. I spoke in this wise, "This friendless individual is the Prince of China and Māchīn, and moreover my father is still sovereign of those realms. He purchased from a merchant for hundreds of thousands of rupees this picture, from beholding which all my senses and tranquillity have left me, and after assuming the garb of a faḳīr, I have searched through the whole world. Now I have found my desired object, which you have in your disposal."

When the blind man heard this, he heaved a sigh, and said, "O dear friend! my daughter is plunged in a grievous calamity. No mortal has the power to wed her, and enjoy the fruition of his marriage." I said, "I am in hopes that you will explain in detail." Then that Persian made known his history in the following manner. "Listen, Prince! I am the chief and the

---

[696] Our expression is "a pin's point."

magnate[697] of this city. My renown was great, and my family illustrious. God Most High has bestowed upon me this daughter. When she reached the age of puberty, the fame of her beauty, and delicacy, and genius, was bruited abroad, and it became known throughout the whole country that, 'in the house of such a person there is a daughter such that the Ḥūrīs of Paradise and the fairies are ashamed when contrasted with her loveliness. As for the countenance of a human being, what is it in comparison with hers?' The Prince of this city heard this eulogy, and, without having seen her, he, even in absence, became her lover. He forbore to eat and drink. He fell sick and took to his bed.[698]

"At length the King learned the circumstance. He called me at night into his private apartment, and cajoled me to such a degree as to gain my consent to contract a marriage-connexion with him. I too had thought that, as a daughter had been born in my house, I ought to affiance her to some one or other, and consequently that I had no better course than to betroth her to the King's son. Meanwhile the King too [thought I] pleads for it. I gave my consent and took leave, and from that very day the preparations for the nuptials went on on both sides. One day in a fortunate moment the ḳāẓī,[699] the muftī, the wise, the pious, and the noble assembled. The marriage was performed, and the jointure fixed. They conducted home the bride with great pomp, and went through all the customary

---

697 اکابر *akābir*, which is properly the plural of اکبر *akbar*, and signifies "grandees," is here, by a strange perversion, used as a singular, and must be so translated.

698 The dictionaries thus render اٹھواٹی کٹھواٹی *aṭhwāṭī kaṭhwāṭī*, on what authority or etymology I know not. I should be inclined to derive the word from اٹھوانا *uṭhwānā*, "to cause to get up," from the root of which comes اٹھ بیٹھ *uṭh baiṭh*, "restlessness." It would then be the state of one wanting to get up and anon to lie down.

699 The ḳāẓī is, as everybody knows, the Muḥammadan judge. The muftī is an officer of still higher rank, being the expounder of the law of which the ḳāẓī sustains the executive.

ceremonies. At night, when the bridegroom sought to consummate the marriage, there arose such an uproar in the apartment that the people who were watching outside were aghast. They tried to open the door of the room, and see what calamity had happened. It was so firmly fastened on the inside that they could not undo it. All of a sudden the cries also grew less. They forced out the hinges of the door, and saw that the bridegroom was lying with his head cut off, and his limbs yet convulsed, and foam was issuing from the mouth of the bride, who was wallowing senseless, with her clothes draggled in that blood and dirt.

"Beholding this disastrous sight, all were distracted. On such a festal occasion this piteous spectacle was disclosed. The King was informed of it, and he hastened to the spot, beating his head. All the pillars of the State were assembled, but no one had sufficient sagacity to penetrate into these circumstances. At last the King, in that state of mental agony, commanded, saying, 'Cut off the head of that unfortunate, ill-omened bride also.' As soon as these words dropped from the King's tongue, the same uproar again arose. The King was terrified, and fled for fear of his life, and ordered them to thrust her forth from the palace. The female attendants conveyed her to my house. These circumstances have been noised abroad in the world, and whoever hears it is dismayed, and in consequence of the murder of the Prince, the King himself, and all the inhabitants of this city, have become my deadly enemies.[700]

"When the mourning was concluded, and the fortieth day had expired, the King asked counsel of the nobles, saying, 'What should be done now?' All replied, 'Nothing more can be done; but as a slight consolation and solace to Your Majesty, be pleased to cause the girl, with her father, to be put to death, and confiscate their property.' When this sentence had been passed against me, the Kotwāl received

---

[700] The use of the singular میرا دشمن *mera dushman*, must immediately strike every one as a mistake. On reference to Mr. Romer's MS., I find that the proper reading is میرے دشمن *mere dushman*, which ought to be restored.

instructions [to carry it out]. He came and surrounded my dwelling on all sides, and caused a trumpet to be sounded at the door, and was about to force an entrance, and execute the King's command. From an unseen quarter, bricks and stones began to shower down in such a way that the whole army was discomfited. Covering their heads and faces, they fled in different directions, and the King, in his palace, heard with his own ears a terrible voice, saying, 'What calamity has fallen on thee? what demon possesses thee? If thou wishest thy own welfare, interfere not in the affairs of this lady, else thou too, for thy hostility, shalt experience just what thy son reaped from his marriage. Now if thou dost molest them, thou shalt suffer for it.'

"The King was seized with a fever from the violence of his alarm. He immediately commanded, saying, 'Let no one meddle with those ill-omened ones, and neither speak to them nor listen to them; but let them remain in their house, and do not inflict any violence on them.' Since that day the rulers, regarding the matter as sorcery, use prayers and amulets, and the wise men practise charms, and all the inhabitants of the city recite the Great Name of God, and the glorious[701] Ḳur'ān. For a long time this spectacle has lasted, but hitherto the secret[702] has in no degree been penetrated, and I too have no insight into it; but I once asked this girl, saying, 'What did you see with your own eyes?' She said, 'I know nothing more; but what I saw was this, that at the time when my husband attempted to have connexion with me, a throne set with jewels suddenly came forth, on which sate a handsome young man, clothed in royal apparel, and with him a great number of persons, in attendance upon him, entered the apartment, and engaged in the murder of the Prince. The person who was the chief came to me and said, "How now, dearest? whither will you fly from me now?" Their forms were like those of men, but their feet appeared to me like those of goats.

---

701 The epithet مجيد *majīd*, is appropriated to the Ḳur'ān.

702 اسرار *asrār* is properly a plural, but is here used as a singular, as اکابر *akābir* was a page or two before.

My heart began to throb, and through terror I fell into a swoon, after which I have no recollection of what happened.'

"Since when my condition is this, that I and my daughter remain in an abject condition in this ruined place. Owing to the wrath of the King, all my former companions keep aloof from me, and when I go out to beg, not a person gives me a kauṛī. Nay, I am not even permitted to stop at the shops. There is not a rag on the body of this unfortunate girl to cover her nakedness,[703] and we can get nothing to eat that we may satisfy ourselves. I ask this of God, that our death may arrive, or the earth open and swallow up this girl, who ought never to have been born. Death is better than such a life. God, perhaps, has sent thee solely on our account, hence thou hast taken compassion on us, and given us a gold coin. Thus, too, I have cooked and eaten a delicious repast, and caused clothes also to be got ready for my daughter. I have offered up thanks at the shrine of God, and uttered benedictions on thee. If the evil influence of a jin, or a fairy, had not fallen upon her, I would have presented her to thee to serve thee as a handmaid, and would regard it as my happiness. This is the story of this fallen person; do not seek after her, and abandon this pursuit."

When I had heard all this recital, I entreated and besought him much, saying, "Accept me as thy son. Whatever may have been predestinated in my fate, that will take place." That old man would not, in any degree, yield his consent. When evening came, I took leave of him and came to the inn. Mubārak said, "Well, Prince! May it be fortunate! God has provided the means at last; at length this toil has not been fruitless." I said, "How many flatteries have I employed to-day; but that false old man consents not. God knows whether he will give her to me or not." The state of my heart, however, was such that I found it difficult to pass the night, and I was thinking, "When will it be morning, that I may go again and present myself?" At times this thought occurred to me, "If he was to become kind and consent, then Mubārak

[703] Forbes has a blunder here, سر *sir*, "the head," for ستر *satr*, "pudenda." People do not wear rags on their bodies to cover their heads; but setting that aside, the plain reading in Mr. Romer's MS. is ستر *satr*, which ought to be restored.

would take her away for Malik Ṣādiḳ." Again I said to myself, "Well! let me only get possession of her, I will persuade Mubārak, and enjoy my happiness." Again I bethought myself of the danger, and said, "Even if Mubārak should consent, I should suffer the same fate from the genii as the Prince underwent, and when will the King of this city be willing that, after his son has perished, another should enjoy the bliss?"

The whole night my sleep was disturbed, and was spent in [considering] the intricacies of my undertaking. When the day had dawned, I took my way. I purchased in the bāzār the choicest pieces of cloth for apparel, and lace, and fringe, as also fruit fresh and dried, and presented myself before the old man. He was much pleased, and said, "There is nothing dearer than life to any one, but if my life could be of service to thee, I would not withhold it, and I would instantly deliver over my daughter to thee; but the fear arises lest thy life should be put in peril, and the stain of this reproach rest on me till the resurrection." I said, "I am now without friends in this town, and you are my father both in a spiritual and a worldly sense. What distresses and afflictions have I not endured, and what blows have I not for a length of time undergone in coming thus far? and [at length] I have found traces of the object I have been in search of. God has also made you kind, that you consent to the marriage, but hesitate on my account. Be just a little and reflect, that no creed admits of rescuing the head from the sword of love, and screening one's life. Come what may, I have altogether given selfish considerations to the winds. I look upon the union with my mistress as life, and have no care whether I live or die; nay, if I become hopeless, I shall die without the intervention of destiny, and in the resurrection shall rise up against you" [*lit.* "shall seize your skirt"].

In short, nearly a month had passed in these disputations, refusals, and acquiescences, and hope, and fear. Every day I hastened to wait on that venerable man, and continued to employ flatteries and entreaties.[704] It happened that the old

[704] بر آمد *bar āmad*, which signifies "egress," makes no sense here, and has doubtless been employed only for the jingle with خوشامد *kh'ushāmad*.

man fell sick. I attended him on his sick bed, and always took his urine to the doctor [for inspection]. I prepared whatever remedies were ordered according to the exact prescription, and gave them to him to drink, and with my own hands I dressed rice and pulse, and other aliment, and gave him a small part of it to eat. One day, being soothed [by my attention], he said, "Young man! thou art very obstinate, although I have told thee all the evils, and recommended thee to desist from this purpose;[705] still, where the inclinations are, that is the whole world, and thou nevertheless desirest to cast thyself, *nolens volens*, into a well. Well! I will mention thee this day to my daughter, and see what she says." O faḳīrs of God! when I heard this good news, I was so elated that my clothes could not contain me. I thanked him respectfully, and said, "Now you have taken thought for my life." I then took leave and went to my lodgings, and discoursed on this subject the whole night with Mubārak. Where was sleep, and where was hunger? In the morning, as soon as it was light, I returned and presented myself, and made my salutation. He said, "There! I give you my daughter. God grant that it may be fortunate. I commit both of you to the protection and safe-keeping of God. As long as I have breath, stay under my eye. When my eyes close, do as you think proper. You are at liberty to choose."

After some days the venerable old man resigned his spirit to his Maker. We wept and lamented him, and performed the duties of shrouding and interring him. After the rites of the third day[706] from the interment, Mubārak put that beautiful girl into a sedan, and brought her to the inn, and said to me, "She is a charge entrusted to you for Malik Ṣādiḳ. Take care; act not perfidiously, and do not throw to the winds all this toil and trouble." I said, "Gossip![707] where is Malik Ṣādiḳ

---

705 There should not be a full stop at باز آ *bāz ā*, for تو بھي *to bhī* must be understood before جي *jī*, as the relative to هر چند *har chand*; or پر *par* may be the relative to هر چند *har chand*, in which case the same remark applies.

706 The rites referred to in this expression are also spoken of at page 140, line 31, *q.v.* Also see the note on the same passage, note 436.

707 We have no equivalent term for کاکا *kākā*, which is a friendly appellation for an elder brother, or the servant of one's father.

here? my heart listens not, why should I wait? Come what may,[708] whether I live or die, I will now enjoy the bliss." Mubārak was vexed and threatened me, saying, "No boyish tricks! now in an instant some terrible catastrophe[709] will occur. Do you think Malik Ṣādiḳ at a distance, that you disobey his commands? At the time of our departure, he explained the whole matter, pointing out the ups and downs from the very first. If you persevere according to his directions, and conduct her there in perfect safety, then he too being a king will perhaps have regard to your labour, and bestow her upon you, then what a happy thing it will be; let but your friendship continue, and you will experience the sweets of it."[710]

At length, confounded by his threats and reproofs, I remained silent. We purchased two dromedaries, and, mounted on camel-saddles, took the way to the country of Malik Ṣādiḳ. As we were going on in a plain, the sound of clamorous outcries began to reach us. Mubārak said, "Thanks to God! our labour has been successful; this is the army of the genii which has arrived." At length Mubārak, having joined their company, inquired, "Whither do you purpose going?" They said, "The King has detached us to come to meet you. Now we attend your orders. If you say the word, we will in a moment transport you to his presence." Mubārak said, "Lo! from what hardships has God brought us successful [*lit.* "with red faces"] into the presence of the King! Now what need is there of haste? If (which God forbid) any interruption should supervene, our labour would be uselessly thrown away, and we should fall under the anger of the King." All said, "Of this the disposal is with you; proceed in whatever manner you

---

708 This is the Urdū translation of the Persian proverb which occurs in the page before, هرچه بادا باد *harchih bādā bād.*

709 This is freely translated. Literally it is, "of something something will take place."

710 A proverb. Forbes, in his vocabulary, has omitted the gender of پیت *pīt*, which, according to Shakespear, is feminine.

please." Although we had every sort of comfort, still we occupied ourselves night and day with travelling.

When we drew near, I, seeing Mubārak asleep, placed my head on the feet of that beautiful girl, and began to tell her, with words of tender entreaty, of the inquietude of my heart, and of my helplessness on account of Malik Ṣādiḳ, saying, "From the day that I beheld your picture I have banished from me sleep and food and rest. And now that God has shewn this day to me, I have still remained an utter stranger." She said, "My heart too is inclined to you, for what troubles have you not undergone for my sake, and by what labours have you brought me hither! Keep God in mind, and do not forget me. Only wait and see what will be disclosed from the curtain of the future." With these words she wept so bitterly that she was choked by her sobs. Here was my state and there her distress. Meanwhile Mubārak's slumber was broken, and seeing the affliction of us two lovers, he began to weep, and said, "Be of good cheer! I have an ointment by me, which I will rub on the body of that delicate lady, and Malik Ṣādiḳ's heart will revolt at its smell, and it is probable he will give her to you."

When I heard this counsel from Mubārak, my heart was encouraged. I clung to his neck, caressed him, and said, "O papa! thou art more than a father to me! Thou hast saved my life already, and now too act in such a manner that my life may be preserved, otherwise I shall perish from this grief." He gave me a vast deal of encouragement.[711] When the day dawned, the voices of the genii began to reach us. I saw then that some attendants of Malik Ṣādiḳ had arrived, and had brought two sumptuous dresses for me, and with them was a sedan covered with a network of pearls. Mubārak rubbed that oil over the lady, and having dressed and adorned her, took her to Malik Ṣādiḳ. When the King saw her, he bestowed much honour on me, and seated me with respect, and said, "I will treat thee in such a manner that no one has to this day ever treated any one

---

[711] There ought to be a full stop at تسلّي دي *tasallī dī.*

so well. The empire of thy father is truly ready for thee, but besides thou art now in the place of my son." He was still in the midst of these courteous expressions, when meanwhile the lady too entered his presence. At the smell of that ointment, his brain was gradually overcome, and his state of mind perturbed. He could not endure the pungency of the odour, but rose and went out and called us both, and turning to Mubārak, said, "How now, sir! you have performed your agreement well![712] I warned you that if you deceived me you would incur my displeasure. What means this smell? Now see what I'll do to you!" He was mightily incensed. Mubārak through fear undid the string which tied his trousers, and shewed [his state of castration], saying, "Health to the King! When by command of Your Majesty we were appointed to this business, your slave at the very first cut off his mark of virility, and having shut it up in a casket, entrusted it sealed up to Your Majesty's treasurer, and after applying the ointment of Sulaimān, set out." When he heard this answer from Mubārak, he directed his looks to me, and frowning, said, "Then this is thy doing!" and getting angry he began to pour out a torrent of invectives.[713] At that time I understood from the language he used that he would probably cause me to be slain outright. When I discovered this from his countenance, I washed my hands of my life, and feeling that there was no hope of surviving,[714] I drew the concealed[715] poniard from Mubārak's belt, and stuck it into Malik Ṣādiḳ's belly.[716] The instant the knife entered, he stooped down and swayed about. I was amazed, and felt sure he was dead. Then I thought that the wound

---

712 The paragraph ought not to end at بجا لائي. *bajā lāe*, but at كرتا هون *kartā hūn*, two lines further on.

713 This is a free translation. The literal one is, "he began to talk idly with his mouth evil and good."

714 This is freely translated. Literally it is, "having lost my life."

715 The dictionaries are silent as to the word سرِ غلاف *sar-i ghilāf*, which signifies a dagger concealed by its sheath.

716 توند *tond* is a vulgar word for belly, and signifies "paunch," "pot-belly." The common words are شکم *shikam* and پیٹ *peṭ*.

was not so very deadly; what could be the reason of it? I was standing looking on, when he, after rolling and wallowing on the ground, assumed the form of a ball and flew up towards the sky.[717] He rose so high that at last he disappeared from sight, and then, after a moment, flashing like lightning and venting some meaningless words in his wrath, he descended and gave me such a kick that I swooned and fell flat on my back, and my life succumbed within me. After, God knows how long, I recovered my senses, and on opening my eyes and looking about me, I found myself lying in such a jungle that there was nothing visible but acacias and the capparis aphylla, and the wild ber-tree. At that time my reason was of no assistance to me as to what I should do or whither I should go. I heaved a sigh of despair, and took my way in one direction. If I saw any human beings anywhere, I asked after Malik Ṣādiḳ, and they, thinking me mad, replied that they had not even heard his name.

One day I too ascended a mountain, and determined to throw myself down and destroy myself. When I was on the point of falling, that same veiled horseman, possessor of the sword Ẕū-l-faḳār,[718] arrived, and said, "Why dost thou throw away thy life? Every sort of affliction happens to man. Thy evil days are now past and thy good ones at hand; go quickly to Rūm. Three persons like yourself have preceded you; join their company and obtain a meeting with the Sulṭān of that country. You will all four obtain your wishes in one and the same place." This is the story of me the faḳīr, which I have narrated. At length, according to the good tidings of my lord, the resolver of difficulties,[719] I have arrived in your presence, O spiritual guides! and have also obtained the honour of waiting

---

717 Forbes has a misprint here, آسما *āsmā* for آسمان *āsmān*.

718 ذوالفقار *Ẕū-l-faḳār* (literally, "possessor of the joints of the back"), was a sword belonging to Muḥammad, and bequeathed by him to Ålī. It had its name either from cleaving the vertebræ of infidels, or from its wavy appearance like vertebræ.

719 مشکل کشا *mushkil kushā*, "resolver of difficulties," is an epithet appropriated to Ålī.

on the King, the shadow of God. All must now receive their consolation.

This conversation was still going on between the four darweshes and Āzād-Bakht, when, in the midst of it, an eunuch came running from the royal seraglio, and performed his obeisance in token of congratulation in presence of the King, and represented as follows, "At this time a prince has been born, before whose beauty the sun and moon are ashamed." The King was astonished, and asked, "In whose pregnancy[720] has this sun appeared? for to outward appearance indeed no one was pregnant." He respectfully stated, "The female slave Māh-rū, who has been for many days under the royal displeasure, and, like the friendless, was keeping in a corner, and near whom none went from fear, nor inquired how she fared: to her this divine grace has been extended, that a moon-like son has been born from her womb."

The King was so overjoyed that it seemed probable he would die of delight. The four faḳīrs also uttered benedictions, saying, "Well, son! may thy house continue populous, and may his step be fortunate! May he grow up to manhood and old age under thy shadow!" The King said, "This blessing is due to your presence, for otherwise this event was not even surmised by me. If you will permit me, I will go and see." The darweshes replied, "In the name of God, go by all means." The King proceeded to the seraglio, took the Prince into his lap, and returned thanks to the Divine Majesty. His mind was tranquillized. He immediately clasped [the child] in his arms, and brought and laid it at the feet of the faḳīrs. The darweshes recited blessings, and by their exorcisms forbade evil spirits to approach it. The King made preparations for a feast. Redoubled music began to sound. [The King] opened the door of the treasury, and by his profuse liberality, made him who

---

[720] Here is another of those equivoques in which Orientals delight. برجِ حمل *burj-i ḥaml* is "the constellation of pregnancy;" برجِ حمل *burj-i ḥamal*, "constellation of the sign Aries."

was in want of a kauṛī the master of a lakh.[721] To all the pillars of the State grants were issued, doubling the grants of land and the dignities they possessed. The army received a gratuity of five years' pay. On the elders and holy men grants of subsistence and deeds of gift were bestowed. The porringers of the indigent, and the cups of the mendicants were filled with a mixture[722] of gold and silver coins, and the revenue for three years was remitted to the peasantry, so that whatever they should sow or plant, they should store both shares (their own and that of the government) in their houses.

Throughout the whole city, in the houses of soldiers and civilians, wherever you looked, was merry-making and the dance. Every one, low or high, was sitting like a temporary king for joy, when, all of a sudden, in the midst of the festivity, arose from the interior of the palace the sound of weeping and beating the breast. Female slaves and Turkish women and armed female attendants and eunuchs, came forth casting dirt on their heads, and said to the King, "Just when, after washing and bathing the Prince, they had put him in the nurse's lap, a piece of cloud came and enveloped the nurse. When, after a moment, we looked, the nurse was fallen down insensible, and the Prince had vanished. We know not what calamity has happened." When the King heard these marvels, he was greatly amazed, and lamentation arose throughout the whole country. For two days not a pot was put on the fire in any one's house; they were grieving for the Prince, and drinking their own blood.

In short, they were weary[723] of their life, living as they did. When the third day came, the same cloud returned and brought a cradle set with jewels, and overlaid with a network of pearls. It deposited the cradle in the palace, and vanished. The people

---

[721] A لکھ *lakh* is "a hundred thousand," and if no noun be expressed, we may add "rupees."

[722] کھچڑي *khichṛī* is a dish made of pulse and rice boiled together, and hence comes to signify any mixture.

[723] لاچار *lāchār*, literally "helpless," an ill-selected word and quite unsuited to this passage.

found the Prince in it, sucking his thumb. The Queen quickly, taking his calamities upon herself, lifted him in her hands, and clasped him to her breast. She saw then that he had on the upper part of his body a vest made of the finest muslin [*lit.* "of flowing water"], with a fringe of pearls sewed on it, and over that he wore a bib of brocade, and on his hands and feet were bracelets covered with jewels, and on his neck was a necklace of nine gems, and a rattle, and a coral to suck, and a clapper made of jewels were laid there. All, through joy, began to go round the infant in token of their devoting themselves for it, and to utter benedictions, saying, "May thy mother find a solace[724] in her child! and mayest thou live to extreme[725] old age!"

The King caused a new and spacious palace to be erected, and having caused carpets to be spread in it, placed the darweshes there. When he was at leisure from the affairs of government, he then came and sate with them, and shewed them every care and attention. But on the Thursday preceding the new moon of each month, the same cloudy fragment came and took away the Prince. After two days it brought back the Prince, and curiosities, and playthings, and presents from every country, and of every kind, such that at the sight of them human reason was amazed. In this same manner the Prince passed happily into his seventh year. Exactly on his birthday, [his father] the King Āzād-bā͟kht said to the fakīrs, "Men of God! no one knows who carries off the Prince and restores him again. It is a great marvel. Let us see what the end of it will be." The darweshes said, "Do this one thing. Write a friendly note to this effect, and put it in the Prince's cradle, 'Seeing your kindness and amity, my heart too has become desirous of meeting you. If, in a friendly manner, you will acquaint me with your circumstances, my mind will be eased, and perplexity will be entirely banished.'" The King, in accordance with the advice

---

[724] This is freely translated. Literally it is, "may thy mother's stomach remain cool."

[725] Forbes, in his vocabulary, has omitted the expression بوڑھا آڑھا *būṛhā āṛhā*, which Shakespear renders "old man," "eldest man." It is to be regretted that these pure Hindī expressions are left without etymology or explanation, for آڑھا *āṛhā* requires both.

of the darweshes, wrote a letter to that effect on paper sprinkled with gold, and placed it in the golden cradle.

The Prince, in accordance with his former custom, disappeared. When it was evening, Āzād-bakht came and sate down on the bedding of the darweshes, and began a conversation. A paper folded up came and fell near the King, who opened and read it, and found it to be the answer to his own note. There were but two lines written in it, and they were as follows:—"Consider me too as anxious to see you. A throne goes to convey you. If you come at the present time, it will be most excellent. Let us meet together, for all things necessary for enjoyment and mirth are ready. Your Highness's place alone is vacant." The King Āzād-bakht, taking with him the darweshes, seated himself on the throne, which, like the throne of the prophet Sulaimān, moved through the air. Proceeding on, they arrived at a place where they saw a lofty edifice, and preparations [for a banquet], but they knew not whether any one was there or not. Meanwhile some one passed a needle smeared with the collyrium of Sulaimān through the eyes of all five. Two drops of tears fell from the eyes of each, and they beheld the court of the fairies, who were standing holding vases for sprinkling them with rose-water, as a mark of courtesy in receiving them, and who wore dresses of every hue.

Āzād-bakht went forward and thousands of the children of the fairies stood facing either way, and in the centre was placed a throne of emerald, on which Malik Shāhbāl, the son of Shāh-rukh, was seated in great pomp, supported by pillows, and a fairy-born girl sate before him, who continued playing with the Prince Bakhtiyār, and on either hand seats of various kinds were spread, on which the nobles of the fairies sate. As soon as Malik Shāhbāl saw the King, he rose quite up, and descending from his throne, embraced him, and taking him by the hand brought him and made him sit beside him on the throne, and a very friendly and affectionate conversation ensued. The whole day laughter, and mirth, and feasting, and fruits, and an entertainment of perfumes went on, and the music and the dancing were listened to. The next day, when the two kings met again, Shāhbāl inquired of the King as to the circumstances of his bringing the darweshes with him.

The King narrated in detail the histories of the four mendicants as he had heard them, and spoke in favour of them, and besought assistance, saying, "They have undergone such great toil and affliction, if now by the favour of Your Highness they could each of them attain their wishes, it would be a most meritorious action, and this friend, too, will all his life be thankful. By Your Majesty's favourable regard all their rafts[726] will cross the stream." When Malik Shāhbāl heard this, he said, "With my head and eyes! I will not fail to meet your request." With these words he cast a wrathful glance towards the devs and fairies, and wrote letters to the chief genii who presided over various places, to the effect that, on seeing the order, they were instantly to transport themselves into the illustrious presence of royalty, and that whoever delayed to come should receive punishment, and should come as a prisoner, and that whoever had a descendant of Adam, whether man or woman, should bring him with him. Further, that whoever kept such person concealed, and it should afterwards be discovered, his wife and children should be crushed to death in an oil-press, and neither his name nor trace should be left.

With this mandate devs were despatched in all directions, while an intimacy arose between the two kings, and words of friendship were exchanged. Meanwhile, Shāhbāl, addressing the darweshes, said, "I myself entertained a strong desire for a child, and had made this covenant in my heart, that if God gave me a son or a daughter,[727] I would give her in marriage to the family of a human king, wherever a son was born." After making this vow I learned that the Queen was pregnant. At length, as they reckoned the hours and months, the days were fulfilled, and my present daughter was born, and in accordance with my covenant I ordered the genii to search, saying to them, to make diligent inquiry through the four quarters of the world, and in whatever emperor or king's house a son was born, they should quickly, but with extreme care, take him up

[726] A favourite metaphor with Orientals, too plain to require explanation.

[727] A faulty sentence. It should be, "would give him or her in marriage whenever a son or a daughter was born to a human king."

and bring him. In accordance with the command the fairies dispersed in all directions, and after a long time brought the Prince to me. I returned thanks to God, and took him upon my lap, and an affection for him stronger than even that for my own daughter sprang up in my heart. I was unwilling to part with him a moment from my sight, but was sending him back because, should not his parents see him, what a condition theirs would be. I therefore sent for the child once a month, and after keeping him a few days, sent him back. If it please God Most High, now that we have met, I will celebrate his marriage. Death, as well as life, is fated to all. Well! while yet living I will see his marriage chaplet."

When King Āzād-bakht had heard the words of Malik Shāhbāl, and had observed his good qualities, he was much pleased, and said, "At first many marvellous perils occurred to my mind from the disappearance and return of the Prince, but I now feel consoled by what Your Highness has said. This boy is now yours; do as seems good to you." In short, the two kings associated with one another, and took pleasure together like sugar and milk. In the space of ten or five days the great Kings of the rose-garden of Iram[728] and of the mountains and the islands (in quest of whom people had been despatched), all came and were present at court. The King first ordered Malik Ṣādiḳ to produce any child of Adam he had by him. He, with much grief and annoyance, yet feeling that he had no alternative, produced that rose-cheeked lady. Then from the King of the country of Ŭmān[729] he demanded the fairy princess (for whose sake the Prince of the country of Nīmroz, riding on the bull, became mad). He too, after many shifts and evasions, produced her. When the King asked for the daughter of the King of Europe and Bihzād

---

[728] Celebrated gardens fabled to have been anciently made in Arabia Felix by one of the giant kings, Shaddād bin Aad or Iram bin Omad. They are described as a perfect model of the voluptuous Paradise which is promised after death to the Muḥammadans.

[729] The southern coast of Arabia extending from Maskat to Adn, *i.e.* from the entrance into the Persian Gulf to the straits of Babelmandel.

Khān, all positively denied having them, and were ready to take the oath of the prophet Sulaimān.

At last, when the turn of the King of the Red Sea to be interrogated came, he held down his head and remained silent. Malik Shāhbāl encouraged him and adjured him, and gave him hopes of promotion, and also urged him with threats and menaces. Then he also joined his hands and made his statement, saying, "Hail to the King! the truth is this, that when the King came to the river to meet his son, and the Prince, from impatience, urged his horse into the water, it happened that I had that day come forth for amusement and the chase. I passed by that spot, and stopping my cortége, surveyed the sight. Meanwhile the Princess too was taken by the mare into the stream. When my eyes fell upon her, I lost the control of my heart, and commanded my fairies to bring the Princess with her steed. After her, Bihzād Khān urged in his horse, and when he also began to sink, I was pleased with his courage and intrepidity. I caused him also to be quickly seized, and taking the two with me, I turned back my cortége; so these two are in perfect health and safety with me."

Having stated these circumstances, he called both into his presence, and the King made great search for the daughter of the Sultān of Syria, and inquired strictly and sternly of all, but no one admitted having her, or knowing anything about her. Then Malik Shāhbāl inquired if any king or chief was still absent, or if all had come. The genii made representation as follows, "Asylum of the world! All have come into the presence but one, Musalsal Jādū, who by magic art has built in the recesses of Mount Caucasus, a fort. He, from pride, has not come, and we, your slaves, have not the power to bring him by force. The place is very strong, and he himself is a great devil."

When Malik Shāhbāl heard this, he was wroth, and despatched a host of genii and ʿifrīts,[730] and fairies, and enjoined them, say-

[730] Forbes in his vocabulary has given this word as عفريت *ʿafrīt*, but Richardson and Shakespear in their Dictionaries make it عِفريت *ʿifrīt*.

ing, "If he present himself by fair means, and bring that Princess with him, then it is well! otherwise overthrow him and bring him with his hands tied behind his back, and after desolating his fortress and his country, cause it to be ploughed up with ploughs drawn by asses." The instant the order was issued, such an army set forth that in the space of half a day they humbled [*lit.* "put a ring in his ear"], and seized the rebel, frantic and furious as he was, and placed him standing in the royal presence, with his hands bound. Though Malik Shāhbāl rebuked him sternly, and interrogated him, that haughty one gave no answer but denial [*lit.* "gave no 'yes' except 'no'"]. At length the King, becoming incensed, commanded them to sever that reprobate limb from limb, and having stripped off his skin, to fill it with chaff; and he then despatched an army of fairies to go to the mountain Ḳāf,[731] and there search for and find [the lady]. That army so deputed searched for and brought the Princess, and conveyed her into the royal presence. All those captives and the four faḳīrs, beholding the justice of Malik Shāhbāl's commandments, offered benedictions and rejoiced, and King Āzād-bakht also was greatly delighted. Then Malik Shāhbāl said, "Cause the men to enter my private hall of audience, and the women to go into the royal seraglio, and give orders in the city for a public rejoicing by fastening up mirrors, and let the preparations for marriage be made quickly; so that the order may be as it were anticipated."

One day, having selected a fortunate moment and an auspicious period, he tied the marriage-knot between the Prince Bak͟htiyār and his own daughter Roshan Ak͟htar;[732] and he united the son of the merchant of Yaman[733] to the daughter of the King of Damascus; and wedded the Prince of Fārs[734] to the Princess

---

731 A fabulous mountain supposed to surround the world and bound the horizon. It rests on the stone Sakhrat, a solid emerald, which imparts the azure colour to the sky. It is also the name of Caucasus, to which the Orientals assign these fabulous attributes.

732 *Vide* note 681. This was the name of Aurangzīb's sister. Bak͟htiyār signifies "fortunate."

733 The first darwesh.

734 The second darwesh.

of Baṣra; and gave the hand of the Prince of Ajam[735] to the Princess of Europe; and joined the daughter of the King of Nīmroz in wedlock with Bihzād Khān; and consigned the Princess of the genii to the Prince of Nīmroz; and celebrated the nuptials of the Prince of China[736] with the old Persian's daughter who had been in the possession of Malik Ṣādiḳ. Each despairing lover by means of Malik Shāhbāl attained his object and his wish. After that he commanded a feast for forty days, and they engaged, night and day, in mirth and festivity.

At length Malik Shāhbāl, having bestowed rarities and presents and wealth on each prince, dismissed them each to his own country. All set off with joy and contentment, and arrived safely and well, and began to govern their kingdoms. But Bihzād Khān and the merchant's son of Yaman alone chose to remain with King Āzād-bakht. At length the latter appointed the merchant's son of Yaman to be the comptroller of his household, and Bihzād Khān to be the general of the army of the Prince, the lord of auspicious fortune, that is to say, Bakhtiyār. As long as they lived they enjoyed happiness.

O God! in the same manner as these four darweshes and the fifth, Āzād-bakht, attained their wishes, in the same manner, according to Thy grace and favour, fulfil the heart's wish of every despairing one! [I ask this] for the sake of the five Holy Persons,[737] the twelve Imāms,[738] and the fourteen Innocents;[739] may the blessing and the peace of God rest upon them! Amen, O God of all worlds![740]

---

[735] The third darwesh. [736] The fourth darwesh.

[737] These are: 1. The Prophet Muḥammad. 2. His daughter Fāṭimah. 3. His son-in-law Alī. 4 and 5. His grand-children, the sons of Alī and Fāṭimah, viz. Ḥasan and Ḥusain. [738] *Vide* note 8.

[739] The fourteen Innocents are the children of Ḥasan and Ḥusain.

[740] It is only fair to that learned Orientalist, Professor Forbes, to say that many of the words which I have noticed as omitted in his vocabulary to the Bāgh o Bahār, have been supplied in his third edition. For the sake of those who have only the first two editions I have, however, retained the notes which advert to these omissions.

CONCLUSION OF THE BOOK.

When by the divine favour this book reached its termination, it occurred to my mind that I would give it such a name also that the date would be found therein. When I made the calculation, I found that I began to write at the close of the year twelve hundred and fifteen of the Hijrah, and by reason of my scanty leisure, it was not finished[741] till the beginning of the year twelve hundred and seventeen. I was meditating thus when my heart suggested,[742] "'Bāgh o Bahār' is a good name, since both the name and the date are combined in this;" whereupon I gave it this very name. Whoever reads this will, as it were, perambulate a garden, nay, a garden is subject to the vicissitudes of autumn, from which this is free. This will bloom perpetually.

When first "the Garden and the Spring" saw light,
Twelve hundred ten and seven years
Were numbered from the holy Prophet's flight.
Here in its name its date appears,
Then ever wander through it, day and night;
For this no wintry autumn fears,
But ever blooms a garden of delight.

With my heart's blood I did it irrigate,
Its leaves, its fruit, my vitals are.
All will forget me when relentless fate
Quenches in death life's fading star,
But this memorial nought shall dissipate,
No chilling blasts its beauty mar,
To all who read, it shall my name relate.

---

741 Forbes in his vocabulary has omitted the word مرتّب *murattab*, "arranged, regulated, prepared."

742 For an explanation of the chronological name, *vide* Preface, p. xi, and for the numerical power of the letters generally, *vide* the Translator's "Grammar," p. 36.

Reader! be this one word in memory borne:
  If somewhere, too, a fault you see,
Think how 'mid flow'rets ever lurks the thorn,
  And man will err, though wise he be:
It fits not clay its fellow-clay to scorn,
  For faults make up humanity,
Nought else is man, of false pretensions shorn.

Hear now, O God! my last, my single prayer,
  'Tis all I wish for and implore;
Keep me each moment in Thy heavenly care;
  Thus may I pass life's changeful store
Of day and night, and not for me prepare
  The grave-night's dread tribunal, nor
Be wroth; but at the last thy suppliant spare!
So in each world be added grace to grace,
For sake of him who sealed the Prophet race.

THE END.

THE PETITION OF MĪR AMMAN, OF DIHLĪ,

WHICH WAS PRESENTED TO THE GENTLEMEN MANAGERS [OF THE COLLEGE OF FORT WILLIAM].

MAY God keep in safety the gentlemen of illustrious rank who rightly appreciate the worthy!

This exile, having heard the command issued by public proclamation,[a] has, with a thousand toils and troubles, turned the Story of the Four Darweshes into the "Bāg͟h o Bahār," in the language of the High Urdū.[b] By the grace of God, and by reason of its being traversed by all gentlemen, it has become verdant.[c] I am now in hopes that I too shall obtain the fruit of it, so that the bud of my heart shall blossom like the rose, for according to the word of the sage Firdausī,[d] which he has written in the "Shāh-nāmah,"

Mighty toil I've borne for years thirty,
I have revived Persia by this Pārsī.
And thus adorning the Urdū tongue,
I have made Bengāl and Hindūstān one.

My lords are themselves able to judge of merit,—there is no need of representation. O God! may the star of their good-fortune remain shining!

---

[a] When the Marquess Wellesley founded the College of Fort William, he issued a proclamation announcing rewards and encouragement for translations from the Persian, Arabic, and other languages into the vernacular dialects of India.

[b] At page 6 of Mīr Amman's preface we have the explanation of the term Urdū which might be termed معلا *muảllā*, "lofty," as being the imperial camp.

[c] An allusion to the chronological title of the book, "Bāg͟h o Bahār," or "Garden and Spring."

[d] Firdausī, the Persian Homer, lived in the reign of Sulṭān Maḥmūd of Ghaznī, in the eleventh century after Christ.

STEPHEN AUSTIN AND SONS, PRINTERS, HERTFORD.